Karoline Fath

Technical and economic potential for photovoltaic systems on buildings

PRODUKTION UND ENERGIE

Karlsruher Institut für Technologie (KIT)
Institut für Industriebetriebslehre und Industrielle Produktion
Deutsch-Französisches Institut für Umweltforschung

Band 25

Eine Übersicht aller bisher in dieser Schriftenreihe
erschienenen Bände finden Sie am Ende des Buches.

Technical and economic potential for photovoltaic systems on buildings

by
Karoline Fath

KIT Scientific Publishing

Dissertation, Karlsruher Institut für Technologie
KIT-Fakultät für Wirtschaftswissenschaften

Tag der mündlichen Prüfung: 5. September 2017
Referenten: Prof. Dr. Frank Schultmann
Prof. Dr. Hans-Martin Henning

Impressum

KIT Scientific Publishing

Karlsruher Institut für Technologie (KIT)
KIT Scientific Publishing
Straße am Forum 2
D-76131 Karlsruhe

KIT Scientific Publishing is a registered trademark
of Karlsruhe Institute of Technology.
Reprint using the book cover is not allowed.

www.ksp.kit.edu

Print on Demand 2018 – Gedruckt auf FSC-zertifiziertem Papier

ISSN 2194-2404
ISBN 978-3-7315-0787-1
DOI 10.5445/KSP/1000081498

Technical and economic potential for photovoltaic systems on buildings

Zur Erlangung des akademischen Grades
Doktor der Ingenieurwissenschaften (Dr.-Ing.)
von der Fakultät für Wirtschaftswissenschaften des
Karlsruher Instituts für Technologie (KIT)

genehmigte
Dissertation
von

M.sc. Wi.-Ing. Karoline Fath

Tag der mündlichen Prüfung:	5. September 2017
Referent:	Prof. Dr. Frank Schultmann
Korreferent:	Prof. Dr. Hans-Martin Henning

Acknowledgements

This thesis has been written during my research at the Institute for Industrial Production (IIP) at the Karlsruhe Institute of Technology (KIT). I would like to express my sincere gratitude towards all persons that I had the pleasure to collaborate with during this time. First of all I thank my supervisor Prof. Frank Schultmann for his feedback and support. I also thank Prof. Hans-Martin Henning for the Korreferat.
I thank Prof. Jay Yang for the research stay at the Queensland University of Technology (QUT) in Brisbane, Australia, and the Karlsruhe House of Young Scientists (KHYS) for the funding. Also, the funding of the German BMBF and the European Commission for the research projects "Solarvalley Mitteldeutschland - BIPV" and "Construct-PV" is gratefully acknowledged. Especially I thank the city of Karlsruhe and the GTA GeoService GmbH for the provision of 3D city models and the LuBW for the provision of cadastral data. At IIP my special thanks goes to Michael Hiete, Julian Stengel, Anna Kühlen, Rebekka Volk, Simon Schulte-Beerbühl and Jens Ludwig for always critical and helpful discussions. During my research I was lucky also to be a member of the group Solar Facades at Fraunhofer ISE. I am grateful to Tilmann Kuhn, Helen Rose Wilson and Wendelin Sprenger. Wendelin's irradiation simulation programs provided a basis for a central part of this thesis.
Last but not least I thank my brother Philipp Fath and Elke Schubert for their endless patience in supporting me technically and my parents, grandmothers, partner and friends for their unceasing understanding and support.

Karlsruhe, February 2018 *Karoline Fath*

Kurzfassung

Die Verknappung fossiler Energieträger macht die Suche nach alternativen Energiequellen zu einem der dringlichsten Forschungsthemen unseres Jahrzehnts. Am aussichtsreichsten ist die Forschung im Bereich der erneuerbaren Energien, wie Wasserkraft, Windkraft, Photovoltaik, Solarthermie und Biomasse. In Deutschland findet seit der Einführung des Gesetzes zur Förderung Erneuerbarer Energien (EEG) ein starker Ausbau dieser Energieträger statt, so dass im Jahr 2016 über 30 % des Bruttostromverbrauchs aus erneuerbaren Energieträgern gedeckt werden konnten.

Der deutsche Gebäudebestand hat einen 40-prozentigen Anteil am Energieverbrauch. Für den Einsatz im Gebäudebereich eignen sich insbesondere Photovoltaikanlagen: Das Fehlen mechanischer Teile macht sie geräuschfrei und wartungsarm. Sie können daher problemlos in dicht besiedelten Gebieten eingesetzt werden, ohne eine Belastung für die Be- und Anwohner darzustellen.

In der Dissertation wird eine Methode für die Potenzialberechnung für Photovoltaikanlagen an Gebäuden entwickelt. Die Erweiterungen der entwickelten Methode im Vergleich zu existierenden Photovoltaikpotenzialstudien wurden einerseits durch den exponentiellen Anstieg der Rechenkapazitäten ermöglicht. Dadurch konnten zeitlich und räumlich hochaufgelöste Einstrahlungssimulationen auf Gebäude- und Stadtteilebene als Grundlage für ähnlich hochaufgelöste Stromerzeugungssimulationen durchgeführt werden. So konnten zum ersten Mal verlässliche Aussagen über den Einfluss von Verschattung und Reflektionen von der Umgebung auf die photovoltaische Stromerzeugung getroffen werden und damit das bisher vernachlässigte oder nur grob abgeschätzte Potenzial für Photovoltaikanlagen an Gebäudefassaden verlässlich bestimmt werden. Diese Analysen dienten dann für eine großflächige Abschätzung.

Andererseits sind die Preise für Photovoltaikanlagen seit der Jahrtausendwende so stark gesunken, dass es an ausreichend bestrahlten Gebäudeflächen jetzt wirtschaftlich sein kann, eine Photovoltaikanlage zu installieren auch ohne öffentliche Förderung. Existierende Potenzialstudien haben nur das theoretische oder technische Potenzial berechnet, da es in der Vergangenheit aufgrund der hohen Investition kein wirtschaftliches Potenzial gab.
Die in dieser Dissertation entwickelte Methodik wurde auf den Gebäudebestand in Deutschland angewendet, für den die erforderlichen statistischen und 3D-Gebäudedaten zur Verfügung standen. Das berechnete theoretische Potenzial für 2015 beträgt 37 700 km^2, das Flächenpotenzial 22 855 TWh, das Elektrizitätserzeugungspotenzial 2923 TWh und das wirtschaftliche Potenzial von 1158 TWh bis 2482 TWh. Außerdem wurde eine Prognose für die Entwicklung des Potenzials bis 2050 berechnet, die von 3015 TWh bis 4210 TWh erzeugte Elektrizität reicht (3095 GW_p bis 4325 GW_p installierte Leistung).
Die entwickelte Methode kann auf andere Länder angewendet werden, wo eine ähnliche Datenbasis verfügbar ist. Die Studie kann auch noch weiter verfeinert werden, wenn detailliertere Daten zur geographischen Verteilung der Gebäude in Deutschland zur Verfügung stehen.

Abstract

Finite fossil resources and the negative effects of their consumption on global climate result in a necessity for the exploitation of alternative energy sources like photovoltaics. Large-scale subsidy programs in Europe have led to their ubiquitous installation: On building roofs and facades, as sunscreens, on noise protection walls, free-standing with or without agricultural usage or simply art objects. In this thesis, a methodology for the potential assessment of photovoltaic installations on buildings is developed. This methodology extends the scope of existing photovoltaic potential studies in multiple ways facilitated by two external developments: On the one hand, the increase in computing power has enabled the researcher in this thesis to perform small-scale and medium-scale irradiation simulations on an individual building and urban district level with an hourly resolution as the basis for equally detailed electrical simulations. In this way, reliable conclusions on the influence of shading and reflections from the surroundings on photovoltaic electricity generation can be drawn. Most importantly, for the first time the so far often neglected or roughly estimated potential on building facades has been included in the analysis and due to the detailed simulation methodology, results are sufficiently reliable to provide a basis for large-scale estimates.

On the other hand, photovoltaic installations have experienced an unprecedented price decline since the millennium. As a result, for a profit-oriented investor it can now be economic to install a photovoltaic plant on a roof or facade even without public subsidies. Previous photovoltaic potential studies just focused on the theoretical or technical potential, i.e. establishing the total of available surface areas and the electricity generation potential, since there was no economic potential without public subsidies due to the high investment.

In this thesis, the developed methodology has been applied to the German building stock for which both the necessary statistical as well as 3D geometrical information has been available. As a result, for 2015 a theoretical potential of 37,700 km^2, a location potential of 22,855 TWh, an electricity generation potential of 2923 TWh and an economic potential ranging from 1158 TWh to 2482 TWh has been calculated. Finally, based on prognoses for the population development and technological improvements in the photovoltaic industry, a prognosis for the potential development until 2050 has been derived ranging from 3015 TWh to 4210 TWh generated electricity (3095 GW_p to 4325 GW_pinstalled capacity).
The methodology developed in this thesis based on detailed irradiation simulations and a combination of geographically referenced and statistical data can be easily transferred to other countries where a similar database is available. Results can also be further refined when more detailed geographic information on the actual building stock in Germany exists.

Contents

List of Figures

List of Tables

List of Abbreviations

2D	2-dimensional
3D	3-dimensional
aa	ambient accuracy - Radiance simulation parameter
ab	ambient bounces - Radiance simulation parameter
AB	apartment block
ABC	activity-based costing
AC	alternating current
ad	ambient division - Radiance simulation parameter
ALK	automated cadastral land register
ar	ambient resolution - Radiance simulation parameter
ATKIS	Official Topographic-Cartographic Information System
BBSR	German Federal Institute for Research on Building, Urban Affairs and Spatial Development
BIM	Building Information Modeling
BAPV	building-added photovoltaics
BIPV	building-integrated photovoltaics
BMUB	German Federal Ministry for the Environment, Nature Conservation, Building and Nuclear Safety
BOS	balance-of-system
CHP	combined heat and power
DC	direct current
DEM	digital elevation model
EC	European Commission
EEG	Renewable Energy Law (German: Erneuerbare Energien Gesetz)

EPBD	Energy Performance of Buildings Directive
Fraunhofer ISE	Fraunhofer Institute for Solar Energy Systems ISE
GDP	gross domestic product
GIS	geographic information system
HR	high-rise buildings
HVAC	heating, ventilation and air conditioning
IEA	International Energy Agency
IRR	internal rate of return
IT	information technology
IWU	Institut Wohnen und Umwelt
JRC	Joint Research Centre
LAU	local administrative unit
LCC	life-cycle costing
LCOE	levelized cost of electricity
LiDAR	light-detection and ranging
LOD	level of detail
MFH	multi-family house
MPP	maximum power point
MWT	Metal Wrap-Through
NPV	net present value
NUTS	Nomenclature des Unités territoriales statistiques
nZEB	nearly-zero energy building
OBIA	object-based image analysis
OECD	Organisation for Economic Co-operation and Development
PR	Performance Ratio
SFH	single-family house
ST	settlement type
STC	Standard Test Conditions
SWCT	SmartWire Connection Technology
TH	terraced house
TCO	total cost of ownership

VAT	value-added tax
WEEE	Waste Electrical and Electronic Equipment Directive

Notation

$^\circ$	degree
a	year
A	ampere
A_{fa}	facade area
A_{fp}	building footprint area
A_{ro}	roof area
A_{total}	total building surface area
$A'_{fa,gt500}$	facade area - technical potential receiving more than 500 kWh/(m^2a) solar irradiation
$A'_{ro,gt500}$	roof area - technical potential receiving more than 500 kWh/(m^2a) solar irradiation
$A'_{total,gt500}$	total building surface area - technical potential receiving more than 500 kWh/(m^2a) solar irradiation
AM	Air Mass
C	Celsius
E_{glob}	global irradiation on a horizontal surface
E_{avg}	area-weighted average irradiation on all building surfaces
$E_{avg,u}$	average global irradiation on building surfaces unshaded
El_{avg}	area-weighted average electricity yield
eta	Efficiency
I	electric current
km^2	square kilometre
kWh	kilowatt-hour
MPP	maximum power point
N_{res}	Number of residential units

pd	population density
P_{ec}	Economic potential
$p_{ec,tech}$	share of economically usable building surface area in technical potential
$p_{ec,total}$	share of economically usable building surface area in total surface area
P_{MPP}	module output power at MPP
$P_{tech,el}$	technical electricity generation potential
$P_{tech,loc}$	technical location potential
P_{theo}	theoretical potential
R_p	parallel resistance
R_s	series resistance
s_{gt500}	share of $A_{gt500,total}$ in A_{total}
TWh	terawatt-hour
TR_{fa}	transparency ratio facade
TR_{ro}	transparency ratio roof
TR_{total}	transparency ratio total
V	electric voltage
V	volt

1 Introduction

1.1 Motivation

Finite fossil resources and the negative effects of their consumption on the global climate result in a necessity for the exploitation of alternative energy sources. Photovoltaic systems are one option for renewable energy generation providing an almost emission free source of renewable electricity. Large-scale subsidy programs in Europe have led to ubiquitous installations and a variety of application areas: On building roofs and facades, as sunscreens, on noise protection walls, free-standing with or without agricultural usage or simply art objects, all with high public acceptance.
Due to a massive increase in production capacities for photovoltaic modules fuelled by public subsidy programs (Hoffmann 2008), the price for photovoltaic installations dropped by 66 % between 2006 and 2013 (Bundesverband Solarwirtschaft 2013). By the end of 2016, in Germany a cumulative photovoltaic capacity of 41 GW_p was installed (Bundesnetzagentur 2017) providing 6.9 % of German electricity consumption (Fraunhofer ISE 2017b). According to the roadmap for the expansion of renewable energy production by the German Federal Ministry for the Environment, Nature Conservation, Building and Nuclear Safety (BMUB), by 2020 51.8 GW_p photovoltaic capacity should be installed and 65 GW_p by the year 2050. Consequently, a quarter of today's installed capacity must be added by 2020 and two thirds by 2050 to meet these objectives. But is there actually enough potential in Germany to reach these objectives? The approval of large-scale free-standing installations has been restricted to a limited number of areas not needed for agricultural purposes (EEG 2017) such that further photovoltaic installations must be realized mainly on buildings.

Similarly to fossil fuels, also in the photovoltaic industry advances in technological development and changes in economic conditions have led to resources becoming reserves.[1] Hence, studies on the photovoltaic potential performed 20, 10 or just 5 years ago are no longer valid due to the outdated technological framework and the underlying fragmented database. Assumptions on module efficiency and investment have to be adapted to the present technological and market conditions. Nowadays, an economic potential for photovoltaic installations without public subsidies exists, since the cost of photovoltaic electricity generation is below the cost of conventional electricity generation (Fraunhofer ISE 2017a). This economic potential has not been calculated yet in existing studies which have focused only on the technical potential. Simulation methods for the solar irradiation and electricity generation are now much more accurate in modeling also complex environmental conditions (Sprenger 2013). Furthermore, an increase in computing power makes the large-scale application of these detailed simulation methods possible in a reasonable time frame (Fath et al. 2015). Above all, with increasing amounts of spatial information being supplied by governmental organizations (INSPIRE 2014) and also becoming publicly available (GODI 2014), research possibilities increase tremendously. Coupling spatial information with statistical information by employing a geographic information system (GIS) provides additional insights not only for researchers but also for public authorities, companies and interested individuals. Nowadays, researchers can access a large database on the German building stock and urban structures including geographically referenced data, as well as affordable GIS software solutions.

1.2 Objective and scope

In this thesis, a new methodology for the assessment of the technical and economic potential of photovoltaic installations on buildings will be developed.

[1] Reserves encompass the potential economically exploitable with today's means and technologies while resources have been identified but cannot be economically exploited, yet (BMWi 2016).

By applying the developed methodology to the German building stock, the following research questions shall be answered:

- Which economic potential for photovoltaic installations exists on the German building stock as of 2015?
- How can the economic potential be expected to develop until the year 2050 considering technical and economic progress?

The developed methodology extends the scope of previously conducted potential assessments by explicitly considering the following aspects in detail:

- both residential and non-residential buildings,
- building roof and facade surfaces,
- effects of shading and reflections on the electricity yield,
- the combination of 3-dimensional (3D), statistical and geographically referenced data and
- the actual economic conditions and their expected future development.

In the following chapters the development and application of the methodology is presented. Finally, the research questions will be answered.

1.3 Structure

For the calculation of the potential for photovoltaic installations on buildings in Germany, Chapter 2 presents the definition of the different potentials for photovoltaic energy generation and a literature review of existing photovoltaic potential studies. In Chapter 3, the basic physical principles underlying photovoltaic electricity generation relevant for the simulations performed in this thesis will be explained. Based on this, in Chapter 4 the developed methodology for the technical potential assessment is presented. In Chapter 5, the methodology for the economic potential assessment is presented and different considered economic scenarios are derived. These developed methodologies are applied to individual buildings in Chapter 6 and urban districts in Chapter 7. For the large-scale analysis, i.e. on the national scale, in Chapter 8 a methodology based on statistical and geographically referenced data employing urban data-mining techniques is developed. In Chapter 9 this methodology is applied to the German building stock in 2015. Based on this, a prognosis for the development of the potential for photovoltaic installations in 2050 is derived. The results of this thesis are summarized and critically discussed in Chapter 10.

2 Literature review

In this chapter, a literature review of existing photovoltaic potential studies is presented. For a clear categorization of these existing studies, first in Section 2.1 the term potential in the context of photovoltaic electricity generation as it will be used throughout this thesis is defined. In Section 2.2, a categorization of photovoltaic potential studies with exemplary references is presented. From this, the academic void addressed and the objective of the potential assessment presented in this thesis is derived. In Section 2.3, the results of existing photovoltaic potential studies for Germany are compared.

2.1 Definition of photovoltaic potential

Since multiple definitions of the potential for renewable energy exist in the literature, for this thesis it was decided to follow the definition of Quaschning (2000), which will be explained in detail in the following sections.

2.1.1 Theoretical potential

All available surfaces receiving solar irradiation in a specified region form the theoretical potential. This thesis focuses on building surfaces, i.e. building roofs and facades. Thus, open areas for the installation of free-standing photovoltaic plants are outside the scope of this thesis and will not be considered further.

2.1.2 Technical potential

Based on the theoretical potential, the technical potential can be derived by first considering the amount of solar irradiation convertible into electricity on available surface areas, resulting in the so-called location potential.

Secondly, when also module and system efficiency are taken into account, the electricity generation potential results, i.e. the electricity generated from the solar irradiation on available surface areas.
Since also 3D models of buildings and urban districts have been used for the location potential assessment performed in this thesis, it is crucial to declare the considered level of detail (LOD) since it strongly influences available surface areas for photovoltaic installations. The LOD in 3D building and city modeling is defined as follows (Biljecki 2013):

1. LOD1 - Buildings modeled as simple blocks without roof shapes; Based on building footprints, i.e. the 2-dimensional (2D) outline of the building ground floor plan, such building models can be automatically created by defining a building height.
2. LOD2 - Buildings with standard roof shapes.
3. LOD3 - Buildings with complicated facades and roof shapes, i.e. including windows, dormers, chimneys, balconies and alcoves.
4. LOD4 - Additionally the interior design of the building is modeled

With increasing LOD, the location potential can be expected to decrease. In the following simulations, all considered buildings were modeled in LOD2. Surrounding buildings not assessed in detail were modeled in LOD1.

2.1.3 Economic potential

The economic potential contains the share of technical potential currently economically exploitable from a building owner's point of view, i.e. considering actual system prices, electricity tariffs and the expected system lifetime. In this thesis, the building owner is considered to be identical with the investor in the photovoltaic plant and the consumer of the generated electricity even though in practice differing business models exist. However, then in the economic potential assessment additional factors like taxes, required profit margins and refurbishment cycles would have to be considered which would considerably increase the uncertainty of results.

This distinction between the theoretical, technical and economic potential is similar to other studies assessing photovoltaic potentials (Wittmann et al. (1997); Quaschning (2000); Hoogwijk (2004); Wouters (2007); Izquierdo et al. (2008); Bergamasco and Asinari (2011); Hossain Mondal and Islam (2011)).

2.2 Categorization and review of solar potential assessments

Since the development of photovoltaic systems, different methodologies have been used for the assessment of the potential for the large-scale implementation of this technology. With increasing computing power, the amount of data which can be processed and the spatial resolution of results has continuously increased. However, a validation of results is seldom feasible.

A comprehensive review of potential assessments is provided by Schallenberg Rodríguez (2013). A review of methodologies employed in solar potential map creation and a technical comparison of them can be found in Ibarra and Reinhart (2011) for six irradiation distribution methods and Jakubiec and Reinhart (2013) for four irradiation distribution methods and a Radiance-based methodology which has also been employed in this thesis.

In the following sections, photovoltaic potential asessments were categorized by the author according to different criteria, extending the general ones used by Hoogwijk (2004), Schallenberg Rodríguez (2013) and Sliz-Szkliniarz (2013) in Section 2.2.1 by methodological (Section 2.2.2) and technical (Section 2.2.3) categories. These categories as well as the defined sub-categories are depicted in the morphological box in Fig. 2.1. These criteria are explained in more detail in the following sections with some references as examples. It should be noted, that these criteria are not fully independent of each other but the author considered them to reflect the main characteristics of photovoltaic potential assessments and therefore suitable for forming a framework to structure the researched literature.

Table 2.1: Morphological box for the categorization of photovoltaic potential studies

Level 1	Level 2	Level 3	Level 4	Level 5
General categorization	Potential considered	Theoretical potential	Open-areas	
			Infrastructure	
			Buildings	Residential
				Non-residential
			Building surfaces	Roof
				Facade
		Location potential	Spatial resolution	
			Temporal resolution	Yearly
				Monthly
				Daily
				Hourly
		Electricity generation potential	Linear approach based on module and system efficiency	
			Also accounting for temperature effects	
			Considering changes in efficiency due to low-level irradiation	
		Economic potential	Levelized cost of electricity (LCOE)	
			Net Present Value (NPV)	
	Geographic area covered	International		
		National		
		Regional		
		Local		
	Spatial resolution of results	National		
		Regional		
		Local		
		Individual building		
Categorization of employed methodology	Statistical methods			
	Bottom-up approaches	Photogrammetric methods		
		LiDAR methods		
		3D city models		
	Hybrid approaches			
Technical categori-zation	Open-source			
	Commercial			

2.2.1 General categorization

Solar potential assessments can be categorized according to general criteria like

- the potential considered[1],
- the geographic area covered and
- the spatial resolution of results.

2.2.1.1 Photovoltaic potential considered

According to the potential definition from Section 2.1, the possibility to derive an actually installable capacity from the photovoltaic potential study increases from the theoretical to the technical and economic potential since an increasing number of variables is considered. However, these variables also increase the uncertainty and expiry of validity of results since they are, except for the location potential[2], subject to structural (i.e. change in available surfaces affecting the theoretical potential), technological (i.e. developments in module and system efficiency affecting the electricity generation potential) and economic (i.e. changes in the investment for a photovoltaic installation and in the electricity tariff affecting the economic potential) developments.

Theoretical potential

The theoretical potential forms the basis for all photovoltaic potential assessments. Therefore it is always explicitly or implicitly defined by stating the surface areas considered suitable according to the scope of the study. Suitable surface areas can be open land for the installation of large free-standing photovoltaic systems (Ruiz-Arias et al. 2012) and/or building surfaces. When building surfaces are considered, studies can be further differentiated according

[1] The categorization of publications was made by the author of this thesis according to the potential definition presented in Section 2.1. Therefore the potential definition in the respective study can deviate from the categorization presented here.

[2] The change in solar irradiation incident on the earth's surface due to global dimming and brightening (Müller et al. 2014) is not considered relevant for the time horizon of this thesis.

to considered building type (residential (Mainzer & Fath et al. 2014), non-residential or both (Kaltschmitt and Wiese 1993b)) and considered building surfaces (building roofs (Hofierka and Kanuk 2009), building facades (Jochem et al. 2011) or both (Enquête-Kommission (2002); Compagnon (2004); Wouters (2007); Redweik et al. (2013); Catita et al. (2014)). In Quaschning (2000), open areas, residential and non-residential buildings and all building surfaces (i.e. roofs and facades) were considered.

Technical potential: Location potential

For the location potential assessment, usually long-term (10 or 20 years) average data from actual measurements for the solar irradiation are used since solar irradiation in one location in a specific year varies with weather conditions. For locations where no measured data is available, irradiation data from the nearest measurement station is interpolated. The location potential can be further differentiated according to the temporal resolution.

Suri et al. (2007) have developed the Photovoltaic Geographic Information System (PVGIS), a European solar irradiation database providing monthly average irradiation data. For Germany, an average annual specific location potential of 780 kWh/kW$_p$, 900 kWh/kW$_p$ and 600 kWh/kW$_p$ results for horizontal, optimally tilted and vertical surfaces (averaged over all compass directions for the surface orientation) respectively.

According to Quaschning (2000), the total annual location potential of solar energy on the territory of Germany (open areas and building surfaces) amounts to 380 PWh (or $3.8 * 10^{15}$ Wh) based on average solar irradiation measurements from 80 meteorological stations throughout Germany.

Technical potential: Electricity generation potential

For the assessment of the electricity generation potential, the solar irradiation on a surface (i.e. the location potential) has to be converted into the electricity generated by the photovoltaic system assuming typical module and system efficiencies. For this conversion, simple linear approaches based on an average efficiency (Quaschning (2000); Theodoridou et al. (2012); Hoogwijk (2004); Mainzer & Fath et al. (2014); Fath et al. (2015)) and also considering temperature effects (Schallenberg Rodríguez 2013) can be employed. Based on highly resolved irradiation data recorded over short periods, changes in system efficiency due to low-level irradiation can also be considered (Jakubiec and Reinhart 2013).

Economic potential

The economic potential is strongly dependent on the date of completion of the study, since here actual photovoltaic system prices, electricity tariffs and possibly public subsidies are taken into account. Since in the past, photovoltaic installations were not economically viable due to high module prices, earlier studies did not consider the economic potential. Due to the introduction of the German Renewable Energy Law(German: Erneuerbare Energien Gesetz) (EEG) (Hoffmann 2008) and a consequent widespread application of this technology, resulting in a massive increase of industrial production capacity in Germany and abroad, particularly China, photovoltaic plant prices have dropped (66 % from 2006 to 2013 (Bundesverband Solarwirtschaft 2013)) to such a level, that now actually an economic potential for photovoltaic installations exists.
The economic potential can be expressed in terms of levelized cost of electricity (LCOE) (Schallenberg Rodríguez 2013) or NPV (Jakubiec and Reinhart (2013); Fath et al. (2015)) of the photovoltaic installation. Considering the LCOE, assuming 100 % self-consumption of the generated electricity, photovoltaic installations with LCOE below the electricity tariff(s)[3] constitute the economic potential. Considering the NPV, photovoltaic installations with a NPV greater than zero form the economic potential from an investor-owner perspective, with

[3] In Germany, private/residential electricity tariffs were 0.25 €/kWh for private households at the beginning of 2012, while commercial enterprises had average electricity tariffs of 0.15 €/kWh in 2013 (BMWi 2013). By the end of 2016, the private/residential electricity tariff rose to 0.33 €/kWh while the commercial electricity tariff remained unchanged (BMWi 2017).

the expected profit being expressed in the choice of the interest rate. Based on finely time-resolved electricity generation and consumption data, also the possible share of self-consumption of the generated electricity can be calculated. With decreasing public subsidies, this information is relevant for an economic layout of the photovoltaic plant, possibly in combination with an energy storage system (Mainzer & Fath et al. 2014).

2.2.1.2 Geographic area covered

Depending on the objective and the employed methodology[4] of the potential assessment, different geographic areas can be investigated.

International

International photovoltaic potential assessments are solely based on readily available statistical data and are mainly targeted at providing the basis for a general comparison between countries. The International Energy Agency (IEA) conducted a potential study for 14 countries based on an average residential area per citizen (IEA PVPS Task 7-4 2002). Hoogwijk (2004) conducted a potential study for renewable energy in OECD countries and based the estimate of the photovoltaic potential on the population density and a country's GDP. Scholz (2012) assessed the potential for renewable energy in European and five North African countries.

National

National photovoltaic potential studies for Germany are also based on statistical data since no complete database for the German building stock exists. However, since at the time of completion of these studies, reliable statistical data were available only for the residential building stock, the potential of non-residential buildings had to be either estimated (Quaschning (2000); Carr and Schmid (2013)) or has been omitted (Mainzer & Fath et al. 2014).

[4] For a categorization of photovoltaic potential assessment methodologies see Section 2.2.2.

Regional

Regional potential assessments are defined here as considering more than one administrative district on a NUTS 2 level (Statistisches Bundesamt 2014a). For the State of Baden-Württemberg in Germany, Räuber et al. (1987) and Kaltschmitt and Wiese (1993b) have performed a regional potential study based on available statistical data for the number of buildings. Gernhardt et al. (1992) performed a similar analysis for the German State of North Rhine-Westphalia. Since 2012, an atlas of the potential for solar energy, based on building roof geometry data captured with light-detection and ranging (LiDAR) technology, and other renewable energy sources has been available online for the whole State of Baden-Württemberg (LUBW 2014).

Local

In local potential assessments, often more detailed information can be employed for an assessment at the individual building level. Wittmann et al. (1997) assessed the photovoltaic potential of a district in the city of Vienna based on orthophotos. Jakubiec and Reinhart (2013) analyzed roof tops in the city of Cambridge, Massachusetts, USA based on LiDAR data. Strzalka et al. (2012) employed a 3D city model generated also from LiDAR data in the assessment of the urban district of Scharnhauser Park in the community of Ostfildern, Germany. With more than 120 German cities offering solar roof cadastres to interested citizens in 2015 (EnBauSa GmbH 2014). and automatic procedures for their creation (SUN-AREA 2017), local solar potential assessments for building roofs are now widespread.

2.2.1.3 Spatial resolution of results

The spatial resolution of results is closely interconnected with the employed methodology and the geographic area covered. Whereas using general national data results only in results aggregated at the national level (IEA PVPS Task 7-4 (2002); Hoogwijk (2004)), Kaltschmitt and Wiese (1993b) actually publish also regional results in their national potential study, while Mainzer & Fath et al. (2014) provide a national study with a resolution on local administrative unit (LAU)[5] 2, i.e. 11,593 municipalities in Germany (German: Gemeinde). From solar cadastres and potential assessments based on 3D city models (Strzalka et al. 2012), even the suitability of individual buildings can be derived.

2.2.2 Methodological categorization

The methodology employed in the photovoltaic potential assessment is highly dependent on available data sources and the geographic scope of the study. In the following sections, different technical methods for solar potential assessments with exemplary references will be presented. Generally, methodologies can be categorized into statistical methods employing available statistical data as a proxy for the photovoltaic potential and bottom-up approaches calculating the potential as an aggregate of individual building assessments.

2.2.2.1 Statistical methods

The assessment of a photovoltaic potential based on readily available statistical data can be seen as a transparent and easily reproducible methodology. It can be applied in assessments with a large variety of geographic scopes, from district to regional (Kaltschmitt and Wiese 1992), national (Lehmann and Peter (2003); Quaschning (2000)) and even international (IEA PVPS Task 7-4 (2002); Hoogwijk (2004)) level. Statistical data used include e.g. the number of residential buildings, the population density and the gross domestic product (GDP). However, from these highly aggregated results, no recommendations for the installation of a specific photovoltaic plant can be derived. Instead, they can be useful for policy recommendations.

[5] The LAU 2 level corresponds to the former NUTS 5 level (Statistisches Bundesamt 2014a). Due to changes in administrative units, the number of considered municipalities depends on the time of study completion.

2.2.2.2 Bottom-up approaches

Bottom-up solar potential assessments are based on the analysis of individual building surfaces (mainly only roofs) to arrive at a total potential of a specified area. Due to the time-consuming efforts for data capturing and processing, these studies have been limited so far to a regional scope.

Photogrammetric methods

In the following, studies based on photogrammetry, both from aerial and satellite images, are presented. Wittmann et al. (1997) have assessed the photovoltaic potential of a district in the city of Vienna, Austria, by means of aerial stereophotogrammetric images. Employing this technique, a 3D model is formed from conventional photographs taken from different viewing angles enriched with information concerning the geographic position.
Also based on stereophotogrammetric methods is the use of ortho-images, i.e. uniformly scaled, non-distortioning aerial images. Such images of the earth's surface are created from stereophotogrammetric images and serve e.g. as the foundation for maps. Bergamasco and Asinari (2011) have assessed the photovoltaic potential of Turin, Italy, using in addition to geographically referenced building footprints an ortho-image of the area assuming darker roof surfaces on the ortho-image to be more affected by shading during the day.
Jo and Otanicar (2011) performed a photovoltaic potential analysis for Chandler, Arizona, using satellite-captured images for the recognition of roof obstructions.

Methods based on Light-detection and ranging (LiDAR) technology

In contrast to photogrammetric methods, laser-scanning data from LiDAR technology is available as point clouds where every point represents an exact position and orientation. Brito et al. (2012) have assessed the photovoltaic potential of a Lisbon suburb using LiDAR data employing the Solar Analyst tool of the ArcGIS software package.

Jakubiec and Reinhart (2013) applied a ray-tracing algorithm to building rooftops constructed from LiDAR data in the city of Cambridge, Massachusetts, USA. The methods described above were based on aerially collected data which so far allowed an assessment only of roof areas. Jochem et al. (2011) developed a methodology for acquiring data by Mobile Laser Scanning, i.e. a laser scanner mounted on a car so that especially the potential on facades can be assessed. However, due to the large amounts of data to be processed, this methodology has only been used in the assessment of one street to date.

3D city models

Resulting from a trend to construct 3D city models for various urban planning and marketing purposes, now an increasing number of solar potential studies is based on these models. Strictly speaking, these 3D city models were also originally built mainly from laser-scanning data. However, here they are listed as a new category since usually in addition to the roof areas also facade areas are available from these models (Redweik et al. (2013); Catita et al. (2014)). Additionally, the detailed knowledge of surrounding buildings and shading conditions allows a very reliable potential assessment (Strzalka et al. (2012); Karteris et al. (2013)).

2.2.2.3 Hybrid approaches

Some authors also pursue hybrid approaches. This means that first a detailed bottom-up analysis on the individual building level is performed. Then, in the next step, the detailed results are up-scaled to a national level often employing a GIS. Wouters (2007) assessed the solar potential differentiated according to urban fabric structures in cities. A building typology was used by Izquierdo et al. (2008) in the assessment of the solar potential of Spain by deriving a representative building typology from statistical, cadastral and CORINE Land Cover data. Hofierka and Kanuk (2009) employed urban zones for the calculation of a national potential based on the potential assessment for the city of Bardejov in Slovakia. Lödl et al. (2010) also used a building typology in the up-scaling of detailed results for one German State to the national level. Scholz (2012) employed the ratio between building area and sealed surfaces in different countries for her international renewable energy potential analysis and optimization model. Karteris et al. (2013) have up-scaled their results with a linear regression model. Hachem et al. (2011) have investigated different neighbourhood designs concerning the effect of building density, orientation and layout on solar energy utilization potential.

2.2.3 Technical categorization

A technical categorization according to the solar irradiation simulation software employed is only applicable for potential assessments based on a bottom-up or hybrid methodology. A detailed review of 28 solar irradiation simulation software programs can be found in Freitas et al. (2015). In the following, only programs employed in large-scale solar potential studies (i.e. urban district or larger) are mentioned. They can be broadly categorized into open-source and commercial applications.

2.2.3.1 Open-source solar irradiation simulation software

The open-source Radiance lighting simulation software was originally developed for architects and designers at Lawrence Berkeley National Laboratory (Ward Larson and Shakespeare 1998). Since it will also be used in this thesis, it is explained in detail in Section 4.1.2. It was already used by Compagnon (2004) for the evaluation of the solar potential of building facade surfaces. It was also used by Hii Jun Chung et al. (2011) in the solar potential assessment of facade surfaces in tropical areas. Jakubiec and Reinhart (2013) have employed Radiance in the solar potential assessment of building roofs in the city of Cambridge in Massachusetts, USA.
Another open-source program is r.sun which was developed by Hofierka and Šúri (2002) and implemented in the open-source software GRASS GIS. r.sun

was used in a solar potential study on building roofs in Bardejov, Slovakia (Hofierka and Kanuk 2009) and for 14 counties in Southeastern Ontario, Canada (Nguyen and Pearce 2010).

The building energy simulation tool EnergyPlus also offers solar irradiation analysis capabilities. Hachem et al. (2011) employed this software in a generic study on solar neighbourhood design.

2.2.3.2 Commercial solar irradiation simulation software

Also commercial GIS software packages provide solar analysis tools. ESRI's ArcGIS Solar Analyst enables users to perform area irradiation and point irradiation simulations on digital surface models (Fu and Rich 1999). The Solar Analyst was employed in conjunction with TRNSYS by Choi et al. (2011) in the analysis of building roofs of the Pennsylvania State University, USA. The freely available program SketchUp also offers solar altitude and shading analysis capabilities (Karteris et al. 2013).

2.2.4 Summary of solar potential assessments' review

An overview of potential studies classified according to the general and methodological criteria is given in Tab. 2.2 and 2.3. For readability reasons, not all have been explicitly mentioned in the explanation of classification categories.

Table 2.2: First part of literature review of solar potential assessments

Authors	Potential considered	Employed methodology	Data sources used	Geographic area covered	Spatial resolution of results	Simulation programs used	Surfaces considered
Aran Carrion et al. 2008	Technical potential for free-standing plants around cities	GIS and PVGIS platform	Map of cities in Andalusia	Andalusia, Spain	Areas	GIS	-
Bergamasco and Asinari 2011	Technical	GIS	Ortho-images	Turin	Individual roofs	Calculated	Roofs
Carr and Schmid 2013	Technical potential	GIS and statistical	GIS, 3D models and statistical data	Germany	Buildings	Roofs	
Catita et al. 2014	Technical potential; Only irradiation, no electricity yield	GIS and SOL-method; LiDAR data	LiDAR data	Test region of campus in Lisbon	Individual roofs and facades	Roof and facade surfaces	
Cheng-Dar and Wang 2006	Technical potential; Economic potential mentioned but not yet economically viable	GIS	Maps of built areas	Rural area of Chigu in SW-Taiwan	Areas	GIS	-
Choi et al. 2011	Technical	GIS system used for solar radiation assessment on DSM	DEM, building footprints	Pollock Commons area at the Pennsylvania State University	building	Solar Radiation tool in ArcGIS and coupled with TRNSYS called PV Analyst	Roof surfaces
Compagnon 2004	Technical	Raytracing	3D models	City	Building	radiance	Roofs and facades
Enquête-Kommission 2002	Technical	Statistical	Statistical	Germany	National	Calculation	Roofs and facades
Fath et al. 2015	Technical	raytracing	3D city model	Urban district	Building surfaces	radiance	roofs and facades
Gernhardt et al. 1992	Technical	Statistical	Statistical	North Rhine-Westphalia	Municipalities	Calculation	roofs and facades
Hofierka and Kanuk 2009	Technical	Shading analysis with r.sun in GRASS GIS, Solar radiation from PVGIS	Aerial images and laser-scanning data	City and up-scaling to national level	Roofs	GIS system	Roof surfaces
Hoogwijk 2004	Economic	GIS	Geographically referenced irradiation and land use data	Global	National	GIS	Roofs, open areas
Hossain Mondal and Islam 2011	Economic	GIS	Geographically referenced irradiation and land use data	Bangladesh	National	GIS	Roofs, open areas
IEA PVPS Task 7-4 2002	Technical	Statistical	Statistical population data	Selected countries	National level	Calculated	Roof and facade surfaces
Izquierdo et al. 2008	Technical	Statistical	GIS and statistical data	Spain	Municipality	GIS and calculation program	Roof surfaces
Jakubiec and Reinhart 2013	Technical with some economic	GIS and ray-tracing	LiDAR data	City	Individual roofs	RADIANCE/-DAYSIM	Roof surfaces
Jo and Otanicar 2011	Technical	GIS	GIS and statistical	Building	Individual roofs	GIS	Roofs
Jochem et al. 2011	Technical	Calculation	LiDAR data	Building	Individual facades	Calculation	Facade surfaces
Kaltschmitt and Wiese 1993a	Economic	Statistical	Statistical	Germany	State	Calculation	Roofs and open areas

Table 2.3: Second part of literature review of solar potential assessments

Authors	Potential considered	Employed methodology	Data sources used	Geographic area covered	Spatial resolution of results	Simulation programs used	Surfaces considered
Karteris et al. 2013	Technical with some economic (consideration of feed-in tariff)	Shading analysis in Google SketchUp, then statistical up-scaling of results	Aerial images	City and up-scaling to national level	Individual roofs	GIS system and Google SketchUp	Roof surfaces on multi-family buildings
Lehmann and Peter 2003	Technical	Statistical	Statistical population data	Europe	National level	Calculated	Roof and facade surfaces
Lödl et al. 2010	Technical	GIS and statistical	GIS and statistical	Germany	State	GIS and statistical	Roofs
Mainzer & Fath et al. 2014	Technical	GIS and statistical data	GIS	Germany	Municipality	GIS and calculation	Roof surfaces
Nguyen and Pearce 2010	Technical	GIS	GIS maps and statistical data	Region in Ontario	1 km^2	r.sun in GRASS GIS	Free-standing plants
Ordonez et al. 2010	Technical	Statistical data combined with shading factors	Aerial images from Google Maps, Shading simulation with AutoCAD, statistical information on the buildings	Andalusia (Spain)	-	AutoCAD	Roof surfaces
Quaschning 2000	Technical	Statistical	Statistical	Germany	National	Calculation program	Roofs, facades, open areas
Ramachandra and Shruthi 2007	Theoretical, i.e. solar radiation on available surfaces	GIS	Measured solar radiation data	Federal state in India	-	GIS	-
Räuber et al. 1987	Technical	Statistical	Statistical	Baden-Württemberg	Municipalities	Statistical	Roofs, facades
Redweik et al. 2013	Technical	Shadow algorithm	3D model	Campus of the University of Lisbon	Building		Roofs, facades
Ruiz-Arias et al. 2012	Technical potential	GIS and European Solar Radiation Atlas	Topographic maps, calculated solar radiation data	Region in southern Spain	Areas	GIS	Open areas
Schallenberg Rodríguez 2013	Economic	GIS	GIS	Canary Islands	Municipality	GIS	Roofs
Scholz 2012	Technical	GIS	GIS and statistical	Europe and Northern Africa	Country	GIS	Roofs, facades and open areas
Sliz-Szkliniarz 2013	Economic	GIS	GIS and statistical	Exemplary regions in Germany and Poland	Region	GIS	Roofs and open areas
Strzalka et al. 2012	Technical	GIS	3D city model	Urban district in Germany	Buildings	GIS	Roofs
Suri et al. 2007	Technical	GIS	Corine Land Coverage data	Europe	National level	Calculated	Roof surfaces
Theodoridou et al. 2012	Technical with adaptations for economic	Photogrammetric and statistical	GIS maps and aerial images	City	Individual roofs	GIS system and PVGIS	Roof surfaces (facade surfaces only in future studies)
Wittmann et al. 1997	Technical	GIS	Photogrammetric data	8th district of Vienna	Individual roofs	CAD program	Roof surfaces
Wouters 2007	Technical	GIS	Geographically referenced data	National	Individual roofs and facades for 20 selected urban districts	GIS	Roofs and facades

2.3 Comparison of solar potential assessments for Germany

After the general review of photovoltaic potential studies, available photovoltaic potential studies for Germany are now presented in detail in this section. Here, the focus is on the different methodologies employed so that a comparison with the methodology developed for this thesis is possible. Since the electricity generation potential is either reported as installed capacity or as generated electricity, for easier comparison of studies in the following both quantities are specified, assuming an average installed capacity of 0.15 kW_p/m^2 (based on a standard 1.7 m^2 crystalline module with an installed capacity of 260 W_p) and an electricity production of 950 kWh/kW_p (Suri et al. 2007). The calculated quantity is indicated by parentheses. An overview of the photovoltaic potential identified in these studies is depicted in Tab. 2.4 and 2.3.

To the author's knowledge, the first German national potential study was conducted by Kaltschmitt and Wiese (1993b). They considered building roof surfaces of residential and non-residential building types based on the average number of apartments in buildings and average apartment floor areas. Average roof tilt angles were calculated based on aerial photographs of more than 500 buildings (Kaltschmitt and Wiese 1992) that were recorded within the framework of the 1000 roof program, an early subvention program for photovoltaic installations which was subsequently extended to become the 100,000 roof program and was eventually replaced by the Renewable Energy law (German: EEG) (Hoffmann 2008). According to these authors, the location potential for solar use on roofs in Germany amounts to approximately 802 km^2 (125 GW_p, 119 TWh/a), with 384 km^2 (60 GW_p, 57 TWh/a) on residential buildings and 418 km^2 (65 GW_p, 62 TWh/a) on non-residential buildings.

Also in the IKARUS project, a potential for photovoltaics was calculated, resulting in an electricity generation potential of 90 GW_p (576 km^2, 86 TWh/a) in 1997 on building roofs. For 2020, this potential is forecasted to increase up to 150 GW_p (960 km^2), equaling 140 TWh/a (Hoffmann et al. 1997).

Quaschning (2000) updated the study by Kaltschmitt and Wiese (1993b) and additionally considered technical obstacles on roofs. Unlike Kaltschmitt and Wiese, Quaschning assumes two quality classes for roofs depending on their deviation from a southern azimuth. Additionally, Quaschning takes the solar potential on facades into account, starting from the building floor area and assuming an average building height. This area is reduced by technical obstacles, shading and regulatory restrictions so that eventually 3 % of the facade area is considered suitable for photovoltaic use. The result is a location and electricity generation potential on roofs of 864 km^2 with 834 TWh/a (878 GW_p) and on facades of 200 km^2 with 153 TWh/a (161 GW_p).
In IEA PVPS Task 7-4 (2002) the photovoltaic potential for 14 countries was calculated based on average available building surface areas (roof and facade) per capita, the population and a utilization factor. For Germany this results into a location potential of 1296 km^2 on building roofs and 486 km^2 on building facades. The electricity generation potential amounts to 159 TWh/a (167 GW_p).
Lehmann and Peter (2003) employed the correlation between the population density and the photovoltaic potential based on the regional potential study by Gernhardt et al. (1992) in their national potential study. They calculated a location potential of 985 km^2 (154 GW_p, 146 TWh/a) on roof and 531 km^2 (83 GW_p, 79 TWh/a) on facade areas in Germany.
More recently, Lütter et al. (2009) calculated the theoretical potential based on the different housing categories, the population density affecting the shading conditions and the number of enterprises. In total, an electricity generation potential of 106 GW_p (675 km^2, 100 TWh/a) results not considering facades or installations in open areas.
Held (2010) did not make new assumptions concerning available surfaces but applied the methodology by IEA PVPS Task 7-4 (2002) with updated population figures. Due to competing usage of surfaces of photovoltaic and solar thermal applications, she divided the theoretical potential in half resulting in a location potential of 648 km^2 (101 GW_p, 96 TWh/a). In contrast to that, Lödl et al. (2010) based his national potential study on a detailed evaluation of the solar

potential of Bavarian houses employing a GIS to digitized cadastral maps. Then he up-scaled the found potential to all of Germany employing statistical data. The main criticism of this method is that the Bavarian building stock cannot be considered representative for all of Germany. From this study a potential of 161 GW_p (153 TWh/a) on building roofs was estimated.

Defaix et al. (2012) estimated the location potential for BIPV installations for all EU-27 countries based on the residential floor area per capita, the total population per country, an average floor number and an average facade area. Using irradiation data by the Joint Research Centre (JRC) (Suri et al. 2007) for each country, the generated electricity is calculated. For Germany, a location potential of 600 km^2 roof and 450 km^2 facade area with an electricity generation potential of 110 TWh/a (116 GW_p) and 40 TWh/a (42 GW_p) respectively results.

Mainzer & Fath et al. (2014) calculated an electricity generation potential of 148 TWh/a with an installable capacity of 208 GW_p (1331 km^2) on roof surfaces of residential buildings taken from statistical data combined with geographically referenced irradiation data.

The results of the photovoltaic potential studies for Germany are summarized in Tab. 2.4. All these publications are (partly) based on statistical data of the German building stock. Differences in the location potential result from different assumptions concerning the number, size and roof area of buildings. Variations in the electricity generation potential are often due to different assumptions regarding the suitability of roof surfaces for photovoltaic applications, i.e. the roof tilt and azimuth angle distribution.

From this comparison, the large spread in the calculated potentials is apparent ranging from a minimum of 90 GW_p when just considering roof surfaces (Hoffmann et al. 1997) to a maximum of more than six times this potential of 569 GW_p calculated by Braun et al. (2012) who considered all building surfaces and open areas in Germany. Therefore a comparison is always only meaningful when additional information on the surfaces considered is provided.

Table 2.4: Comparison of photovoltaic potential studies for Germany [6]

Study	**Location potential** $[km^2]$	**Electricity generation potential** $[GW_p]$	$[TWh/a]$
Kaltschmitt and Wiese (1993b)	802	(125)	(119)
Hoffmann et al. (1997) (Potential in 1997)	(576)	90	(86)
Hoffmann et al. (1997) (Potential in 2020)	(960)	150	140
Nitsch and Fischedick (1999)	838	(131)	(124)
Quaschning (2000)	1064	(1039)	987
Enquête-Kommission (2002)	1095	(171)	164
IEA PVPS Task 7-4 (2002)	1782	(203)	128
Lehmann and Peter (2003)	1516	(237)	(225)
Wouters (2007)	1760	(275)	(261)
Lütter et al. (2009)	(675)	106	(100)
Held (2010)	648	(101)	(96)
Lödl et al. (2010)	(1030)	161	(153)
Braun et al. (2012)	3642	569	(541)
Defaix et al. (2012)	1050	(158)	150
Carr and Schmid (2013)	(1280)	200	(190)
Mainzer & Fath et al. (2014)	(1331)	208	148
Minimum	(576)	90	(86)
Maximum	3642	569	(541)

2.4 Summary and discussion

To summarize the literature review, no large-scale study based on detailed irradiation simulations is available at present, neither for Germany nor for

6 Values in squared brackets were derived from the published values assuming an average installed capacity of 0.15 kW_p/m^2 and an electricity production of 950 kWh/kW_p.

any other country. Instead, large-scale studies are mainly based on statistical data concerning the building stock, which in Germany is associated with high uncertainty due to incomplete and old data, as will be explained in more detail in Section 6. Additionally, studies based on statistical data have either neglected or just roughly estimated the potential for photovoltaic installations on building facades due to even more difficult data procurement than for roofs. Also, in general the focus of existing potential studies was on the correct simulation of the location potential without detailed electricity yield simulations.[7] Last but not least, since there was no economic potential for photovoltaic installations, most studies just calculated a technical potential which some authors have already identified as a weakness of existing studies (Nguyen and Pearce (2010); Choi et al. (2011)). However, due to the dramatic module price decrease in the past now an economic potential can be calculated.

In order to remedy the weaknesses of existing studies, for this thesis a hybrid approach based on 3D building data, statistical and geographically referenced information has been developed. For the irradiation simulation, the open-source program Radiance was used, which in a comprehensive comparison of solar simulation methodologies by Freitas et al. (2015) was considered to be among the best software tools for considering inter-reflections and multiple reflections. Since Radiance is freely available, the developed methodology can be easily applied to other geographic areas. For the electricity generation simulation, a special program developed at Fraunhofer ISE was employed (see Section 4.2) since according to Freitas et al. (2015) "it is essential to provide and account for ambient temperature and/or module temperature when estimating PV production." In this way, a realistic estimate of generated electricity, especially relevant for extreme shading and temperature conditions as can be expected for photovoltaic installations mounted on building facades, can be calculated also accounting for the evolution of system efficiency from 9 % in 1992 (Kaltschmitt and Wiese 1992) to an assumed industrial average of 13 % in 2015 (Mayer et al.

[7] Choi et al. 2011 was one of the few authors conducting detailed electrical simulations by employing the TRNSYS 4 and 5-parameter PV array performance model.

2015). The increase in computing power allows an application of these detailed simulations at a small and medium-scale level, i.e. on an individual building and at an urban district level. Additionally, the investment for a photovoltaic plant has dramatically decreased (Bundesverband Solarwirtschaft 2013) making their installation profitable also in non-optimally irradiated locations like shaded areas and building facades. On top of that the cut in feed-in tariffs for the generated electricity leads to an increased profitability in the case of self-consumption in comparison to feeding into the electricity grid. As a result, investors now seek a better match of the supply and the demand curve instead of maximum electricity generation which also favors the installation of east or west-oriented and facade-mounted photovoltaic modules.

Based on statistical and geographically referenced data, urban data mining techniques and a GIS are employed both to identify similarities in building stock between municipalities and to transfer results to municipalities. Considering both present and future technical and market conditions, one prognosis for the state-of-the art and another prognosis of the economic potential for photovoltaic installations on all building surfaces in Germany result.

3 Photovoltaic electricity generation on buildings

In this chapter, an overview of the fundamental principles of photovoltaic electricity generation relevant for the simulations performed in this thesis is given. For this, first some general terminology used in this thesis and often used interchangeably shall be defined according to Muneer et al. (2004):

- *Solar radiation*: Qualitative term for energy emanating from the sun
- *Irradiation*: Cumulative energy incident on a surface $[Wh/m^2]$
- *Irradiance*: Instantaneous power incident on a surface $[W/m^2]$

3.1 The photovoltaic effect

Photovoltaic electricity generation denotes the direct conversion of solar energy into electricity (Kaltschmitt 2007). The extra-terrestrial solar irradiance is denoted by the solar constant E:

$$E = 1367 \frac{W}{m^2} \tag{3.1}$$

On its way through the earth's atmosphere, the solar radiation is influenced by reflections, absorption and scattering effects depending on the length of the path denoted by the Air Mass (*AM*) resulting in an attenuation of the radiation and a change in the spectrum. $AM = 1$ denotes vertical path for the radiation through the atmosphere, i.e. the shortest possible route. In the Standard Test Conditions (STC) for a photovoltaic module, irradiation with a spectrum according to $AM = 1.5$ is used (Wagner 2010).

The irradiation incident on a surface on earth consists of a *direct* and a *diffuse* component amounting together to the *total* irradiation which is also called *global* irradiation (Sprenger 2013). The share of direct and diffuse irradiation to the total irradiation is important for the photovoltaic electricity yield calculation. The photovoltaic effect causing the electricity generation in a photovoltaic module is based on the photo effect, i.e. the "energy transfer from photons to electrons contained inside material" (Kaltschmitt 2007). Depending on the type of material, this energy transfer from the photon is sufficient to raise the electron to a higher energy level, i.e. from the so-called valence band to the conduction band, resulting in the creation of an electron-hole pair. This is the case for semiconductors and makes the material electrically conductive (Quaschning 2011). By the addition of atoms which readily donate or accept electrons in the semi-conductor material, so-called doping, an electrical field between the layers is created. Therefore, when irradiation impinges on the doped material, the generated electron-hole pairs are separated by the electric field. Now, when the layers are electrically connected, an electric current flows (Kaltschmitt 2007). In general, all semi-conductive materials from group IV in the periodic table possess the characteristics described above (Quaschning 2011). However, in the following, due to their widespread application, only photovoltaic cells and modules based on crystalline silicon will be considered further.

3.2 Photovoltaic electricity generation

A photovoltaic system consists of multiple parts, of which the photovoltaic modules are the most evident. Nevertheless, for the efficient functioning of the modules and the grid connection, an inverter is another indispensable device. Additionally, the individual parts have to be interconnected by cables and the modules have to be securely mounted on a sub-structure (Quaschning 2011). These components of a photovoltaic system will be presented in more detail in the following sections. The cabling as well as further metering equipment is generally summarized as balance-of-system (BOS) and considered as a flat addition to the investment for the photovoltaic system components. Therefore they are omitted from the following detailed description.

3.2.1 Photovoltaic modules

A photovoltaic module consists of electrically interconnected crystalline silicon cells. These cells have at present production-induced maximum dimensions of 156 mm x 156 mm due to the necessary material purity level. The cells have electrical contact fingers on the front and back surfaces for the electrical connection of the oppositely doped layers. Module efficiency is optimized by finding a trade-off between shading, resistance and material consumption associated with the width of the front contact fingers (Quaschning 2011). New interconnection technologies with a multitude of very thin wires, so-called SmartWire Connection Technology (SWCT) (Meyer Burger 2016), or with cell contacts on the back, so-called Metal Wrap-Through (MWT) (Fraunhofer ISE 2016), are now being developed also to minimize the negative effects of cell breakage and shading from contact fingers respectively.

A photovoltaic cell is characterized by the dependence of electric current (I) on electric voltage (V), the so-called I-V characteristic, an example of which is depicted in Fig. 3.1. The I-V curve varies depending on the solar irradiation incident on the module plane. On module data sheets typically the I-V curve at STC is given, i.e. with a spectrum of AM 1.5, a temperature of 25°C and an irradiance of 1000 W/m^2. For cells connected in series, the electric current is the same in all cells and is determined by the cell generating the least current, whereas the cell voltages are added. Therefore, in the case of partial shading, the power of all cells connected in series with the shaded cell(s) is affected (Quaschning 2011). The output power P determined by Eq. 3.2 is reached at the point, where the area under the I-V curve is maximized. This operating point is the so-called maximum power point (MPP).

$$P = V * I \tag{3.2}$$

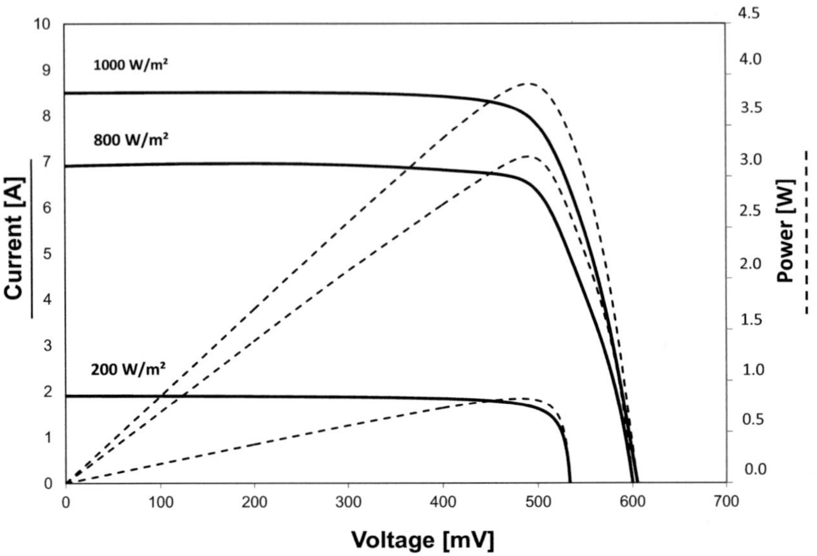

Figure 3.1: Typical I-V characteristics of a crystalline photovoltaic cell for different levels of solar irradiation

Standard, industrially produced photovoltaic modules optimized for maximum power generation consist of 60 cells and typically have dimensions of 1 m x 1.7 m. Here, 20 cells are connected in series, resulting in 3 strings which are connected in parallel and secured against the negative effects induced by partial shading with 3 by-pass diodes.

Different models exist to calculate the electricity yield. Since the electrical characteristics of a photovoltaic cell are similar to those of a diode, the simplest approach is the so-called *single-diode model* (Quaschning 2011). In this model, the illuminated solar cell is represented by a diode connected in parallel with an energy source, the output of which is linearly dependent on the irradiation. In an extension to this model, resistances from contacts, cables, the semiconductor material and leakage currents at the photovoltaic cell edges can be included by series and parallel resistances (Kaltschmitt 2007). This model is sufficient to describe the dependence of the I-V curve on the temperature and the irradiance for monocrystalline silicon within 1.5 % for a range of normal operating conditions (Sprenger 2013).

An improved description of photovoltaic electricity generation can be achieved by the so-called *two-diode model*, where another diode with different electrical characteristics is connected in parallel to the first diode. However, this model is mainly only applicable to crystalline modules. For thin-film modules operating in partial-load mode, significant deviations exist. The *two-diode model* can also be extended by an additional energy source representing the electrical behavior at large negative voltages (Sprenger 2013).

In this thesis, the *Heydenreich model* will be employed which is "a pure power model, describing the dependency of module output power P_{MPP} on incoming irradiation and module (or ambient) temperature" (Heydenreich et al. 2008) since this was considered to reflect all the relevant influential factors considered in this thesis. This model will be described in detail in Section 4.2.

3.2.2 Inverter

For the feeding of the electricity generated by the photovoltaic modules into the grid, the inverter converts the generated direct current (DC) into alternating current (AC). Additionally, inverters contain a so-called MPP tracker which constantly monitors and controls the performance of the photovoltaic system such that at every time step the generated power is maximized. For performance reasons, inverters have to be adapted to the size and type of the installed system since they are typically optimized for a certain input voltage range. Operating conditions near the lower limit of their input voltage range due to low irradiance or shading result in partial load operation of the inverter and therefore reduced efficiency (Wagner 2010).

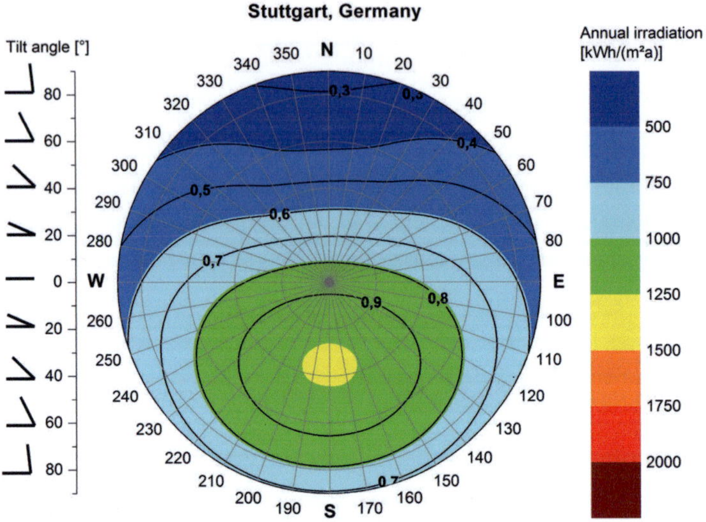

Figure 3.2: Annual solar irradiation for different orientations and inclination angles in Stuttgart, Germany (Kuhn & Fath et al. 2014)

3.2.3 Influence of module orientation and inclination

The radiation incident on the photovoltaic module is directly dependent on module orientation and tilt angle. In Figs. 3.2 and 3.3, the annual solar irradiation in Stuttgart and Madrid respectively for different orientations and inclination angles is depicted (Kuhn et al. 2014).

In Germany, south-oriented modules with a tilt angle of 30° to 35° receive the maximum annual solar irradiation. As can be seen from the diagrams, even a north-oriented facade (90° tilt angle) receives approximately 30 % of the total annual irradiation. However, this is only true for fixed mounted systems. With a tracking system, requiring additional energy, solar irradiation can be further increased (Fath 2013).

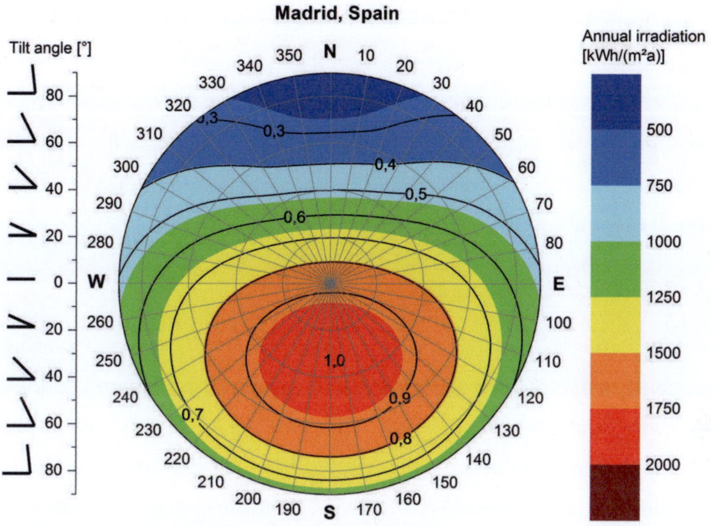

Figure 3.3: Annual solar irradiation for different orientations and inclination angles in Madrid, Spain (Kuhn & Fath et al. 2014)

3.3 Building integration of photovoltaic modules

Building-integrated photovoltaic (BIPV) systems are defined here as photovoltaic modules installed on buildings that assume the function of a conventional building material while simultaneously generating electricity from solar energy. Contrary to building-added photovoltaics (BAPV) systems which are mainly installed on building roofs, building-integrated photovoltaics (BIPV) systems are also used in building facades.[1] For large commercial buildings, especially offices, on the facade often more space for the installation of a photovoltaic plant is available than on the roof. However, due to lower levels of solar irradiation resulting from the inclination angle also electricity generation will be reduced in comparison to a roof-top installation.

[1] In this thesis, building surfaces with an inclination angle below 85° are considered roofs.

BIPV has long led a niche existence in the prospering photovoltaic market. While the market for BAPV systems, mainly roof-top installations, experienced sky-rocketing installation numbers and prices dropping to a level which many European photovoltaic module producers could not keep up with, the market for BIPV modules is still dominated by small companies with modules produced with much manual labor.

Effect of BIPV on building energy demand

Since in this thesis, the focus is on photovoltaic systems on buildings, this section shall be devoted to the special case of semi-transparent photovoltaic modules integrated into windows or glass facades. In this case, apart from the generated electricity and the substituted building material, the photovoltaic modules also influence building energy consumption due to the absorption of solar irradiation and conversion into electricity. The resulting change in lighting (because of the opacity of the photovoltaic components), heating and cooling (because of the solar heat gain (Fung and Yang 2008)) energy demand has to be considered in the planning of the system and in the economic assessment.
Since this effect due to its complexity will not be considered in the national potential calculation presented in this thesis, here at least a detailed overview of available studies on this topic shall be presented.
For an in-depth analysis of the change in building energy demand induced by a semi-transparent photovoltaic system, thorough experiments (Li et al. (2009); Polo and Sangiorgi (2014)) or building energy simulations are necessary employing specialised software like *EnergyPlus* (Miyazaki et al. (2005); Khai (2014)), *EnergyPlus* in connection with *Radiance/Daysim* (Didoné and Wagner 2013), *TRNSYS* (Moor et al. 2012) or ESP-r (Mende et al. 2011).
Since building energy simulations due to the large number of parameters involved cannot be generalized and will also differ strongly between structural building types, climatic regions, occupancy behavior (residential: Wong et al. (2008); non-residential: Miyazaki et al. (2005); Khai (2014); Lu and Law

(2013)), module transparency ratio[2] and type of module integration (roof: Li et al. (2009); facade: Chae et al. (2014)) (to name just a few), in the following only the studies relevant for the Central European climate shall be presented in more detail, since results of analysis performed for other climatic zones cannot be transferred to the focus area of this thesis.

Generally speaking, the majority of the studies presented above has focused on the physical quantification of the impact of semi-transparent BIPV on building energy demand.

Mende et al. (2011) have analyzed with *ESP-r* the effect of module transparency ratios, ranging from 29 % to 74 %[3] due to varying cell spacing, on the energy demand of a 16.7 m^2 office container located in Freiburg, Germany, resulting in an overall improvement of the building's primary energy balance from the generated electricity and saved cooling demand despite higher lighting and heating demand for almost all analyzed system configurations. These results were analyzed economically by Fath et al. (2013), resulting in the highest NPV for systems with a small transparency ratios (e.g. 29 %) where cooling demand was minimized and was not fully outweighed by additional lighting demand. However, these building energy demand cost savings could at the time of this study not compensate the cost surcharge for the photovoltaically active component in comparison with conventional building materials.

In a different study also performed with *ESP-r*, Fath et al. (2012a) have analyzed the economic impact of innovative angle-selective semi-transparent PVShade® modules (Frontini 2011) integrated as a pilot installation in the spandrel area of a 118 m^2 seminar room located in Freiburg, Germany. Covering about one third of the 27 m^2 glazed area oriented south-east, final energy consumption for heating was increased by 116 kWh/a while cooling demand was reduced by 35 kWh/a resulting in a total final energy demand increase of 2 % compared

[2] Studies on the effect of opaque modules on building energy demand have been excluded from this list.

[3] Due to the large computing effort connected with building energy simulation, only a selected number of discrete transparency ratios could be considered.

with a conventional insulating glazing. Due to the installation of the BIPV modules in the spandrel area, changes in lighting demand were not considered. Moor et al. (2012) have applied *TRNSYS* to analyze the shading impact of BIPV on cooling demand in an office located in Austria resulting in a 15 % to 90 % reduction depending on the type of BIPV integration with still "good" to "optimum" natural lighting conditions. However, a thorough description of the parameters used in the economic assessment in this study is missing.

In contrast to the simulation studies presented before, Polo and Sangiorgi (2014) have conducted a one-week experimental study to analyze the change in heating and lighting demand due to semi-transparent BIPV modules employing four different photovoltaic technologies integrated in the whole window area (floor to ceiling) of a 10 m^2 office located in North Italy. As a result, in this fall test week only mono-crystalline modules generated enough electricity to balance supply and consumption from lighting and heating. However, from this study, no conclusions on the building energy demand effect of BIPV in comparison to traditional building materials can be drawn.

4 Methodology for technical potential assessment

According to the definition presented in Section 2.1, based on the theoretical potential, the technical potential for photovoltaics can be calculated. The corresponding methodology is presented in this chapter since it is directly linked to the previous chapter on photovoltaic electricity generation on buildings. The methodology for the theoretical potential calculation will be explained at the appropriate place at the beginning of the chapters on individual building assessment (Chapter 6), urban fabric structure assessment (Chapter 7) and the national potential assessment (Chapter 8).
The technical potential can be further differentiated into the location potential, i.e. the incoming solar irradiation on available surfaces (here: building roofs and facades) and the electricity generation potential, taking photovoltaic module and system efficiency additionally into account. In the following sections, first the methodology for the location potential assessment applying the validated lighting simulation tool Radiance is explained (Section 4.1). Then, the electricity generation potential can be calculated according to the methodology described in Section 4.2. This serves as the basis for the economic potential assessment methodology described in Chapter 5.

4.1 Location potential assessment

In this thesis, the location potential, i.e. the solar irradiation incident on available surfaces, was assessed with Radiance. Radiance is a lighting simulation tool originally developed for architects and designers at Lawrence Berkeley National Laboratory by Greg Ward Larson in the early 1990s (Ward Larson and Shakespeare 1998). Radiance was originally developed for UNIX systems (Jacobs 2012) and is now freely available from `http://radsite.lbl.gov/radiance/HOME.html`. Radiance is capable of processing different optical properties, like reflectance and transmittance for each defined surface (Jakubiec and Reinhart 2013). In the following sections, the necessary input data will be explained in detail as well as the irradiation simulation approach chosen.

4.1.1 Input data

4.1.1.1 Description of geometry in Radiance

For the irradiation simulation, a 3D geometric model of the building surfaces under analysis is needed. Building models converted to the Radiance file format $*.rad$ are simple text files where all model surfaces are listed as polygons defined by the x, y and z coordinates of their n corner points. They are characterized by a material descriptor with reflective and transmissive properties (Jacobs 2012).

```
Material polygon xx
0
0
9
    0    0    0
    1    0    0
    0    1    0
```

Figure 4.1: Description of a triangle in Radiance.

Unlike in a GIS, no meta-information is available for the described polygon in the Radiance file format. I.e., from this format in the case of a 3D city model, it is no longer possible to attribute surfaces to individual buildings. Therefore, for the large-scale potential assessment, a special database containing the assignment of surfaces to buildings had to be developed.

Since here a large range of buildings is analyzed, for which detailed information on used building materials was not always available, the following standard optical properties were used, assuming all building and surrounding surfaces to be Lambertian diffusers with a 20 % reflectance that is unvarying spatially and temporally (Jakubiec and Reinhart 2013).[1]

```
void plastic Material
0
0
5 0.2 0.2 0.2 0 0
```

Figure 4.2: Description of material in Radiance.

For solar irradiation simulation, the $*$.*rad* text file(s) describing the geometry is/are converted into the machine-readable *octree* format using the Radiance command *oconv* (Sprenger 2013).

4.1.1.2 Definition of sensor points

Since Radiance employs a backwards ray-tracing algorithm for the irradiation simulation, discrete sensor points including a viewing direction have to be positioned on the surfaces under analysis (Compagnon 2001). For the large-scale potential assessment, an automated procedure for the positioning of sensor points on all model surfaces based on triangulation has been developed and implemented by the author of this thesis, distributing the sensor points evenly across all building surfaces in a 1.5 m mesh corresponding approximately to the size of a standard photovoltaic module. In order for the sensor points to be illuminated, they have to be placed with a minimal distance in front of the surface, i.e. in the normal direction of the surface towards the outside and not directly in the surface plane. However, no information on the surface orientation is available from the $*$.*rad* file. Depending on whether the corner points of the polygon are listed in clockwise or counter-clockwise direction, a different

[1] The albedo can vary up to 0.6 or 0.7 in the case of snow (Nguyen and Pearce 2010). However, since the number of days with snow is limited in the analyzed locations, a temporally unvarying albedo of 0.2 is a conservative but valid assumption. Nguyen and Pearce (2010) have calculated that the effect of ground reflections on the electricity yield was in the range of Wh while the effect of beam and diffuse radiation was in the order of kWh.

normal vector results. Therefore, in the first step, sensor points are positioned on both sides of the building surface, i.e. in the negative and positive directions of the normal vector as depicted in Fig. 4.3.

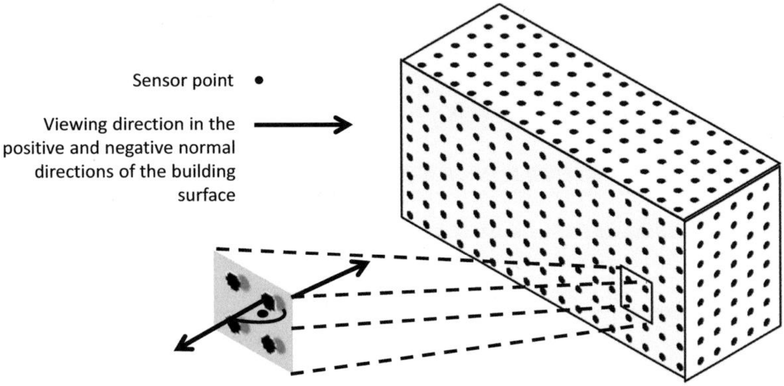

Figure 4.3: Definition of sensor points and viewing direction

In the next step, a single *rtrace* command for all defined sensor points and the *octree* file created from the geometrical information defined in the $*.rad$ file is performed to check which sensor points are illuminated (i.e. facing outward). For this command, the $-I$ option is used such that irradiance instead of radiance is computed (Radiance-online 1997). The other *rtrace* parameters used in this simulation are specified in Tab. 4.1.
1 ambient bounce (*ab*) indicates that direct and diffuse irradiation without reflections, e.g. from the ground or surrounding buildings have been considered, which is sufficient for differentiating between sensor points located inside or outside a building. For performance reasons, Radiance interpolates between sensor points in the indirect irradiation calculation when the relative maximum error is smaller than the ambient accuracy (*aa*), here 0.1. Depending on the maximum dimensions (D_{max}) of the analyzed geometry, the minimum distance for interpolation (S_{min}) can be calculated according to Eq. 4.1 with the ambient accuracy (*aa*) of 0.1 and the ambient resolution (*ar*) of 25 (DesignBuilder 2014).

$$S_{min} = D_{max} * \frac{aa}{ar} \tag{4.1}$$

All sensor points for which the irradiance is equal to zero are assumed to be positioned on the inside of a building surface and are excluded from further analysis. As a result, sensor points positioned outside all building surfaces with their x, y and z coordinates and viewing direction r, g and b in the direction of the building surface normal are available as input for the irradiation simulation.

Table 4.1: Simulation parameters for the identification of illuminated and non-illuminated sensor points on building surfaces

Parameter	Abbreviation	Value
Ambient bounces	ab	1
Ambient divisions	ad	1024
Ambient accuracy	aa	0.1
Ambient resolution	ar	25

4.1.1.3 Angular response properties

The angular response (AR) properties due to solar irradiation incident at an angle θ were calculated according to Eq. 4.2 (Martin and Ruiz 2001, Martin and Ruiz 2013).

$$AR(\theta) = \frac{A(\theta)}{A(0)} = \left[\frac{1 - exp(-cos(\theta)/a_r)}{1 - exp(-1/a_r}\right] \tag{4.2}$$

a_r is the dimensionless angular loss coefficient which was fitted empirically by Martin and Ruiz. Here, in all simulations, a crystalline silicon module without a special antireflective coating was used, assuming an air/glass/ZnS/Si configuration resulting in an a_r of 0.169. The angular response is depicted in Fig. 4.4. As in Sprenger (2013), here also no effect from the spectral distribution of the incident light on the angular response was considered, with $AM = 1.5$ being assumed.

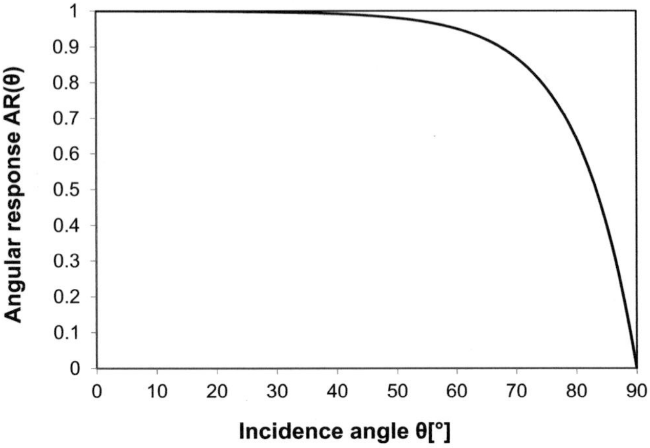

Figure 4.4: The angular response AR versus the incidence angle θ according to Martin and Ruiz (2013) with $a_r = 0.169$.

4.1.1.4 Meteorological data

As further input for the irradiation simulation meteorological data from the METEONORM database version 7.0 was used, representing an average for the years 1981 to 2000 for the respective building location (Meteotest 2011). This data includes hourly global and diffuse irradiation values on a horizontal plane, direct normal irradiation and the ambient temperature.

4.1.1.5 Building location information

For all buildings, the exact location based on the building address and aerial images was determined such that location latitude and longitude as relevant input parameters for *gendaylit* (Section 4.1.2) were available. The time zone was $-15°$ for all considered buildings since they were all located in Germany.

4.1.2 Solar irradiation simulation

Since Radiance consists of more than 100 individual sub-programs, one has to clearly define the irradiation simulation approach chosen. In this thesis, solar irradiation on all surfaces in an hourly resolution has been simulated using the *gendaylit* sub-program.

gendaylit generates an angular distribution of direct and diffuse irradiation for a given location at a certain time following the Perez model for sky luminance distribution (Delaunay et al. 2014). The Perez model creates a sky luminance distribution pattern from standard irradiance measurements (Perez et al. 1993). In an extensive review of solar irradiation simulation models, the Perez model was identified as "widely used and cited among the best performing models" (Freitas et al. 2015).

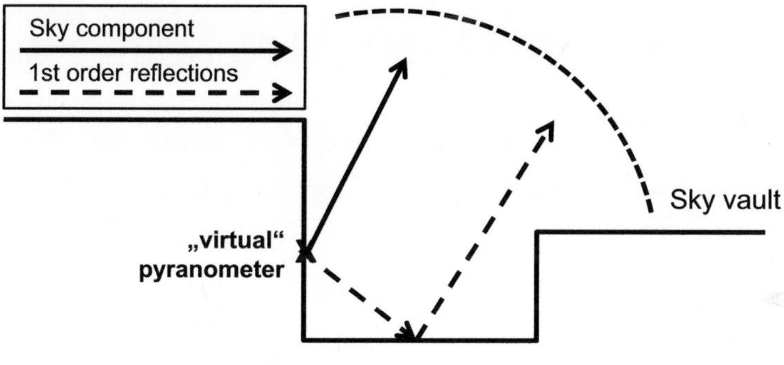

Figure 4.5: Types of rays traced by Radiance to compute irradiance values (Compagnon 2000)

Unlike other solar irradiation assessments, in Radiance it is possible to consider also the reflected component of the solar irradiation as depicted in Fig. 4.5. This is especially relevant for urban environments and facade installations, where the reflected irradiation from other buildings can account for a significant share of incoming irradiation (Sprenger 2013).

Since Jakubiec and Reinhart (2013) have conducted a similar assessment for rooftops in Massachusetts, here also their approach employing another Radiance-based program, *Daysim*, shall be mentioned briefly. *Daysim* divides the sky generated with *gendaylit* into discrete patches for the calculation of daylight coefficients (Tregenza and Waters 1983). This procedure reduces calculation time if inner reflections like a room with a window and a blind system are considered in addition to outer reflections (Reinhart and Walkenhorst (2001); Huang and Wu (2014)). Since here only outside building surfaces are considered and since calculating purely with *gendaylit* results in no loss of accuracy caused by the division of the sky into patches, the *gendaylit* approach was chosen here. In the irradiation simulation, the parameters displayed in Tab. 4.2 have been used as a compromise between accuracy and calculation speed. Three ambient bounces (*ab*) indicate that direct and diffuse irradiation as well as first-order reflections, e.g. from the ground or surrounding buildings have been considered. Since in the present thesis also facades are treated, this was considered relevant, since in Sprenger (2013) solar irradiation on a south-facing facade increased by 12 % when additional reflections from the ground were considered. However, the increase in solar irradiation from reflections cannot be generalized and therefore has to be modeled for every considered case separately. From each sensor point, 1024 rays (ambient divisions - *ad*) have been sent out to be traced back to a light source, thereby considering all objects with a solid angle larger than 0.0061 sr when viewed from the sensor point (DesignBuilder 2014).

Table 4.2: Simulation parameters for irradiation analysis on building surfaces

Parameter	Abbreviation	Value
Ambient bounces	ab	3
Ambient divisions	ad	1024
Ambient accuracy	aa	0.1
Ambient resolution	ar	256

The sky generation procedure with *gendaylit* and the ray-tracing procedure with Radiance were automated by Sprenger (2013) with the program *td_rtrace.py* and used by the author of this thesis. With *td_rtrace.py*, a one-year hourly

irradiation simulation for a given geometry with defined sensor points and a weather file is performed. *gendaylit* is called for every time step, resulting in an hourly irradiation time series for every sensor point for a whole year.
In order to be able to differentiate between the effects of shading and reflections from the surroundings and the effects of a non-optimally oriented building surface area, additionally the same irradiation simulation has been performed for a single sensor point on each building surface without taking information about the surroundings into account. In the following, the irradiation values resulting from this analysis will be denoted by the index u for *unshaded*. In this way, a comparison between e.g. the irradiation on an unobstructed, east-oriented facade surface area and an obstructed east-oriented facade surface area at the given location is possible. Thus, a reduced irradiation can be directly attributed to the geometrical configuration of the considered and surrounding buildings.

4.2 Electricity generation potential assessment

Based on the hourly irradiation time series for every sensor point, the electricity generation potential can be calculated in the next step. For this purpose, first the hourly irradiation time series on the sensor points had to be adapted and then the electricity yield simulation could be performed.

4.2.1 Preparation of irradiation data

For the calculation of the electricity generation potential, the irradiation time series had to be aggregated since the simulation of the generated electricity for every sensor point would imply the installation and system connection of individual photovoltaic modules which is not feasible in practice. Instead, for the work reported in this thesis, it was assumed that one interconnected photovoltaic system is installed on each building surface, i.e. the average irradiation on the building surface determines the electricity yield.[2] Since in practice, strongly shaded areas will not be covered with photovoltaic modules or not connected electrically (installation of so-called dummy modules for architectural reasons), initially sensor points where the annual solar irradiation falls below 500 kWh/(m^2a) were filtered out. This threshold value was chosen based on economic considerations (see Chapter 5), since a photovoltaic module receiving less than 500 kWh/(m^2a) will influence the total profitability of the plant negatively and result in an underestimation of the electricity generation potential.[3] The area represented by the strongly shaded sensor points was deducted from the total surface area.

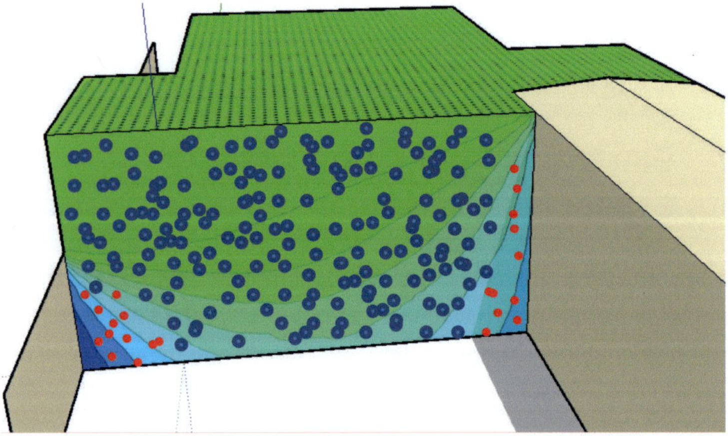

Figure 4.6: View of sensor points and filtered areas (marked in red)

[2] As explained in Section 3.2.1, the photovoltaic module receiving the least irradiation determines the system electricity yield. Therefore, in practice the electric circuit is designed such that photovoltaic modules receiving a similar amount of irradiation are interconnected. Since a detailed electrical design exceeds the scope of this thesis aiming at the calculation of a national potential, here the average solar irradiation on the building surface is considered in the calculation of the electricity generation potential, assuming a well-designed electric circuit.

[3] The author is aware of introducting economic considerations into the calculation of the electricity generation potential but still considers it a necessary measure to define boundary conditions for practical reasons.

Then, in the next step, the hourly solar irradiation on every building surface was calculated as the average irradiation on all sensor points with a yearly total irradiation above the threshold value stated above. This hourly irradiation time series per building surface was then employed in the calculation of the electricity generation potential.

4.2.2 Calculation of electricity yield

As mentioned already in Section 3.2.1, for the calculation of the electricity generation potential the electricity yield is calculated according to the Heydenreich model. For this, validated routines of the Zenit electricity generation simulation program developed at Fraunhofer ISE were used (Fraunhofer ISE (2007); Müller et al. (2009); Müller et al. (2014)). Zenit simulates the electricity yield of a photovoltaic system based on hourly irradiation and temperature input data employing the Heydenreich model (Heydenreich et al. 2008) and the sky luminance distribution on the tilted module surface based on the Perez model (Perez et al. 1993).
For the electricity generation potential assessment presented here, it was not necessary to calculate the sky luminance distribution first, since the solar irradiation on the sensor points had alrady been calculated in the location potential assessment (see Section 4.1). Therefore only the validated routines for simulating the electricity yield based on the Heydenreich model were used. Negative effects on the photovoltaic system's electricity yield from module mismatch, cable losses, reflections and spectral effects are accounted for in Zenit by the flat reduction factors listed in Tab. 4.3. Additionally, a ratio of the inverter power to the installed capacity of the photovoltaic plant of 1.0 has been assumed.

Table 4.3: Flat reduction factors for electricity yield implemented in Zenit

Loss factor	Value [%]
Losses due to module mismatch	0.8
Cable losses	2.5
Generalized losses of diffuse irradiation	3.5
Spectral losses	1.0

The fundamental equation of the Heydenreich model is cited as Eq. 4.3 (Heydenreich et al. 2008):

$$\eta_{MPP,25}(G_{mod}) = a * G_{mod} + b * ln(G_{mod} + 1) + c \left[\frac{ln^2(G_{mod} + e)}{G_{mod} + 1} - 1 \right] \quad (4.3)$$

$\eta_{MPP,25}$ is the efficiency at 25°C, G_{mod} is the total irradiation on the module surface and a, b and c are dimensionless module-specific model parameters. They can be calculated by entering $\eta_{MPP,25}$ at three different irradiation levels G_{mod} in Eq. 4.3 and solving the system of linear equations.

Table 4.4: Exemplary Heydenreich parameters for a mono-crystalline module

Parameter	Value
a	0.007413
b	-9.580626
c	-166.731275
γ	-0.4%/K

Here, the Heydenreich parameters for a mono-crystalline module listed in Tab. 4.4 were used, the normalized efficiency of which at different levels of solar irradiation is depicted in Fig. 4.7.

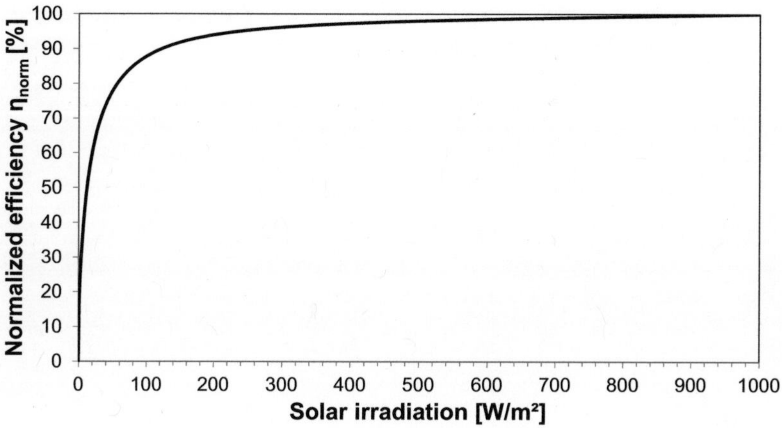

Figure 4.7: Normalized efficiency of a mono-crystalline module depending on the solar irradiation

The output power is calculated according to Eq. 4.4.

$$P_{mod} = \eta_{MPP}(G_{mod}, T_{mod})G_{mod}A_{mod} \tag{4.4}$$

P_{mod} is the module DC output power and A_{mod} is the area of one module or of a 1 kW system.
The temperature effect on module performance is modeled by Eqs. 4.5 to 4.7:

$$T_{PV} = T_{amb} + 0.030 * G_{mod} \tag{4.5}$$

$$\eta_{mod} = \eta_{mod,25} * (1 + \gamma * (T_{PV} - 25)) \tag{4.6}$$

$$P_{mod} = \eta_{mod}/100 * G_{mod} * (1 - Loss_{spectral}) \tag{4.7}$$

T_{PV} is the temperature of the photovoltaic module, T_{amb} is the ambient temperature, γ is the module temperature coefficient and $Loss_{spectral}$ are the spectral losses. Here, a ventilated installation situation has been assumed for all simulations, resulting in a generalized coefficient $\Delta T/E$ of 0.030 K/(W/m^2) being used in the calculation of module temperature (Eq. 4.5).

5 Methodology for economic potential assessment

After the calculation of the electricity generation potential, as an extension to many existing potential studies in this thesis, also the economic potential is assessed. In this chapter, the methodology as well as the relevant influential factors are presented. Since these influential factors are partly based on assumptions, sensitivity analyses are crucial.

As defined in Section 2.1, in this thesis the economic potential is calculated from a building owner's point of view, assuming him to be identical with the investor in the photovoltaic plant and the consumer of the generated electricity.[1] Here, the owner is assumed to be economically motivated, i.e. the photovoltaic installation will only be realized when it is profitable. However, it should be noted that in practice, a range of other reasons for the installation of a photovoltaic plant exists, like the public display of a sustainable business orientation generally associated with the generation of renewable electricity, independence from the electricity grid or architectural reasons. However, the share of photovoltaic plants installed for these qualitative reasons[2] is hard to estimate quantitatively and therefore omitted here. Looking at the course of photovoltaic installed capacity and its direct dependence on the development of public subsidies, which were then crucial for the profitability of the plant, the assumption of the vast majority of installed plants for profit reasons is considered to be valid.

[1] For readability reasons in the following sections, only the term owner will be used encompassing both natural and legal entities.

[2] Here, qualitative reasons are considered to be the antonym to the easily quantifiable profit reason. Depending on the focus of the study, possibly qualitative reasons can also be quantified. However, the procedure is not as straightforward (Maria Cristina Munari Probst 2011).

For an economically oriented owner, the following mutually exclusive general investment alternatives form the basis for the following calculations:

- *General alternative 1:* Consumption of electricity from the grid, i.e. no investment in a photovoltaic plant.
- *General alternative 2:* Investment in and installation of a photovoltaic plant and self-consumption of the generated electricity.

For alternative 1, in alignment with the focus of this assessment, it is assumed that the amount of electricity consumed from the grid considered here is equal to the amount possibly generated by the photovoltaic installation. Generally, for the majority of the German building stock it can be assumed that considering the balance for a whole year not 100 % of the electricity consumption can be supplied by a photovoltaic installation, especially without battery storage systems which are outside the scope of this thesis. The economic valuation of the generated electricity by the photovoltaic installation is explained in detail in Section 5.2.4.
Additionally, in the special case of installing the photovoltaic plant on a building, associated effects have to be included in the economic considerations:

- *Building installation alternative 1:* Investment in and mounting of a traditional, non-active building material and consumption of electricity from the grid, i.e. no investment in a photovoltaic plant.
- *Building installation alternative 2a:* Investment in and mounting of a traditional, non-active building material and investment in and mounting of a standardized building-added photovoltaic installation and self-consumption of the generated electricity.
- *Building installation alternative 2b:* Investment in and mounting of a building-integrated photovoltaic installation and self-consumption of the generated electricity. No investment in a traditional building material for the surfaces covered by the photovoltaic installation.

Since the focus of this thesis is on the potential of photovoltaic installations on buildings, in the following only the *building installation alternatives 1*, *2a* and *2b* will be considered.

In the case of traditional, non-active building materials installable on building roofs and/or facades with similar functional characteristics, i.e. concerning cleaning, repair and insulation properties, the comparison of the purchasing price is sufficient for an investment decision. Then, the material with the lowest initial investment will be chosen, assuming all follow-up cost to be identical and therefore not decisive in the profitability calculation.

However, a photovoltaic plant generates electricity over the system lifetime. Therefore, simply comparing the purchasing price of the *building installation alternatives 1*, *2a* and *2b* is not a suitable approach. Instead, in the economic assessment, the whole system lifetime including the value of the generated electricity has to be considered. Incorporating the cost and revenues associated with an asset over the system lifetime into the economic assessment is already common practice for other long-term investments.

The terms life-cycle costing (LCC) or total cost of ownership (TCO) have evolved since the 1970's for this explicit consideration of cost associated with an asset during the operation and possibly at the end-of-life stage in addition to the purchasing price (Hunkeler et al. 2008). According to Geißdörfer (2009), the American Ministry of Defence already then introduced a LCC assessment in the procurement of new weapon systems. Later, the Gartner Group, specialized in the introduction of information technology (IT) systems, introduced a so-called TCO model. They had recognized that the cost of introducing a new IT system was several times higher than the purchasing price of the desktop computers, due to installation, training and maintenance cost.

Since then, a variety of LCC-oriented methodologies with different application areas and including different cost components has been developed. Geißdörfer et al. (2009) has compared 20 TCO/LCC methodologies concerning their suitability for forming the basis for a standardized LCC methodology. He has also identified the main difference between LCC and TCO methodologies:

While TCO methodologies are mainly treated in Anglo-Saxon publications, LCC methodologies originated in German articles (Geißdörfer 2009). The main conceptual difference exists with regard to the indirect cost, i.e. cost that cannot be directly attributed to the object under consideration like administration or planning. In the mechnical engineering industry, where some of the LCC concepts evolved, indirect cost for administration or planning is negligible in comparison with the direct cost associated with industrial manufacturing machinery like energy, material and maintenance cost. Therefore in LCC, these costs are omitted. In contrast to that, in the computer industry, the cost for training and maintenance cannot be attributed to a physical desktop computer and is therefore indirect cost. In TCO models this indirect cost is explicitly considered (Geißdörfer 2009).

For photovoltaic installations which are the focus of this thesis, the quantification of indirect cost for administration is connected with great uncertainty and therefore omitted. In the case of the installation by a photovoltaic system provider, the planning cost can be assumed to be included in the purchasing price of the system and therefore part of the direct cost. Consequently, the methodology applied here belongs to the LCC category which is therefore the focus of the following review of methodologies. Additionally, methodologies especially applicable to buildings, installations in/on buildings or photovoltaic components will be considered.

5.1 Review of methodologies

As in financial theory, the major difference between LCC methodologies lies between those based on activity-based costing (ABC) and classic investment appraisal methods.

In ABC, all costs associated with the production of a product, such as energy, material and labor input, are taken into account, usually considering just a single period. In the case of necessary production equipment, the value of the machinery is divided by its lifetime. Additionally, financing cost and interest

can be considered. An example for a methodology based on activity-based costing is the SEMI Standard E35-0307 “Guide to calculate cost of ownership (COO) metrics for semiconductor manufacturing equipment”, which is also applied in the photovoltaic industry (Jimenez and Williams 2011).
With this methodology, the production cost e.g. of a photovoltaic module[3] from the perspective of the component producer can be calculated. However, the owner will have to consider in his calculation the price of the photovoltaic modules, i.e. the production cost supplemented by the profit margin of the producer, and the inverter, cabling and sub-structure. Additionally, the consideration of dynamic effects, like changes in energy generation due to degradation and energy cost, will be cumbersome to consider as average values in a single-period assessment. Since the focus of this thesis is on the owner, LCC methodologies based on ABC will not be considered further.
In contrast to ABC, for the comparison of different long-term investment alternatives, LCC methodologies based on investment appraisal methods like the NPV, the annuity or the internal rate of return (IRR) were developed. In these methodologies, the cost and revenues associated with the product over the total system lifetime are considered as well as dynamic effects like changes in interest rate and energy cost. The LCC methodology is now also considered in sustainability assessments, since the economic dimension is one of the three pillars of sustainability, as presented in the German sustainability assessment framework for public buildings (BMVBS 2011a).
For the LCC calculation of a photovoltaic installation on a building, different standards are applicable:

- ISO 15686-5: Standardized Method of Life Cycle Costing for Construction Procurement - Buildings & constructed assets - Service life planning - Part 5: Life cycle costing

[3] Since the photovoltaic modules are the most prominent component of a photovoltaic plant, they are mentioned here as representative of necessary components for photovoltaic installations. The statements can be analogously transferred to the inverters, being also a necessary electrical component of a photovoltaic plant.

- DIN EN 15459 - Energy performance of buildings - Economic evaluation procedure for energy systems in buildings
- VDI 2067 - Economic efficiency of building installations - Fundamentals and economic calculation
- EN 60300-3-3 Dependability management - Part 3-3: Application guide Life cycle costing

All standards provide a more or less detailed framework for calculating the LCC for buildings (ISO 15686-5), energy installations in buildings (DIN EN 15459, VDI 2067) or products in general (EN 60300-3-3). All standards list the investment appraisal methods mentioned above as possible metrics for the LCC and some of them give recommendations on the most appropriate one, either the NPV (ISO 15686-5) or the annuity method (DIN EN 15459; VDI 2067). In the following, due to its status as a European standard and its focus on energy installations in buildings, the LCC calculations will be performed according to DIN EN 15459. However, it should be noted that despite the different calculation structure, calculations according to all standards eventually should yield the same result due to the strong similarities in methodologies.

5.2 Cost breakdown structure according to DIN EN 15459

According to DIN EN 15459, the LCC are composed of the initial and the replacement investment and the periodic variable cost. They are summarized in the total cost according to Eq. 5.1. The nomenclature is listed in Tab. 5.1.

$$C_G(\tau) = C_I + \sum_j \left[\sum_{i=1}^{\tau} (C_{a,i}(j) * R_d(i)) - V_{f,\tau}(j) \right] \tag{5.1}$$

Table 5.1: Nomenclature used in economic potential assessment (DIN EN 15459:2008-06). In the last column, the values used in the investigated economic scenarios are listed.

Notation		Unit	Values for investigated scenarios
C_I	investment at i = 0	€	
C_r	variable cost	€/a	
C_m	maintenance cost	€/a	
C_o	operating cost	€/a	
C_e	energy cost	€/a	0.15, 0.20, 0.25, 0.30, 0.35, 0.40
C_{ad}	additional cost for insurance, taxes	€/a	
$C_p(i)$	replacement cost at time i	€	
$C_{R,i}(j)$	periodic replacement cost at time i	€	
$C_a(i)$	sum of annual variable cost	€/a	
R_i	inflation rate	%/a	1.5
R_d	interest rate	%	2, 5, 8
R	interest rate in agreement with financing body	%	
R_R	real interest rate	%	
$a(n)$	annuity factor	-	
$R_{e,k}$	cost development rate for energy of type k	%/a	1.5
R_o	cost development rate for personnel	%/a	1.5
R_p	cost development rate for products	%/a	1.5

Notation		Unit	Values for investigated scenarios
R_m	cost development rate for maintenance	%/a	1.5
R_{ad}	cost development rate for additional cost	%/a	1.5
R_{deg}	module degradation rate	%/a	0.25
E_a	electricity yield	kWh/a	
$\tau_n(j)$	life expectancy for component	a	
$f_{pv}(n)$	present value factor ($f_{pv}(n) = 1/a(n)$)	-	
τ_0	base year for calculations	-	
τ	time horizon of calculations	a	20, 25, 30
$V_f(j)$	residual value	-	
Present value	sum of all discounted cash flows for the base year	€	
Nominal value	value of cash flows at time of their occurrence	€	
$C_G(\tau)$	total cost or LCC - sum of the present value of all cash flows including the investment	€	

The annuity can be calculated according to Eq. 5.2.

$$AC = C_r + \sum \left(a(i) * \left(\sum_j V_0(j) \right) \right) + a\left(\tau_{building}\right) * \sum_j V_0(j) \tag{5.2}$$

The variable costs C_r are calculated according to Eq. 5.3.

$$C_r = (C_e + C_o + C_m + C_a d) \tag{5.3}$$

According to DIN EN 15459, a 6 step-procedure is to be performed for the LCC or annuity calculation. This procedure will be applied in the following to the photovoltaic plants considered in this thesis. When a single definite value is not available for a required parameter, the following calculations will be performed for a defined set of values. A summary of the values used to define investigated scenarios is given in Tab. 5.1.

5.2.1 Financial data

5.2.1.1 Time horizon of calculations

The time horizon of the calculations (τ) is equal to the expected lifetime of the photovoltaic system. In DIN EN 15459 a life expectance of 15 to 25 years is defined only for solar (thermal) collectors. For photovoltaic plants, economic assessments are usually performed for 20 years since this is the duration of the feed-in tariff guaranteed by the EEG. In practice, by now module producers provide a performance guarantee of up to 30 years with 80 % to 86 % of the original performance (SolarWorld 2015). Therefore in the following calculations, values of 20, 25 and 30 years will be considered for τ.

5.2.1.2 Rates

The financial rates for interest (R_d), inflation (R_i) and cost development for energy (R_e), personnel (R_o), products (R_p), maintenance (R_m) and additional cost (R_{ac}) are highly uncertain since here financial, market and learning effects as well as those from individual preferences accrue. Therefore in the following calculations, values of 2 %/a , 5 %/a and 8 %/a are assessed for the interest rate R_d. The development of the other cost categories is considered to be subject to the same general price increase thereby ignoring abrupt changes due to technological improvements or learning effects.

$$R_i = R_e = R_o = R_p = R_m = R_{ac} = 1.5\,\%/a \tag{5.4}$$

5.2.2 General information

5.2.2.1 Definition of plant

The LCC calculations are performed for photovoltaic installations on buildings in Germany. All buildings are assumed to have also an existing connection to the electricity grid, such that the installation of the photovoltaic plant only affects the variable energy cost and not the fixed cost.

5.2.2.2 Project surroundings

Since here a general methodology for the LCC calculation of photovoltaic plants is demonstrated, peripheral project conditions like the building location cannot be specified. Concerning the structural requirements, all considered buildings are assumed to fulfill the structural requirements associated with the additional load of a photovoltaic plant. In the up-scaling of the found potential to national scale, possible limitations caused by this assumption will be assessed in detail.

5.2.2.3 Meteorological data

For all simulations, average meteorological data for the years 1981 to 2000 were used as described in Section 4.1.1.4 (Meteotest 2011).

5.2.2.4 Limitations concerning the energy supply

In Germany, no regulative limitations concerning the energy source for the electrical energy supply exist. Here it is assumed that the electricity generated by the photovoltaic plant replaces electricity supplied by the grid for the owner. I.e., in the economic assessment the generated photovoltaic electricity is valuated at the owner's electricity procurement price. Alternative electricity suppliers in buildings like a combined heat and power (CHP) plant are not considered.
Apart from the visibility of the photovoltaic modules on the roof and/or on the facade, no other impacts on the building or its users are assumed to exist since the photovoltaic modules do not produce any noise or emissions when in

operation. The inverters are assumed to be mounted in a previously available space and thereby do not interfere with other building uses.

5.2.3 Photovoltaic plant properties

5.2.3.1 Investment

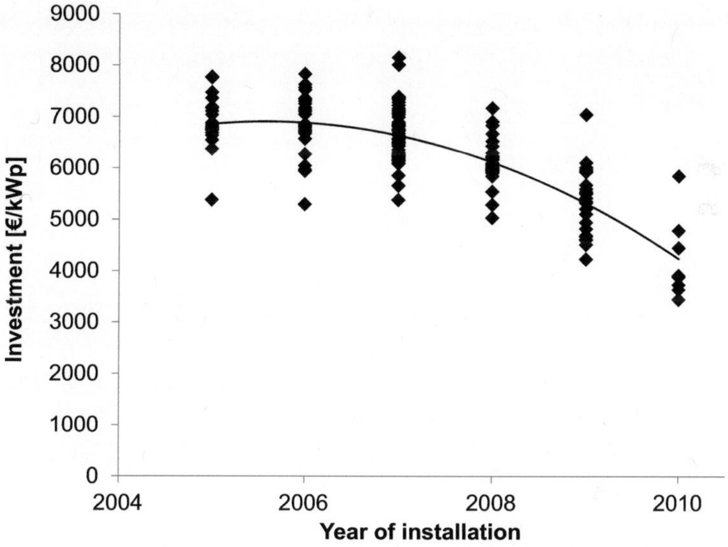

Figure 5.1: Specific investment for 171 photovoltaic plants installed within the framework of the CONCERTO project in 58 communities in 23 countries (Fath 2013)

The investment into the photovoltaic plant is the major cost component, since variable costs during system lifetime are very low due to the lack of moving parts. Photovoltaic installations have experienced a price decrease of 66 % alone from 2006 to 2013 (Bundesverband Solarwirtschaft 2013). The investment is usually given as specific investment in €/kW_p, including all cost associated with the installation of the photovoltaic plant like planning, module, inverter, cabling and mounting cost. In the investment, no value-added tax (VAT) is considered since in Germany this can be refunded when installing a photovoltaic plant.

The investment strongly depends on plant size, location, type of mounting and the year of construction (IEA PVPS Task 2 2007). In Fig. 5.1, the specific investment for 171 photovoltaic plants installed within the framework of the CONCERTO project funded by the European Commission (EC) is depicted (Fath 2013). Due to the varying installation conditions in different locations and the large price variations from month to month, even the specific investment for installations in the same year differs considerably. Therefore market overviews or price indices have to be carefully examined concerning these characteristics for the considered systems.

Roof-mounted installation

Since the majority of photovoltaic plants is installed on building roofs, studies on average specific investments are usually only valid for these installations. In 2007, the analysis of the investment for 33 photovoltaic plants installed in Germany between 2005 and 2007 resulted in an annual mean investment reduction rate of 0.046 €/W_p for systems with an installed capacity between 1.5 and 12 kW_p (IEA PVPS Task 2 2007).
According to IRENA (2012), systems had on average a specific investment of 3777 \$US/kW_p (2 to 5 kW_p installed capacity) and 3600 \$US/kW_p (5 to 10 kW_p) in 2011. Taking the midpoint of the installed capacity range results in an average price decrease of 0.044 \$US/W_p, which is still comparable to findings of IEA PVPS Task 2 (2007). However, since 2011, crystalline module prices have decreased by 50 % (pvXchange 2014) thereby strongly reducing the share of module cost in total investment. Therefore more recent publications were sought for the investment estimate.
Kost et al. (2013) assume a specific investment of 1300 €/kW_p to 1800 €/kW_p for small plants ($< 10\,kW_p$) and 1000 €/kW_p to 1700 €/kW_p for large plants ($< 1000\,kW_p$) in a regularly updated comparison of LCOE for different renewable energy technologies. However, in the urban areas considered in this thesis, no surfaces for large scale installations are available. A distribution of

the possibly installable photovoltaic plant sizes in an urban area assessed by the author of this thesis is depicted in Fig. 5.2 (Fath et al. 2015). Therefore, a better differentiation of the investment for small plants (< 50 kW_p) was necesssary.

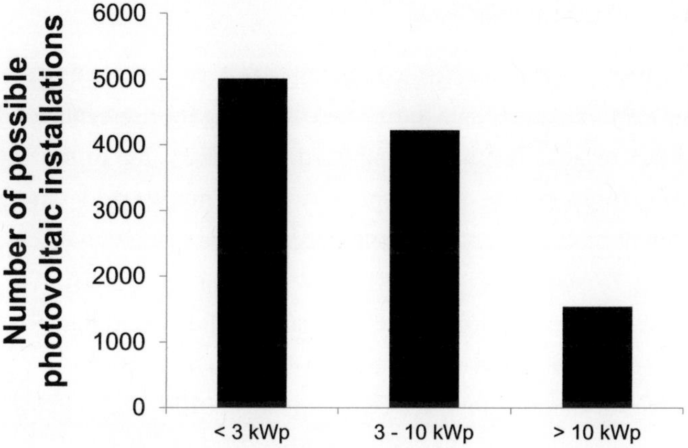

Figure 5.2: Number of possibly installable photovoltaic plants according to the location potential assessment in the urban area of Karlsruhe (Fath et al. 2015)

In a survey of photovoltaic system installers, EuPD research has found a price spread of 1350 to 2500 €/kW_p (< 3 kW_p), 1250 to 2000 €/kW_p (3 to 10 kW_p) and 1000 to 1900 €/kW_p (10 to 100 kW_p) at the beginning of 2013. The PV-Preisindex (2015) then stated an average investment of 1500 to 1570 €/kW_p for systems with less than 100 kW_p. At the end of 2015 / beginning of 2016, according to PV-Preisindex (2015), average plant prices had decreased by approximately 20 % to around 1250 €/kW_p. Transferring this decrease to the prices of the plant categories of EuPD, results in the following average specific investment for roof-mounted installations (I_{roof}), which will form the basis for the economic potential assessment:

- 1425 €/kW$_p$ in the case of less than 3 kW$_p$ installed capacity,
- 1300 €/kW$_p$ in the case of 3 to 10 kW$_p$ installed capacity and
- 1140 €/kW$_p$ in the case of more than 10 kW$_p$ installed capacity.

Facade-mounted installation

For facade-mounted installations, considerable research concerning the price increase due to increased module, fitting and mounting requirements for structural and aesthetic reasons has been conducted. However, due to the small number of installations for this plant type, no average market prices are available. Instead, the published investment surcharges range from 760 €/kW$_p$ (James et al. (2011); Tritsch (2011)) to 2330 €/kW$_p$ (Fath et al. 2012b). Assuming an average module efficiency of 15 % of crystalline silicon modules (Wirth 2014), this results in a specific investment of 114 €/m^2 to 350 €/m^2.
Since the facade solution analyzed by Fath et al. (2012b) with semi-transparent building-integrated photovoltaic modules can be considered at the high end and since the photovoltaic industry is already making efforts towards reducing this large price difference[4], a price surcharge of 1000 €/kW$_p$ or 150 €/m^2 for industrially produced, crystalline silicon modules for facades was chosen here. The resulting specific investment (I_{facade}) for different installed capacity classes is depicted in Tab. 5.2. For better comparison with traditional building materials, in Tab. A.1 in the Annex the investment in €/m^2 is depicted, always assuming a module efficiency of 15 %.

Building-integrated installation

Instead of just being attached to or mounted on a building, photovoltaic modules can also be used like conventional building materials, i.e. assuming the functions of a traditional building material like rain protection or solar control (see also Section 3.3). In this specific case of a building-integrated photovoltaic plant (BIPV), in an economic assessment, the cost of the replaced building material

[4] See for example the European project "Construct-PV" at `www.constructpv.eu`.

has to be considered as a reduction of the total investment as well (IEA PVPS Task 7-5 2002). Since a variety of building materials can be used, here an investment range for the substituted building material of 50 €/m^2 to 100 €/m^2 is assumed, covering typical roof cladding materials like bituminous membranes, metal sheets or clay tiles, and plaster, metal or fibre cement cladding for the facades. The investment for high-quality glass or natural stone facades starts at 300 €/m^2 and can reach more than 1000 €/m^2 (BKI 2010). However, this case was not considered so as not to distort results. Since the economic calculations are performed for the photovoltaic installations, where the investment is given in €/kW$_p$, the cost for the traditional, non-active building materials must be expressed in this unit, corresponding to 330 €/kW$_p$ to 660 €/kW$_p$. The resulting specific investment (I_{BIPV}) is documented in Tab. 5.2. Again, in Tab. A.1 in the Annex the investment in €/m^2 is depicted.

Table 5.2: Specific investment for different plant types and size categories; The asterisks (*) mark the specific investment utilized in the scenario 'Very optimistic BIPV investment scenario' in Section 5.6.

P [kW$_p$]	I_{roof} [€/kW$_p$]	$I_{roof,BIPV}$ [€/kW$_p$]	I_{facade} [€/kW$_p$]	$I_{facade,BIPV}$ [€/kW$_p$]
$P < 3$	1425	765 - 1095*	2425	1765 - 2095
$3 \leq P < 10$	1300	640 - 970*	2300	1640 - 1970
$P \geq 10$	1140	480 - 810*	2140	1480 - 1810

5.2.3.2 Periodic replacement cost

Since the time horizon of calculations τ (see Section 5.2.1.1) was chosen to be equal to the expected lifetime of the photovoltaic system, no periodic replacement cost are considered in the following calculations.

5.2.3.3 Operating cost

Due to a lack of movable parts, photovoltaic installations are almost maintenance free. Therefore, specific operating costs C_O of 50 €/a for a 1 kW_p plant have been assumed in the calculations, including also the insurance cost.

5.2.4 Energy cost

Contrary to other building installations, a photovoltaic plant does not consume but generate electricity. Consequently, the energy cost can be considered to be negative. However, for easier readability, the value of the generated electricity will be considered in the following calculations.
In 2000, the EEG was introduced in Germany, guaranteeing priority access to the grid for renewable energy plants and fixed feed-in-tariffs (FITs) for 20 years. Since the implementation of the EEG, FITs have been adapted downward to decreasing module prices. Since both the average household and commercial electricity tariffs exceed the FIT, photovoltaic plants can be economic even without subsidies when a large share of self-consumption can be ensured. Assuming 100 % self-consumption, average energy costs for electricity C_e of 0.15 €/kWh for non-residential and 0.25 €/kWh for residential buildings are used in the economic assessment of the generated electricity. In the urban areas under consideration, it is assumed that always enough consumers for the generated electricity are present since "self-consumption" in Germany legally also includes the transfer of generated electricity to nearby buildings. Furthermore, the economic potential assessment conducted here encompasses also non-optimally oriented and tilted photovoltaic plants exhibiting a different generation profile than optimally south-oriented installations. Therefore peak electricity generation is lower and electricity generation is more evenly distributed during the day, allowing a greater share of self-consumption.
Due to module degradation, the electricity yield can be expected to decrease by a degradation rate R_{deg} of 0.25 %/a (Kiefer et al. 2010).

5.2.5 LCC calculation

5.2.5.1 Replacement cost

According to DIN EN 15459, the replacement cost are the sum of the periodic replacement cost (see Section 5.2.3.2). Since no periodic replacement cost are considered, the total replacement cost can be omitted here.

5.2.5.2 Residual value

Since 2012, photovoltaic modules are also covered by the European Waste Electrical and Electronic Equipment Directive (WEEE), stating that the recycling of photovoltaic modules is the module producer's legal obligation.[5] Since the value of the module materials is sufficient to cover the disposal and recycling cost, for the economic calculations performed here from the owner's perspective, this means that photovoltaic modules can be recycled for free, i.e. both the modules' residual value and disposal cost equal zero.
Additionally, it should be noted that in the case of multi-functional products like building-integrated photovoltaic installations, the system lifetime of the building product is comparable with traditional building materials. I.e. even if the module stopped generating electricity after a maximum of 30 years, it would still be able to fulfill the functions of a traditional building material.

5.2.5.3 Calculation of the LCC

For the building owner, the investment in the photovoltaic plant, i.e. *building installation alternatives 2a* and *2b*, will only be realized when one of them is more profitable than *building installation alternative 1*, i.e. no investment in a photovoltaic plant and consumption of electricity from the grid. Consequently, the following condition has to hold:

$$C_G(\tau)_{BuildingInstallationAlternative1} > C_G(\tau)_{BuildingInstallationAlternative2} \tag{5.5}$$

[5] For this, the photovoltaic industry has founded a recycling organization called "PVCycle".

Following the initial description of the *building installation alternatives* at the beginning of this chapter, Eq. 5.5 can be reformulated as follows when the value of the generated electricity from the photovoltaic plant is evaluated with the building owner's normal electricity price:

$$-C_G(\tau)_{BuildingInstallationAlternative2} > 0 \tag{5.6}$$

A photovoltaic installation exhibiting a NPV above zero is considered to be included in the economic potential, i.e. the value of the generated electricity over the system lifetime is expected to exceed the initial investment I_0 and the discounted annual operating cost.

$$C_a(i) = E_a * (1 - R_{deg})^i * C_e * (1 + R_e)^i - C_o * (1 + R_o)^i \tag{5.7}$$

Additionally, the LCOE is calculated according to Eq. 5.8 (Konstantin 2013).

$$LCOE = \frac{\sum_{i=1}^{\tau} \frac{C_o*(1+R_o)^i}{(1+R_d)^i}}{\sum_{i=1}^{\tau} \frac{E_a*(1-R_{deg})^i}{(1+R_d)^i}} \tag{5.8}$$

The LCOEs represent the average electricity tariff during the whole considered time horizon for which the plant owner could sell his electricity in order to have LCC of zero when the interest rate is also taken into account. Since the LCOE constitutes an average value for the whole considered time horizon, it should not be confused with the electricity tariff used in the LCC calculation, since this value is only valid for the first year of operation and is then affected by the assumed energy price changes.

5.3 Results of LCC calculation and sensitivity analysis

Since the economic parameters considered in the LCC calculation are uncertain, results are always displayed for a range of the economic parameters considered in the following sections. In the literature, investments and electricity yields for photovoltaic installations are usually stated as specific values, i.e. per kW_p installed capacity of the photovoltaic system. Therefore, the following input values and results are always specific per kW_p installed capacity although in the text for readability reasons the term "specific" was omitted. For better comparison with traditional building materials, in parentheses also the investment in €/m^2 is depicted. An overview is depicted in Tab A.1 in the Annex.
The depicted electricity yield is always stated as the electricity yield in the first year of the operation of the plant, i.e. this does not specify a total electricity yield for the whole system lifetime. The electricity yields in the years following the installation are affected by degradation (see also Eq. 5.7).

5.3.1 Comparison of the impact of time horizon, interest rate and electricity tariff on LCC

In Fig. 5.3, the NPV is plotted versus electricity yield for a specific investment of 1300 €/kW_p (195 €/m^2) for the range of time horizons, interest rates and electricity tariffs considered in this thesis. From this diagram, clearly the large impact of the electricity tariff, interest rate and time horizon considered (in this order) on the LCC of the photovoltaic installation is visible.

5.3.2 Impact of electricity tariff on LCC

In Figs. 5.4, 5.5 and 5.6, the LCC (as quantified by the NPV for the specified time horizon) for a range of specific investments and electricity yields at an interest rate of 5 % for electricity tariffs of 0.15 €/kWh, 0.25 €/kWh and 0.35 €/kWh are depicted. While for a specific investment of 1300 €/kW_p (195 €/m^2)

at an electricity tariff of 0.15 €/kWh, 970 kWh/kW_p are necessary for the investment to break even, at an electricity price of 0.25 €/kWh or 0.35 €/kWh this threshold drops to 580 kWh/kW_p or 420 kWh/kW_p respectively.

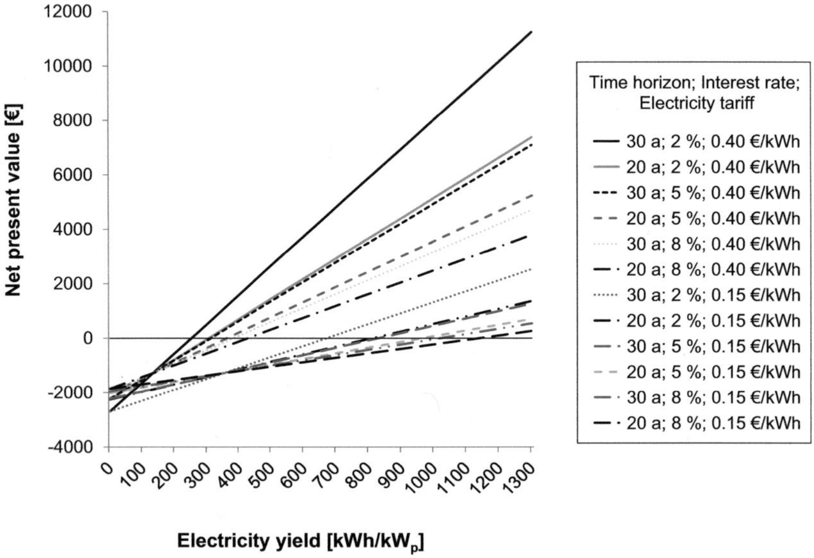

Figure 5.3: Net present value versus electricity yield for a specific investment of 1300 $€/kW_p$ (195 $€/m^2$) for different time horizons, interest rates and electricity tariffs.

5.3.3 Impact of interest rate on LCC

In Fig. 5.7 the LCC are plotted versus electricity yield for a selection of specific investments considered in this thesis as shown in Tab. 5.2 and different interest rates. For systems with a specific investment of 2425 $€/kW_p$ (364 $€/m^2$) at an interest rate of 2 % and an electricity tariff of 0.15 €/kWh at least 1220 kWh/kW_p generated electricity is necessary for the investment to break even over a system lifetime of 20 years. By contrast, for plants with a specific investment below 480 $€/kW_p$ (72 $€/m^2$), ceteris paribus only a specific annual electricity yield above 520 kWh/kW_p is necessary for the investment to break even. Comparing the NPV or LCC for the same specific investment at different interest rates, its effect on LCC is clearly visible. The higher the interest rate, the lower is the impact of the electricity yield on LCC, since all future cash inflows from the generated electricity are more strongly discounted. Viewed from a different angle, this means that in periods of low interest rates, the installation of a photovoltaic plant becomes even more profitable when a certain level of electricity yield can be achieved.

From Figs. 5.3 to 5.7, clearly the large impact of the selection of the economic parameters in the economic potential assessment is visible. Therefore in the following chapters, the economic potential will be generally analyzed with respect to the impact of these influential factors.

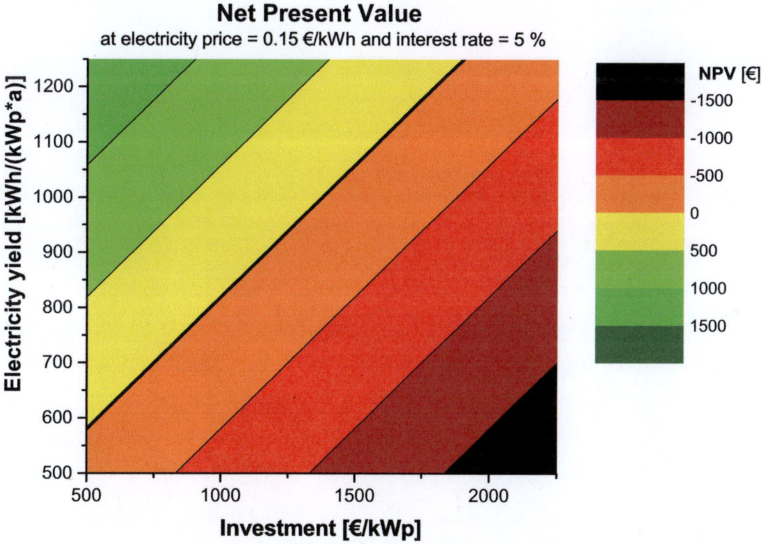

Figure 5.4: LCC at electricity price of 0.15 €/kWh

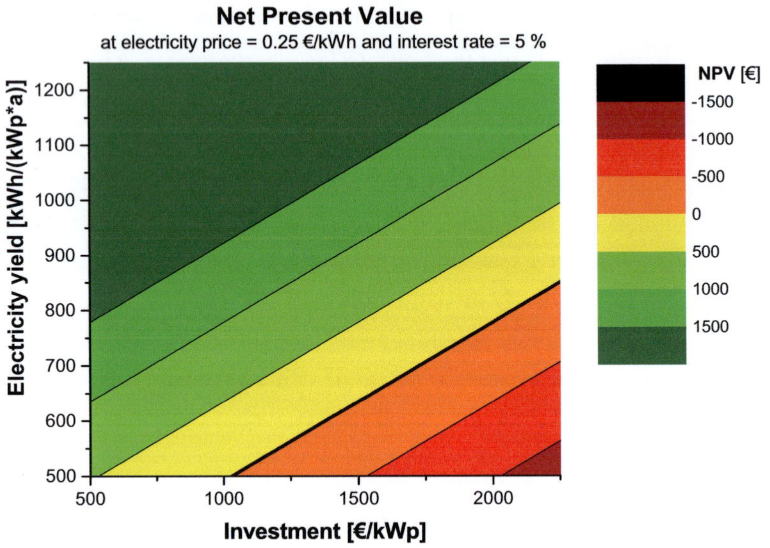

Figure 5.5: LCC at electricity price of 0.25 €/kWh

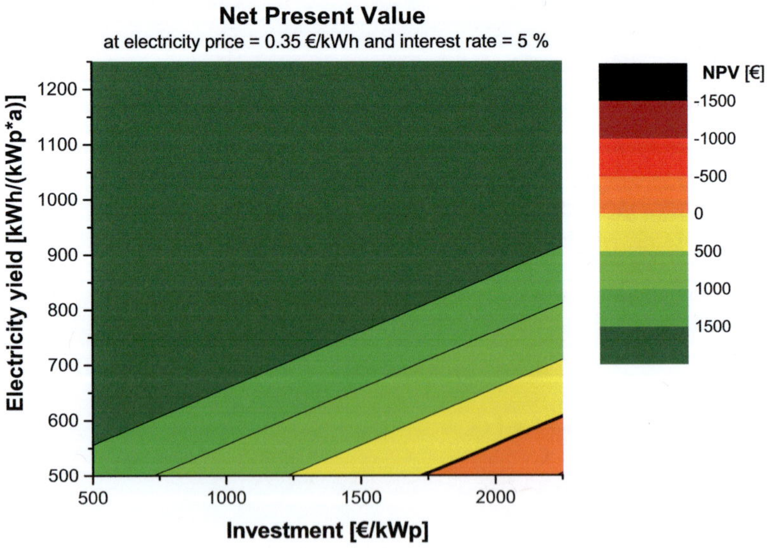

Figure 5.6: LCC at electricity price of 0.35 €/kWh

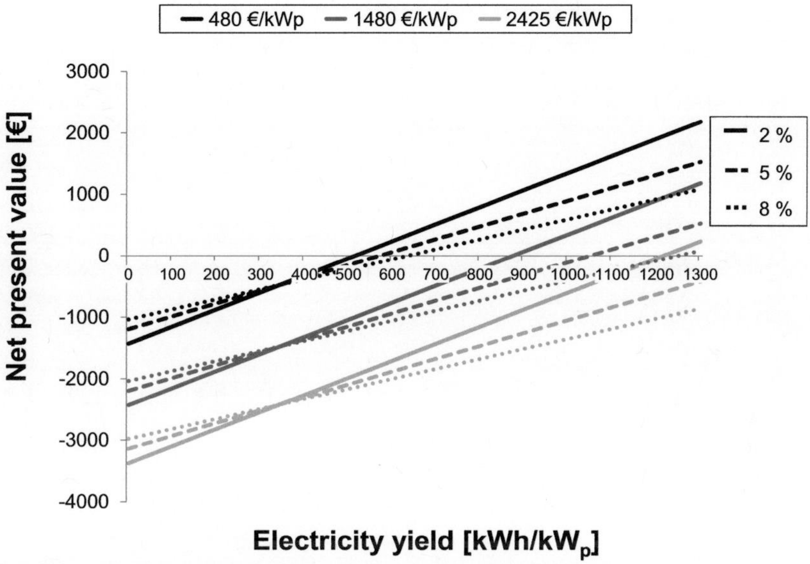

Figure 5.7: Net present value for different specific investments and different interest rates at different electricity yields at an electricity tariff of 0.15 €/kWh

5.4 Results of LCOE calculation and sensitivity analysis

In Fig. 5.8, the LCOE is plotted versus electricity yield for an investment of 1300 €/kW$_p$ (195 €/m^2) for the range of time horizons and interest rates considered. The interest rate has the main influence on the LCOE. At an electricity yield of 1000 kWh/kW$_p$ and an interest rate of 2 %, the LCOE amounts to 0.14 €/kWh, while at an interest rate of 8 %, this amounts to 0.19 €/kWh, both calculated for a time horizon of 20 years.

In Fig. 5.9, the dependence of the LCOE calculated according to Eq. 5.8 on electricity yield is shown for a time horizon of 20 years for a selection of investments and different interest rates at different electricity yields.

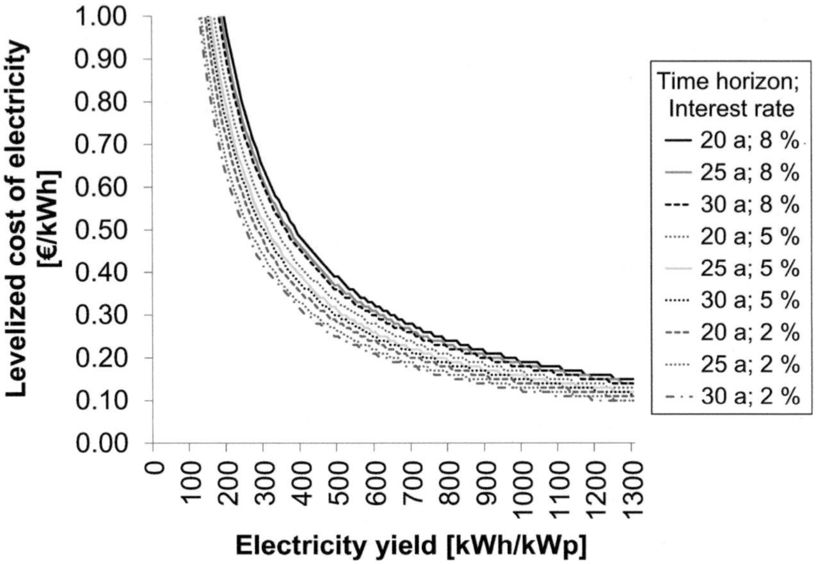

Figure 5.8: Levelized cost of electricity versus electricity yield for an investment of 1300 €/kW$_p$ (195 €/m^2) and different time horizons and interest rates.

Since the operating costs were assumed to be equal for all analyzed scenarios, the investment is the main determinant of the LCOE. For an investment of 480 €/kW$_p$ (72 €/m^2) and an interest rate of 2 %, the LCOE for an electricity yield of 580 kWh/kW$_p$ to 610 kWh/kW$_p$ amounts to 0.15 €/kWh, which is a little higher than the 520 kWh/kW$_p$ necessary for the investment to break even at an electricity tariff of 0.15 €/kWh (see Section 5.3.3). As explained already in Section 5.2.5.3, the reason for this is the fact that the electricity tariff considered in the LCC calculation is subject to price increases during the system lifetime, while the LCOE constitutes an average value for the whole considered time horizon.

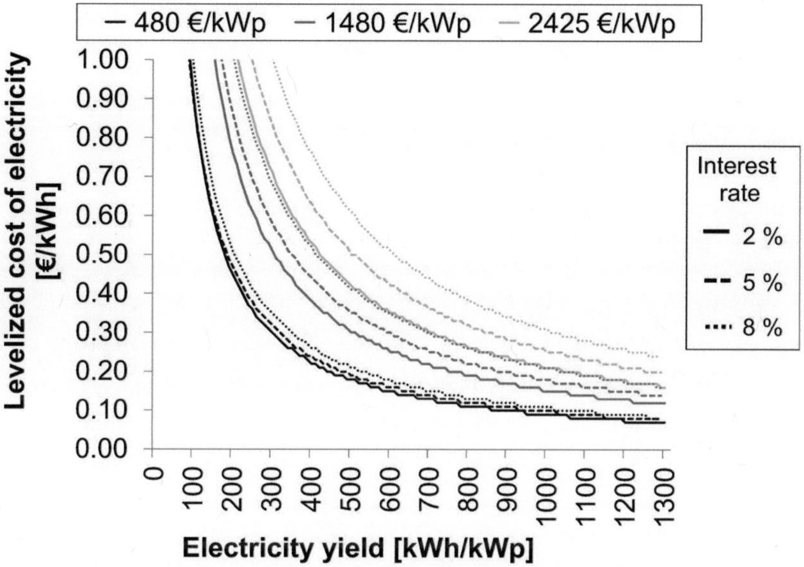

Figure 5.9: Levelized cost of electricity versus electricity yield for different investments and different interest rates.

5.5 Legal situation in Germany affecting the economic potential

In Germany, since 2000 the main determinants of the economic potential for photovoltaic installations have been the feed-in tariffs fixed in the EEG.
Since the assumption of 100 % self-consumption of the generated electricity and therefore a valuation of the generated electricity with the electricity tariff has a large impact on the economic potential, some other interpretations shall be presented in the following.
In reality, depending on the building type and the surface area suitable for the installation of a photovoltaic plant, 100 % instantaneous self-consumption is not always feasible. In this case, the photovoltaic plant owner has two options: He can either use the generated electricity for e.g. heating purposes or feed the

electricity into the grid.[6] However, for both cases here it is assumed that the plant owner is not remunerated for the generated electricity. Nevertheless, the methodology developed in this thesis still allows the economic potential to be determined under these circumstances.

Example 1 - 50 % self-consumption of generated electricity and no feed-in tariff

Assuming that the owner can consume only 50 % of the generated electricity, again only this share can be valuated with the electricity tariff, of e.g. 0.25 €/kWh. In order still to determine the economic potential, the electricity tariff can be multiplied with the share of self-consumption, resulting in an average electricity tariff of 0.125 €/kWh. Thus, to determine the potential, from e.g. Fig. 5.9, only the installation of a photovoltaic plant with a specific investment of less than 480 €/kW$_p$ (72 €/m^2) will be profitable when the electricity yield is at least 720 kWh/kW$_p$ and the interest rate is 2 %.

Example 2 - 50 % self-consumption of generated electricity and feed-in tariff of 0.10 €/kWh

Assuming that the owner can consume only 50 % of the generated electricity, again only this share can be valuated with the electricity tariff, of e.g. 0.25 €/kWh. The other 50 % of the generated electricity are assumed to be fed into the grid at an electricity tariff of 0.10 €/kWh.[7] In order to determine the economic potential for the owner, the share of the self-consumed electricity can be assessed with his electricity tariff of 0.25 €/kWh while the remaining share can be valuated with the feed-in tariff of 0.10 €/kWh. From this, an

[6] Another option is the installation of a battery storage system. However, due to the still developing market for battery storage systems at the time of completion of this thesis, this option was considered to be outside the scope of this research.

[7] In Germany, feed-in tariffs for renewable energy plants have been fixed since 2000 in the EEG for a period of e.g. 20 years for photovoltaic installations. However, since its introduction, the EEG has been subject to multiple changes and finally a strong decrease of electricity tariffs. Therefore, for this research it was decided not to consider a feed-in tariff in the calculations since the resulting economic potential would be quickly outdated.

average electricity tariff of 0.175 €/kWh for all the electricity generated by the photovoltaic installation results. Thus, to determine the potential, from e.g. Fig. 5.9, only the installation of a photovoltaic plant with a specific investment of less than 1480 €/kW$_p$ (222 €/m^2) will be profitable when the electricity yield is at least 880 kWh/kW$_p$ and the interest rate is 2 %.

Example 3 - 100 % self-consumption of generated electricity and obligation to pay the reduced EEG apportionment

Since the introduction of the EEG 2014, the owner of a photovoltaic installation has been obliged to pay the reduced EEG apportionment for self-consumed electricity. This was considered necessary to ensure that owners of photovoltaic installations still contribute to the maintenance and renewal of the electricity grid, which they still use as a backup and an outlet if electricity generation exceeds their demand. Therefore, the plant owner on the one hand saves electricity costs corresponding to his generated electricity. On the other hand, he additionally has to pay the reduced EEG apportionment to the distribution grid operator which amounted in 2016 to 35 % of 0.0635 €/kWh.[8] Thus, he did not save 0.25 €/kWh for every self-generated kilowatt-hour, but this tariff has to be reduced by 0.02 €/kWh resulting in a net valuation of the generated electricity of 0.23 €/kWh. Again, determining the economic potential, from e.g. Fig. 5.9, the installation of a photovoltaic plant with a specific investment of less than 1480 €/kW$_p$ (222 €/m^2) will only be profitable at an interest rate of 2 % when the electricity yield is at least 700 kWh/kW$_p$.

5.6 Conclusion and scenario consideration

5.6.1 Economic scenarios

In total, 648 scenarios for the economic potential assessment were considered, as depicted in Tab. 5.3. It was considered necessary to simulate this large

[8] The EEG apportionment on self-consumed electricity generation is adapted stepwise annually, starting from 30 % in 2015, 35 % in 2016 up to 40 % in 2017 (EEG 2014).

number of scenarios due to the volatile nature of economic parameters and the long-term perspective (until 2050 - see Section 9.4) of this thesis.

Table 5.3: Number of economic scenarios considered

Time horizon τ		Interest rate R_d3		Energy cost C_e		Invest- ment C_I		Total number of scenarios
3	*	3	*	6	*	12	=	648
20, 25, 30 [a]		2, 5, 8 [%]		0.15, 0.2, 0.25, 0.3, 0.35, 0.4 [€/kWh]		see Tab. 5.2		

Considering roofs and facades separately and irradiation classes from 0 to 1300 kWh/kW_p in 10 kWh steps results in 126,360 combinations of time horizon, interest rate, elecitricty price, investments, plant types and irradiation classes. 70,098 of these combinations have a positive NPV and can therefore be considered further in the economic potential assessment. However, for readability reasons, in the following the three scenarios depicted in Tab. 5.4 will be discussed explicitly while the other considered scenarios will be depicted as a range of possible potential development.

Table 5.4: Three considered main scenarios

	High potential	**Status quo**	**Low potential**
Interest rate	$\geq 2\,\%$	$\geq 2\,\%$	$\geq 5\,\%$
Time horizon [a]	≤ 30	≤ 25	≤ 20
Electricity price [€/kWh]	≤ 0.35	≤ 0.25	≤ 0.15

In Fig. 5.10, the share of parameter combinations with a positive NPV per irradiation class in the three considered scenarios is depicted. This figure should be interpreted as follows: For the *High potential* scenario, i.e. assuming interest rates of 2 % or more, a plant operating time horizon of up to 30 years and electricity tariffs of up to 0.35 €/kWh, 54,834 parameter combinations (i.e. scenarios) exist with a positive NPV of which

- one was realized at an electricity yield between 100 kWh/kW$_p$ and 200 kWh/kW$_p$, i.e. irradiation class 100 kWh/kW$_p$ and
- 9 % were realized at an electricity yield between 600 kWh/kW$_p$ and 700 kWh/kW$_p$, i.e. irradiation class 600 kWh/kW$_p$.

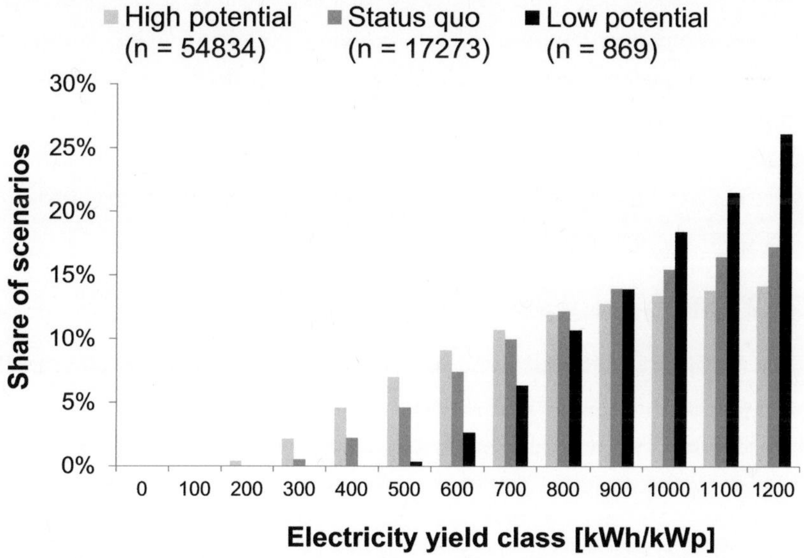

Figure 5.10: Share of combinations of interest rate, time horizon and electricity price per irradiation class in the considered scenarios

From this figure, it is visible that for the *Low potential* scenario,[9] it is only economic to install a photovoltaic plant on building surfaces where it will generate more than 500 kWh/kW$_p$. Since for the electricity yield calculation, sensor

[9] In this scenario, interest rates of 5 % or more, a plant operating time horizon of up to 20 years and electricity prices of up to 0.15 €/kWh are assumed.

points on building surfaces had to be aggregated, those receiving an amount of irradiation below a threshold value sufficient for generating at least 500 kWh/kW$_p$ have to be filtered, since they will actually influence the economic potential negatively in all considered scenarios. Since the relationship between the solar irradiation and the electricity yield is dependent on a range of influential factors like module efficiency, temperature and the solar incidence angle (see Section 3.2) that were considered in the electricity generation potential calculation this procedure would have been far too complex for an initial filtering of sensor points. Therefore here a simplified approach of a linear relationship between the solar irradiation [kWh/(m^{2}a)] and the electricity yield [kWh/(kW$_p$a)] was chosen. Thus, before taking the average of the hourly irradiation values on the sensor points on one building surface, sensor points receiving a solar irradiation of less than 500 kWh/(m^{2}a) were filtered out and therefore omitted from further analysis. The building surface area available for a photovoltaic installation is consequently reduced by the respective area.

5.6.2 Investment scenarios

Since the focus of this thesis is on the economic potential of photovoltaic installations on buildings, with the investment being one of the main determinants for this, additionally four investment scenarios will be considered in the analyses of Section 6.2.3.3 and Chapter 9:

1. Conventional investment scenario: Investment in roof and facade installations corresponding to I_{roof} and I_{facade} in Tab. 5.2.
2. BIPV investment scenario: Investment in roof and facade installations corresponding to $I_{roof,BIPV}$ and $I_{facade,BIPV}$ in Tab. 5.2.
3. Optimistic BIPV investment scenario: Investment in roof and facade installations corresponding to I_{roof} in Tab. 5.2.
4. Very optimistic BIPV investment scenario: Investment in roof and facade installations corresponding to $I_{roof,BIPV}*$ in Tab. 5.2.

6 Potential for photovoltaic systems on individual buildings

As described in Chapter 1, the assessment of the potential for photovoltaic installations on buildings in Germany is divided into three steps. In this chapter, the first step, the assessment of the potential on individual buildings is presented. Since it is not possible to analyze every single building in Germany to reach the objective of this study, i.e. the assessment of a national photovoltaic potential, the commonly used approach in building stock analysis of employing a building typology has been chosen. For this purpose, existing typologies for residential (Section 6.1.1) and non-residential buildings (Section 6.2.1) are reviewed concerning their suitability for a photovoltaic potential assessment. For residential buildings, from the analysis of an existing building typology, a solar residential building typology with the attributes relevant for the large-scale potential asssessment conducted in Chapter 8 is deducted (Section 6.1.2). For non-residential buildings, from existing typologies no differentiation concerning the solar potential can be derived (Section 6.2.3). Therefore, in Section 6.2.4 for further usage in Chapter 8, a cluster analysis for the creation of a solar non-residential building typology is performed.
Additionally, for the national potential assessment it is of major importance to have an indication of the number of buildings per identified building type. Therefore, this aspect is also considered in the following review of existing building typologies.

6.1 Residential buildings

In Germany, detailed information exists about the residential building stock consisting of 18.4 mio buildings (Statistisches Bundesamt 2013). Data on the location (assignment to a municipality), type, age and size of every residential building in Germany was collected during a national census in 2011. Before the census in 2011, data on the number of residential buildings originated from assessments in 1987 for former West Germany and 1995 for former East Germany. Until the census in 2011, the current residential building stock was estimated based on these assessments and the annual numbers of newly constructed and demolished buildings (Statistisches Bundesamt 2014b). In the course of the years, this approach led to deviations of approximately 500,000 apartments (Jensen 2013).

6.1.1 Residential building typology

A detailed building typology exists for residential buildings (Institut Wohnen und Umwelt 2005) and has already been used often for building stock analysis (McKenna et al. (2013); Stengel (2014)). In the course of analysing the census conducted in 2011, this building typology was revised by adding building types for the most recent building age classes (Loga et al. 2015). As a result, for 40 building type and age combinations, detailed information on building shape, size, materials and energy-relevant attributes exist. The following four building types are differentiated (Loga et al. 2015):[1]

- Single-family house (SFH)
- Terraced house (TH)
- Multi-family house (MFH)
- Apartment building (AB)

The building age categories are not defined by time periods of equal duration, but instead are set according to historic events that had a major impact on the

[1] A typical building is not defined for every building size in every age category.

energy-relevant quality of the building stock, like for example the reconstruction of cities after two World Wars in the 1950s with limited resources, urban expansion during the “Wirtschaftswunder" (English: Economic miracle) in the 1960s, urban renewal after an economic crisis in the 1970s resulting in the first Thermal Insulation Ordinance[2] and finally urban development after German reunification in the 1990s (Breuer (2010), Kohler et al. (1999)). Thus, buildings falling into the same building age category exhibit similar energy-relevant and architectural properties. The following building age categories are denoted by the following suffixes (Loga et al. 2015):

- A - before 1859,
- B - 1860 - 1918,
- C - 1919 - 1948,
- D - 1949 - 1957,
- E - 1958 - 1968,
- F - 1969 - 1978,
- G - 1979 - 1983,
- H - 1984 - 1994,
- I - 1995 - 2001,
- J - 2002 - 2009,
- K - 2010 - 2015 and
- L - 2016 and later.

In Figs. 6.1 to 6.4, the attributes relevant to the photovoltaic potential of a building, i.e. total building surface A_{total}, roof A_{ro} and facade A_{fa} area, are summarized for every building age category of the four building types (Loga et al. 2015). Since the sample size in each category is not known, it is not possible to analyze the statistical significance of the differences between categories. Therefore further analysis will be conducted to test a possible alternative summary of building type and age combinations.

[2] In German: 1. Wärmeschutzverordnung.

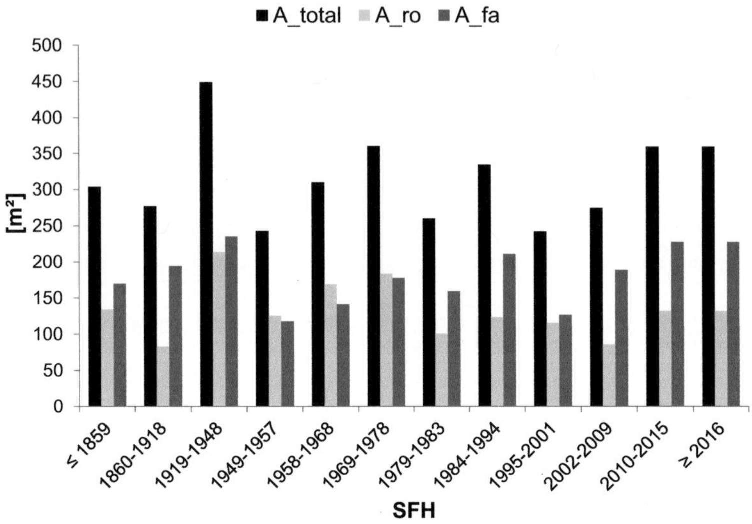

Figure 6.1: Total building surface A_{total}, roof A_{ro} and facade A_{fa} area for all SFH building age categories (Loga et al. 2015)

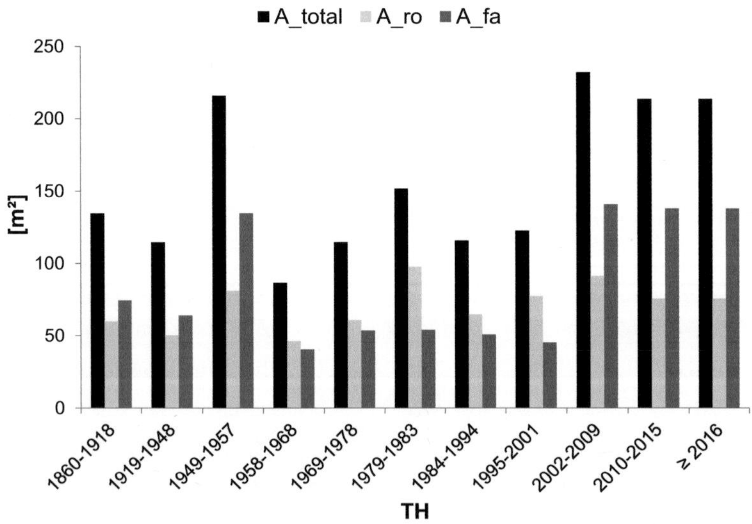

Figure 6.2: Total building surface A_{total}, roof A_{ro} and facade A_{fa} area for all TH building age categories (Loga et al. 2015)

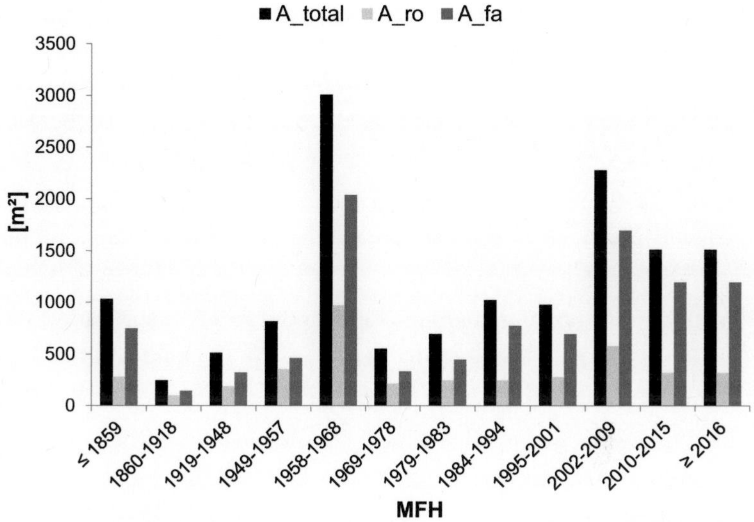

Figure 6.3: Total building surface A_{total}, roof A_{ro} and facade A_{fa} area for all MFH building age categories (Loga et al. 2015)

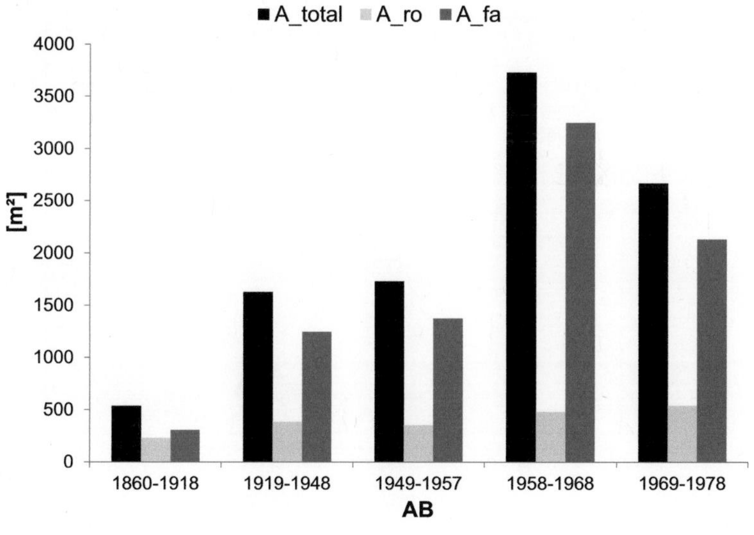

Figure 6.4: Total building surface A_{total}, roof A_{ro} and facade A_{fa} area for all AB building age categories (Loga et al. 2015)

6.1.2 Creation of a solar residential building typology

The 40 building type and age combinations of the residential building typology presented in the previous section are considered by the author to be too detailed and too similar in attributes relevant for the photovoltaic potential. In this section, it is analyzed, how these categories can be regrouped for the creation of a solar residential building typology containing only attributes relevant for the photovoltaic potential.

In Figs. 6.5 to 6.8, boxplot diagrams for the total building surface area A_{total}, the facade area A_{fa}, the share of the facade area in the total building surface area and the facade area transparency ration TR_{fa} are presented for the four building types aggregating all available building age categories. The results of the analysis of the roof area A_{ro} for the four building types is similar or complementary and therefore not listed here explicitly. The boxplot diagrams can be found in the Annex in Figs. A.1 and A.2.

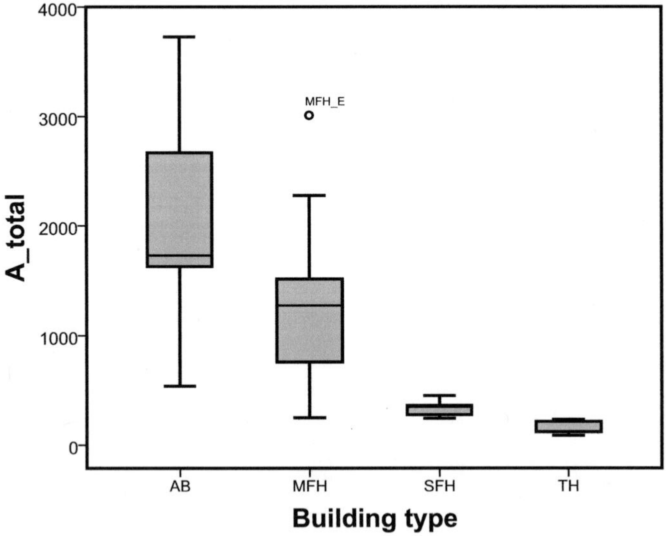

Figure 6.5: Total building surface area A_{total}

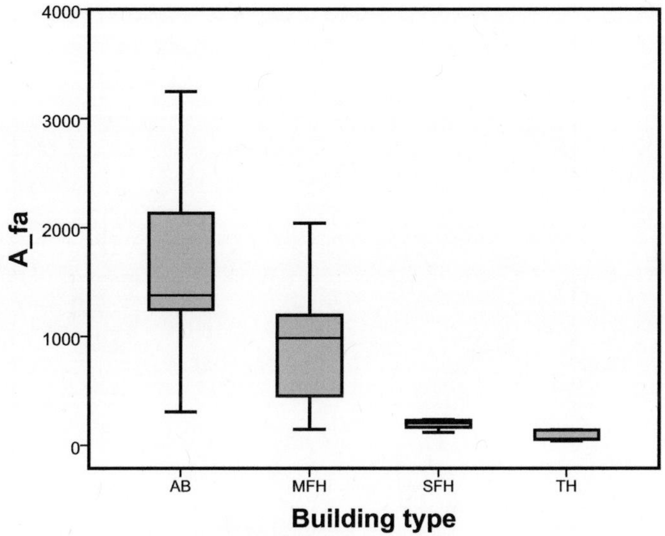

Figure 6.6: Facade area A_{fa}

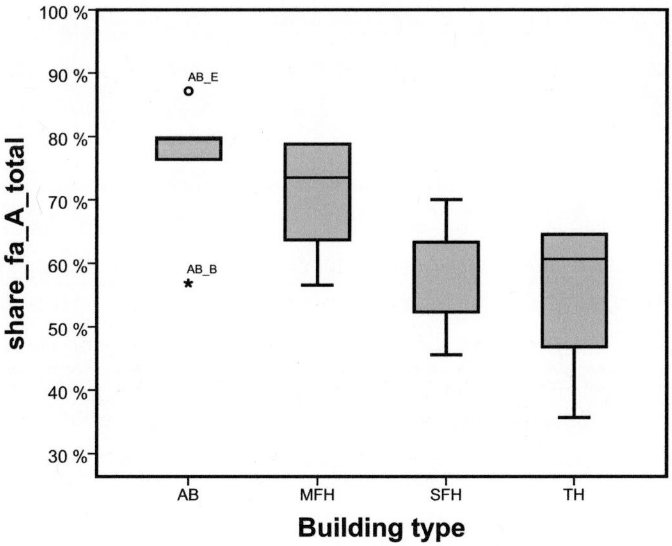

Figure 6.7: Share of facade area in total building surface area

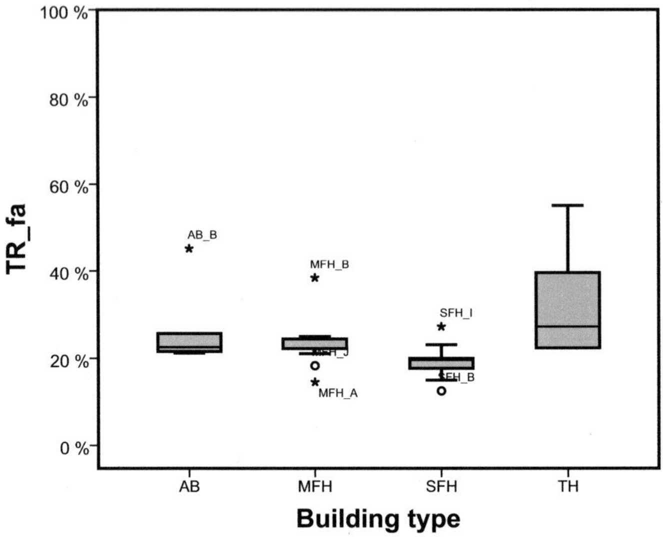

Figure 6.8: Facade transparency ratio TR_{fa}.

For the creation of a solar residential building typology with quantative attributes for typical buildings, first outliers and extreme values should be eliminated. From the boxplot diagrams, a first visual identification of outliers and extreme values for the four building types is possible.[3] According to Hair (2010), observations with a standardized z-score above 2.5 should be considered outliers, which was taken as the normative criterion here. Standardizing by the z-transformation converts the value of all attributes such that the mean is 0 and the standard deviation is 1. The standardized z-scores were calculated according to Eq. 6.1 with z being the standardized value, x being the non-standardized value of the attribute, μ being the average of the attribute and σ being the standard deviation (Bacher et al. 2010).

[3] The boxplot diagrams were automatically generated with the SPSS program. For a definition of outliers and extreme values in SPSS see Brosius (2013).

$$z = \frac{x - \mu}{\sigma} \tag{6.1}$$

This analysis results in the building categories MFH_E and AB_F being identified as outliers such that they will be considered separately. MFH_E and AB_F are classified as very large buildings, so that this more meaningful description will be used further. Thus, six residential building categories are differentiated in the following analysis for which the specification and the average attributes values are documented in Tab. 6.1.

Table 6.1: Average values of selected attributes for the six residential building categories formed; *N* denotes the number of building type and age combinations summarized in the building category.

	N	Year of construction	A_{total}	A_{ro}	A_{fa}	TR_{fa}
SFH	16	all	326	133	193	19 %
TH	15	all	171	72	99	32 %
MFH	15	< 1958; > 1968	1148	296	853	24 %
MFH$_{\mathbf{large}}$	1	1958 - 1968	3010	971	2039	25 %
AB	3	< 1958	1298	323	975	30 %
AB$_{\mathbf{large}}$	2	1958 - 1978	3199	510	2689	23 %

For this residential building typology, an estimate of the number of buildings per building type according to the census in 2011 exists (Diefenbach 2013). This estimate will be used in up-scaling the individual building results to a national potential in Chapter 8. High-rise residential buildings are not considered due to their limited occurrence.

6.2 Non-residential buildings

Compared to residential buildings, non-residential buildings are much more heterogeneous. Also, no national census for non-residential buildings has been performed since 1950 (Gierga and Erhorn 1993). As a consequence, no non-residential building typology with an indication of buildings per building type exists. Therefore, in the following section, initially existing non-residential building typologies are reviewed concerning their suitability for utilization in a photovoltaic potential study. Based on the result of this analysis, a new photovoltaic building typology containing the attributes relevant for the large-scale potential asssessment will be developed.

6.2.1 Review of non-residential building typologies

Since there has been no national census of the non-residential building stock since 1950, existing non-residential building typologies with indicators of resource or energy consumption and estimates of the number of buildings are always based on an incomplete database (Gierga and Erhorn (1993); Sonntag and Mittner (1993); Kohler et al. (1999); BMVBS (2011b); Gruhler and Böhm (2011); BMVBS (2013)). Additionally, none of these studies has treated the embedding of the building in the urban context in detail which would allow conclusions to be drawn on possible solar gains. Therefore, for a long time only estimates ranging from approximately 3 million (BMVBS 2013) to a total of 20 million non-residential buildings (Behnisch 2008) existed for the non-residential building stock .
A large-scale assessment of the number of buildings is the IÖR-Monitor by the Leibniz Institute of Ecological Urban and Regional Development (IÖR) offering indicators on land-use development in Germany, including information on general and residential building density in various urban structures based on the building footprints provided by the AdV (Leibniz-Institut für ökologische Raumentwicklung 2014). However, since the building type is not specified and the urban land-use structures only differentiate between 'Residential area', 'Combined use area', 'Specific functional area' and 'Industry, commercial area' (Meinel et al. 2013), this database was considered not to be sufficiently detailed. The most complete database of buildings in Germany consists of the so-called cadastral data, which however are split between the 16 federal states. They have just recently been summarized by the Working Committee of the Surveying

Authorities of the States of the Federal Republic of Germany (AdV) such that now a database with a total of 50.5 million geographically referenced building footprints for all German buildings (i.e. residential and non-residential) exists. Even though this database still lacks information on building type (AdV 2014b), from this it can be concluded that approximately 32.1 million non-residential buildings exist. Furthermore, the AdV is preparing a national database with 3D building models in LOD 1, i.e. simple building block models without exact roof shapes, but using an approximate building height (Westenberg and Will (2013); AdV (2014a)). However, the cost of this data hinders wide-spread usage (Esch and Tum 2013). Since this database was not available for this study, a different approach for estimating the number of non-residential buildings in Germany will be employed (see Chapter 8).

In order to make results comparable, it was decided to use the cadastral non-residential building typology (ALK). There, 78 building types are differentiated (Landesvermessungsamt Baden-Württemberg 2005). Since the definitions there are often quite similar, for the purposes of this study it was decided to reduce the number of building types. Therefore they were categorized into the 8 first-level building categories for non-residential buildings[4] used in BMVBS (2013) and supplemented by the building categories 'Agricultural', 'Other' and 'Residential'. In Tab. 6.2, this assignment of ALK building categories to BMVBS (2013) categories is depicted.[5] Unlike the residential building typology (Institut Wohnen und Umwelt 2005), no detailed information on factors influencing the suitability for the installation of a photovoltaic system like building sizes, surface area or location are available for these non-residential building categories, such that the author decided to create her own building typology, from which the economic potential for a photovoltaic installation on a non-residential building can be derived.

[4] These 8 building categories are further separated into 23 sub-categories in BMVBS (2013). However, this level of differentiation was considered too detailed for the analysis performed here.

[5] For readability reasons, the building category 'Other', where 28 building types were summarized, was omitted since this category was considered to be too heterogeneous.

Table 6.2: Categorization of ALK building types according to the BMVBS (2013) building typology with additional building categories 'Agricultural' and 'Residential' without buildings falling into the 'Other' building category

BMVBS (2013)	ALK
Education	School Research University Childcare center Court City hall
Offices & Administration	Administrative Fire department Prison Police Mail Mixed residential and administrative building Office Mixed residential and office
Commercial & Industrial	Factory Warehouse Workshop Energy supply Sewage plant Waste incineration
Healthcare	Hospital Rehabilitation Sanatorium

BMVBS (2013)	ALK
Sports	Sports hall Swimming pool Sports facility
Culture	Library Museum Entertainment building Community building
Hospitality & Food Services	Restaurant Hotel Hostel
Agricultural	Operation building Forestry Barn and stall Mixed residential and agricultural Agricultural
Residential	Nursing home Residential Weekend house
Trade & Service	Commercial Trade exhibition Mixed residential and commercial

6.2.2 Non-residential buildings database

During the work on this thesis, for research purposes the author had access to a database of approximately 100 planned building projects with detailed geometry and builiding usage data from a commercial enterprise in the construction industry. Since this number of buildings is far from being representative for the German non-residential building stock, special care has been devoted in the selection process for further analysis to achieve a range concerning building type, location and geometry.

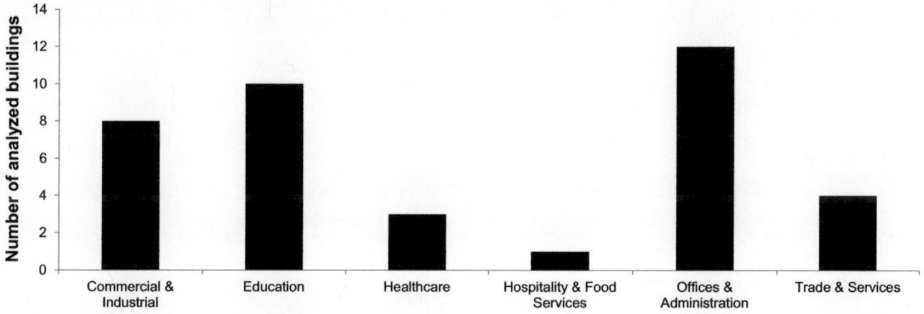

Figure 6.9: Analyzed buildings according to BMVBS (2013) building categories

Eventually, a total of 38 buildings were collected, for which the following detailed information on factors subjectively considered to influence the photovoltaic potential were available:

- Location,
- building type,
- building surface areas,
  - roof area,
  - facade area,
  - share of transparent surfaces,
  - orientation,
  - tilt angle,

- number of storeys and
- settlement type.

This data was entered in a database. The frequency distribution of the analyzed buildings according to the BMVBS (2013) building categories is shown in Fig. 6.9. In order to prevent bias from specific regional construction types, a regional distribution of the analyzed buildings has been sought.

6.2.3 Photovoltaic potential assessment

In this section, based on the quantitative data from the previously described non-residential buildings database, the solar potential according to BMVBS (2013) building categories is assessed concerning the suitability for further usage in Chapter 8. Here, the potential assessment developed in this thesis is demonstrated in detail. Since this typology does not prove suitable, the author of this thesis created her own solar non-residential building typology (Section 6.2.4).

6.2.3.1 Theoretical potential

For the assessment of the theoretical potential and for further usage in the technical potential assessment, a 3D building model for each of the 38 selected buildings was created. The 3D building model was created manually in SketchUp in LOD2 from architectural plans, aerial and terrestrial images and available 3D models in the AutoCAD file format. Concerning this re-modeling of buildings with an already existing 3D model it should be noted that 3D modeling for construction planning and 3D modeling for solar irradiation simulation are two application areas utilizing different software tools with limited compatibility. E.g. 3D models for building planning comprise a higher LOD to be useful for the intended purpose and also contain additional information like material type, connection with other building elements or cost, then also called Building Information Modeling (BIM). By contrast, for solar irradiation simulation, only exterior surface areas and their material properties are relevant.

All additional information increases file sizes and calculation times without generating additional insights. The SketchUp models of the buildings were transformed to the Radiance file format *.*rad* for further analysis.
From these 3D models, some attributes like building surface areas could be retrieved automatically. Other attributes were calculated by hand from the available planning documents. The descriptive statistical parameters of the 38 analyzed buildings when analyzed as a single sample set are listed in Tab. 6.3.

Table 6.3: Descriptive statistical parameters of 38 analyzed buildingswith the standard deviation given as percentage of the average value

	Minimum	**Maximum**	**Average**	**Standard deviation**
A_{total} [m^2]	1985	73,921	14,429	113 %
A_{ro} [m^2]	620	54,979	6580	163 %
A_{fa} [m^2]	1184	31,783	7850	96 %
A_{fa}/A_{total}	26 %	88 %	60 %	24 %
A_{ro}/A_{total}	12 %	74 %	40 %	37 %
TR_{total}	5 %	80 %	36 %	51 %
A_{fp} [m^2]	620	46,766	5520	153 %

From the standard deviation amounting to more than 100 % of the average value, the heterogeneity of the analyzed building database is clear. Therefore, the buildings were clustered according to the BMVBS (2013) building categories. The resulting standard deviations as a percentage of the average value are listed in Tab. 6.4. It ranges from a minimum of 11 % for the share of facade area to total building surface area (education buildings) to a maximum of 180 % for the total roof area (offices & administration buildings). In Figs. 6.10 to 6.13, boxplot diagrams for the statistical distribution of these attributes are depicted. The total building surface area constitutes the theoretical potential.

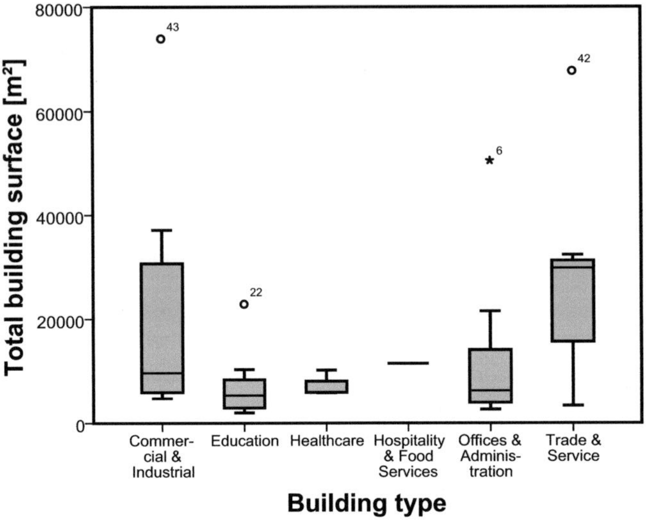

Figure 6.10: Total building surface area according to building types

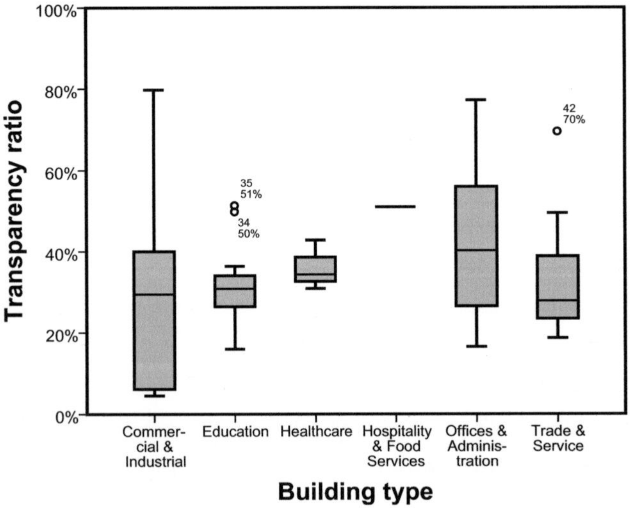

Figure 6.11: Transparency ratio of total building surface according to building types

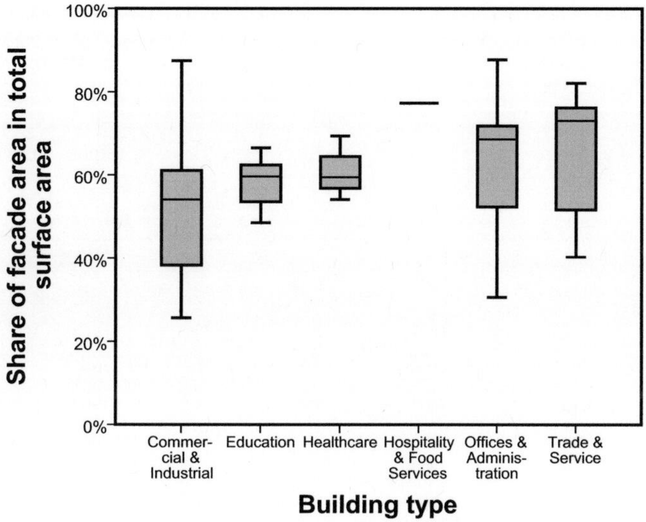

Figure 6.12: Share of facade area in total building surface area according to building types

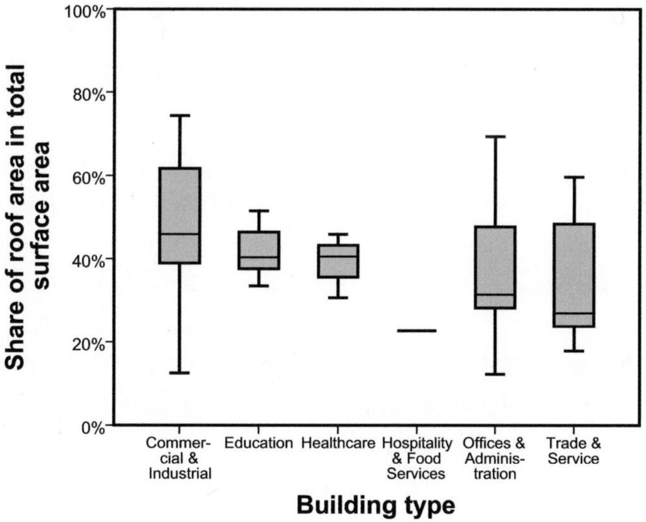

Figure 6.13: Share of roof area in total building surface area according to building types

Table 6.4: Standard deviation as percentage of the average for the theoretical potential according to BMVBS (2013) building categories; The building category 'Hospitality & Food Services' is not depicted, since here only one building has been analyzed. *N* denotes the number of buildings analyzed in this category.

Standard deviation [%] of	Commercial & Industrial	Education	Healthcare	Offices & Administration	Trade & Service
A_{total}	108	85	34	116	74
A_{ro}	142	74	14	180	110
A_{fa}	79	92	47	81	65
A_{fa}/A_{total}	37	11	13	24	26
A_{ro}/A_{total}	40	15	20	42	46
TR_{total}	88	34	17	43	54
A_{fp}	133	74	37	99	91
N	8	10	3	12	4

6.2.3.2 Technical potential

Location potential

To determine the location potential, as defined in Section 2.1.2, the solar irradiation convertible into electricity on available surface areas has to be assessed. Unlike the theoretical potential, for the location potential also shading from surrounding buildings is relevant. But, almost no documentation about them existed in the analyzed database so that their location and height had to be estimated from aerial images, allowing only a modeling in LOD1 (see Section 2.1.2). However, for the analysis of their shading effects on the considered buildings, this LOD is considered sufficient.

Thus, as has been described in Section 4.1, the following analysis steps have been performed for all 38 considered buildings for the irradiation simulation employing the lighting simulation tool Radiance:

1. Creation of a 3D building model in LOD2 in SketchUp
2. Conversion to the Radiance file format
3. Positioning of sensor points in the normal direction on both sides of every building surface
4. Identification of illuminated sensor points for usage in further analysis
5. Simulation of the hourly-resolved irradiation for one year on every sensor point including shading and reflections from the surroundings
6. Integration of the hourly time series to an annual irradiation total
7. Calculation of the area-weighted average annual solar irradiation of all building surfaces representing the location potential

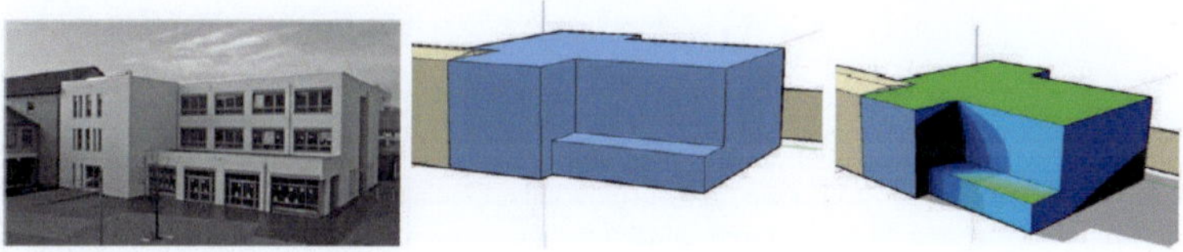

Figure 6.14: Modeling of an exemplary building. Left: View on original building. Middle: LOD2 model of building. Right: Cumulative (annual) result of irradiation simulation.

In Fig. 6.14 an exemplary assessment of a building is depicted, starting from modeling the original building in LOD2 and then performing an irradiation simulation on all building surfaces.

In Fig. 6.15, the location potential is depicted in relation to the global horizontal irradiation of the building location. From this, no correlation between the global horizontal irradiation and the location potential can be deducted. Therefore it can be concluded that the building characteristics like the number of storeys and shape have a greater influence on the location potential than the geographic location within Germany with a limited range of solar irradiation levels.

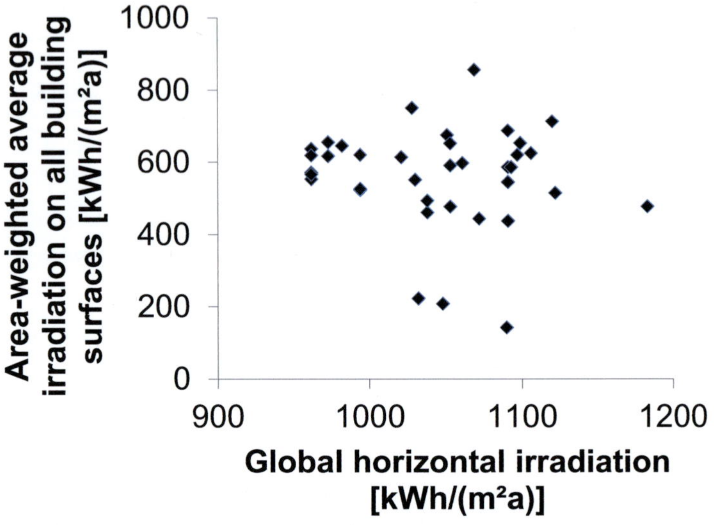

Figure 6.15: Annual global irradiation on a horizontal surface and area-weighted average irradiation on all building surfaces of 38 considered buildings

Electricity generation potential

For the calculation of the electricity generation potential, the electricity yield for every building surface was simulated according to the methdology described in Section 4.2:

1. Calculation of the cumulative annual irradiation on every sensor point
2. Filtering of sensor points with an irradiation below the threshold value of 500 kWh/(m^2a) (see Section 5.6)
3. Calculation of the average hourly irradiation of remaining sensor points
4. Calculation of the hourly-resolved specific electricity yield for every building surface (in kWh/kW_p)
5. Calculation of the area-weighted average electricity yield of all building surfaces for one building, constituting the electricity generation potential for that building

In Fig. 6.16, the electricity generation potential with respect to the annual global irradiation on a horizontal surface at the building location of all 38 considered buildings is depicted. In Fig. 6.17 the location potential and the electricity generation potential of the 38 considered buildings are depicted.

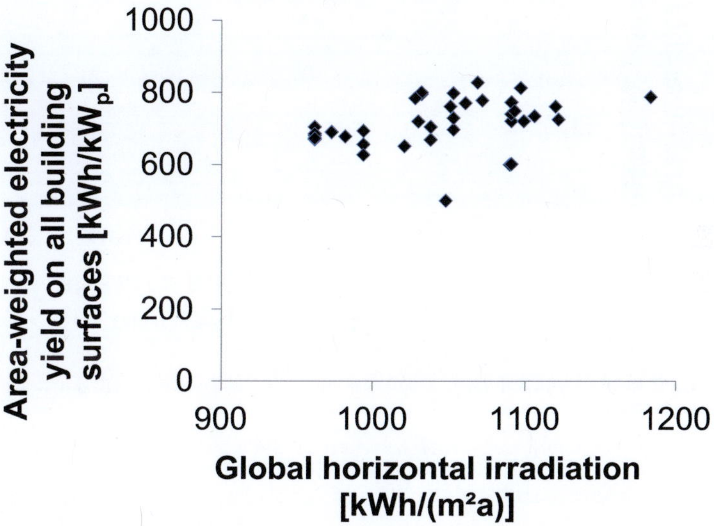

Figure 6.16: Annual global irradiation on a horizontal surface and area-weighted average electricity yield on all surfaces of the 38 considered buildings

While for the location potential, no correlation between the annual global horizontal irradiation and the average irradiation on all building surfaces could be detected, for the electricity generation potential a weak correlation of 0.34 with both the annual global horizontal irradiation and the area-weighted average irradiation results. One explanation is the fact that building surface areas with an irradiation below 500 kWh/(m^2a) were filtered out so that these strongly shaded areas due to exterior influences like surrounding buildings or building architecture do not have a negative impact on total electricity yield.

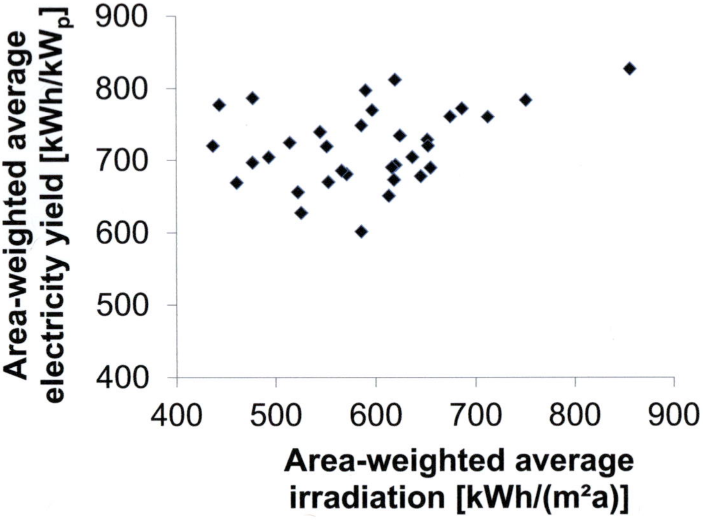

Figure 6.17: Area-weighted average irradiation and electricity yield on all surfaces of the 38 considered buildings

6.2.3.3 Economic potential

For the economic potential assessment, as described in Section 5, due to the large uncertainty inherent in economic parameters, 648 scenarios were considered. These were summarized in three economic scenarios (see Tab. 5.4). Additionally, since the investment for a photovoltaic installation depends on a large range of influential factors, three investment scenarios (see Section 5.6.2) were considered.

Based on the electricity yield calculation for every building surface for the electricity generation potential, it was considered in the next step for the economic potential assessment for every building surface whether it is economic to install a photovoltaic plant there, or not. For this, a size-dependent investment was considered (see Tab. 5.2). Then, the NPV was calculated for the 648 scenarios of economic and investment parameter combinations. When the NPV was positive

for a building surface (i.e. greater than 0 €, see Section 2.2.1.1), these building surfaces were included in determining the economic potential for photovoltaic electricity generation of this building.
In Fig. 6.18, the economic potential of the 38 analyzed buildings is depicted for the scenario combination *Status quo* and *Conventional investment*:

- Economic scenario *Status quo* (see Tab. 5.4), i.e.
  - Interest rate 2 % or more
  - System lifetime up to 25 years
  - Electricity tariff up to 0.25 €/kWh
- *Conventional investment scenario* (see Section 5.6.2), i.e.
  - I_{roof} from Tab. 5.2
  - I_{facade} from Tab. 5.2

In order to allow a comparison between buildings, the economic potential is depicted as the share of the theoretical potential, i.e. total building surface area, in the first bar of the bar graph and as the share of the technical electricity generation potential, i.e. without building surface areas receiving less than 500 kWh/(m^{2}a), in the second bar.
Fig. 6.19 illustrates the economic potential of the 38 buildings also for the economic scenario *Status quo*, but considering the *BIPV investment scenario*, i.e. with a material substitution worth 50 €/m^2 or 330 €/kW$_p$.
For the share of the economic potential in the theoretical potential, an average increase of 4 % for the *BIPV investment scenario* in comparison to the *Conventional investment scenario* results. For the share of the economic potential in the building surface area considered for the electricity generation potential, an average increase of 9 % can be observed. Generally speaking, it can be noted that the share of the economic potential in the theoretical potential or the electricity generation potential shows a large spread from 1 % to 76 % (average of 37 %) and 20 % to 98 % (average of 73 %) respectively for the *Conventional investment scenario*. For the *BIPV investment scenario* it ranges from 1 % to

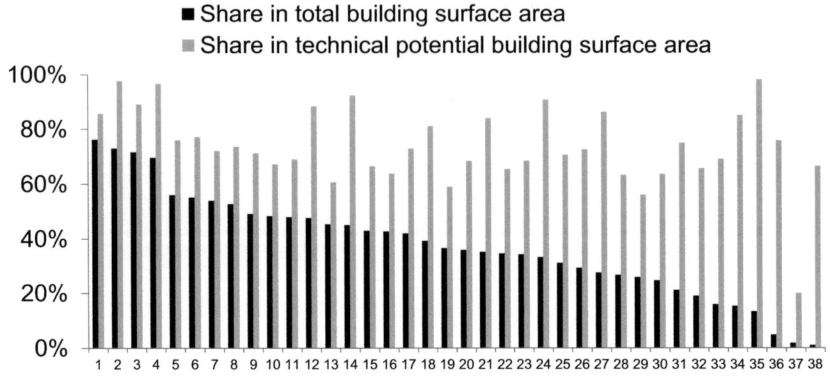

Figure 6.18: Economic potential of 38 analyzed buildings for the economic scenario *Status quo* and the *Conventional investment scenario*

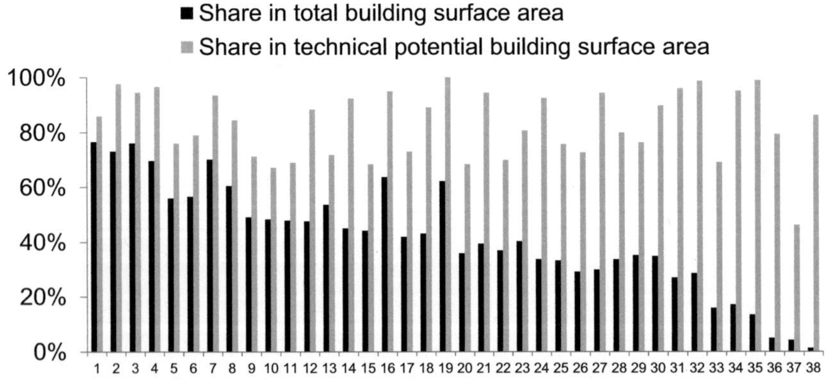

Figure 6.19: Economic potential of 38 analyzed buildings for the economic scenario *Status quo* and the *BIPV investment scenario* assuming a material substitution worth 50 €/m^2 or 330 €/kW$_p$

77 % (average of 41 %) and from 46 % to 100 % (average of 83 %). However, from the standard deviation of 50 %[6] (47 %) for the theoretical potential or 19 % (15 %) for the electricity generation potential in the case of the *Conventional investment scenario* (*BIPV investment scenario*), the large heterogeneity of results is obvious.

6.2.3.4 Conclusion on potential assessment

The analysis of the non-residential buildings' investigated and calculated potential was performed according to BMVBS (2013) building categories for the theoretical potential and for each building individually for the technical and the economic potential. However, all statistical values illustrate the large heterogeneity even when building types are summarized according to the BMVBS (2013) building categories. From this analysis, it is clear that the building type does not have a dominating effect on the potential of a building for the installation of a photovoltaic plant. Non-residential buildings are so heterogeneous that even within one building type, all kinds of different construction types exist. One supporting argument for this statement is also the fact that a non-residential building with a certain usage can be converted for a different type of usage without essentially changing the parameters used in the presented methodology to characterize a building type.

Therefore, in the following assessment, it does not make sense to differentiate between BMVBS (2013) building types. The methodology proposed in the following section is different to what is commonly found in literature when building stock analysis is performed: The analysis is based on the hypothesis that for a non-residential building, the suitability for photovoltaic applications is not dependent on the building type but on the size, the surface area, the ratio of facade and roof surfaces and the location, i.e. the shading situation. Under this assumption, in the following section, the analyzed buildings will be ordered into groups which will then serve as the archetypes for the calculation of the

[6] Standard deviation is given as percentage of the average value.

potential for photovoltaic installations on non-residential buildings. These more homogeneous groups of non-residential buildings will be formed employing the statistical methodology cluster analysis.

6.2.4 Cluster analysis for the creation of a solar non-residential building typology

6.2.4.1 Introduction to cluster analysis

Cluster analysis is an explorative methodology based on statistical analysis, in which similar groups of data within data sets are identified. It is the objective of cluster analysis to maximize heterogeneity between groups and homogeneity within groups which are then called clusters. Similarities within and between clusters are measured by proximity measures. For the creation of clusters different clustering algorithms can be chosen (Bacher et al. 2010).
According to Backhaus et al. (2008) the following steps should be performed in cluster analysis:

1. Specifying the problem
2. Defining the objects to be classified
3. Selection of attributes
4. Selection of measures of distance
5. Selection of grouping algorithm
6. Conducting the grouping
7. Selection of number of clusters
8. Analysis and interpretation of results

For the creation of a solar non-residential building typology using the existing non-residential buildings database, these steps have been performed in this order and are described in the following sections. All presented analysis has been conducted with the statistical software package IBM-SPSS 20.0.0.

6.2.4.2 Cluster analysis of non-residential buildings database

1. Specifying the problem and objective of the cluster analysis

In this cluster analysis, non-residential building types for the creation of a solar building typology which can later be used for up-scaling the results to a national potential are to be identified. It is therefore necessary to select attributes affecting the photovoltaic potential of a building like available surface areas and shading conditions. As stated earlier, the economic potential depends on a large range of economic parameters which cannot be attributed to buildings. Therefore, the cluster analysis will include only building-specific characteristics.

2. Defining the objects to be classified

The non-residential buildings database described in Section 6.2.2 forms the basis for this analysis. The objects to be classified comprise 38 non-residential buildings, for which all attributes including the theoretical and technical potential are available.

3. Selection of attributes

In this analysis, non-residential buildings shall be classified according to attributes influencing their photovoltaic potential. From the attributes collected in Section 6.2.2, the ones listed in Tab. 6.5 have been chosen as possibly influencing the photovoltaic potential.

Table 6.5: Attributes and nomenclature used in cluster analysis

Notation	Attribute	Unit
Location characteristics		
pd	Population density	[persons/km^2]
Theoretical potential		
A_{fp}	Building footprint area (i.e. 2D outline of building ground floor plan)	[m^2]
A_{ro}	Roof area	[m^2]

Notation	Attribute	Unit
A_{fa}	Facade area	[m^2]
A_{total}	Total building surface area (Roof and facade)	[m^2]
TR_{ro}	Transparency ratio for roof	[-]
TR_{fa}	Transparency ratio for facade	[-]
TR_{total}	Transparency ratio for total building surface	[-]
Technical potential		
E_{glob}	Global horizontal irradiation	[kWh/(m^{2}a)]
E_{avg}	Area-weighted average irradiation on all building surfaces	[kWh/(m^{2}a)]
$E_{avg,u}$	Average global irradiation on unshaded building surfaces	[kWh/(m^{2}a)]
El_{avg}	Area-weighted average electricity yield	[kWh/kW$_p$]
$A'_{ro,gt500}$	Roof area receiving more than 500 kWh/(m^{2}a) solar irradiation	[m^2]
$A'_{fa,gt500}$	Facade area receiving more than 500 kWh/(m^{2}a) solar irradiation	[m^2]
$A'_{total,gt500}$	Total building surface area (Roof and facade) receiving more than 500 kWh/(m^{2}a) solar irradiation	[m^2]

Some attributes relevant for the theoretical potential were calculated according to Eqs. 6.2 to 6.5.

$$A_{total} = A_{ro} + A_{fa} \tag{6.2}$$

$$TR_{ro} = \frac{A_{ro} - A_{ro,opaque}}{A_{ro}} \tag{6.3}$$

$$TR_{fa} = \frac{A_{fa} - A_{fa,opaque}}{A_{fa}} \tag{6.4}$$

$$TR_{total} = \frac{A_{total} - A_{total,opaque}}{A_{total}} \tag{6.5}$$

The global horizontal irradiation and the area-weighted average irradiation, both shaded and unshaded (Section 4.1.2), are naturally influenced by the building location. Therefore, their direct utilization in the cluster analysis would lead to erroneous results due to the differing sum of horizontal solar irradiation (from 962 kWh/(m^{2}a) to 1183 kWh/(m^{2}a) for the analyzed buildings). Therefore, the global horizontal irradiation E_{glob} was used to standardize the area-weighted average irradiation on all building surfaces according to Eqs. 6.6 and 6.7, thereby making this attribute independent of geographic location.

$$E_{avg,n} = \frac{E_{avg}}{E_{glob}} \tag{6.6}$$

$$E_{avg,u,n} = \frac{E_{avg,u}}{E_{glob}} \tag{6.7}$$

According to Backhaus et al. (2008), no strongly correlated attributes should be used in the cluster analysis, since they will distort the result of the analysis. For the correlation analysis, Pearson's correlation coefficient calculated according to Eq. 6.8 has been used.

$$r(x,y) = \frac{cov(x,y)}{\sigma(x)\sigma(y)} = \frac{\sum(x-\bar{x})(y-\bar{y})}{\sqrt{\sum(x-\bar{x})^2\sum(y-\bar{y})^2}} \tag{6.8}$$

For this analysis, a threshold value for the correlation coefficient of 0.85 has been defined. Pairs of attributes with a correlation coefficient above this value have to be either excluded from the analysis or summarized by other variables. The correlation of the listed attributes is documented in Fig. 6.6. For further analysis, the strongly correlated attributes A_{total}, $A_{total,opaque}$, $A_{fa,opaque}$ and $A_{ro,opaque}$ have been excluded from further analysis. For TR_{total} and TR_{fa} showing a strong mutual correlation, the selection of the attribute to be excluded from further analysis was arbitrary. Here, it was decided to exclude TR_{fa}, so that the following attributes result for clustering:

Table 6.6: Correlation analysis of selected attributes. Correlation coefficients above 0.85 are marked in red.

	pd	A_fp	A_ro	A_fa	A_total	TR_ro	TR_fa	TR_total	A_ro,opaque	A_fa,opaque	A_total,opaque	E_avg,n	E_avg,u,n	A'_total,gt500	El_avg
pd	1.00	-0.08	0.03	0.20	0.13	-0.07	0.10	0.11	0.04	0.15	0.10	-0.18	0.04	-0.07	-0.08
A_fp	-0.08	1.00	0.61	0.57	0.68	-0.17	-0.43	-0.41	0.60	0.67	0.74	0.31	0.29	0.85	0.23
A_ro	0.03	0.61	1.00	0.53	0.89	-0.20	-0.19	-0.35	0.99	0.48	0.91	0.05	0.23	0.45	0.00
A_fa	0.20	0.57	0.53	1.00	0.86	-0.16	-0.19	-0.18	0.50	0.95	0.80	0.01	0.17	0.48	-0.13
A_total	0.13	0.68	0.89	0.86	1.00	-0.20	-0.22	-0.31	0.87	0.80	0.98	0.03	0.23	0.53	-0.07
TR_ro	-0.07	-0.17	-0.20	-0.16	-0.20	1.00	0.33	0.61	-0.27	-0.19	-0.29	-0.09	0.00	-0.25	-0.20
TR_fa	0.10	-0.43	-0.19	-0.19	-0.22	0.33	1.00	0.89	-0.21	-0.44	-0.35	-0.34	-0.22	-0.41	0.02
TR_total	0.11	-0.41	-0.35	-0.18	-0.31	0.61	0.89	1.00	-0.39	-0.39	-0.46	-0.28	-0.19	-0.40	-0.09
A_ro,opaque	0.04	0.60	0.99	0.50	0.87	-0.27	-0.21	-0.39	1.00	0.45	0.90	0.07	0.23	0.47	0.03
A_fa,opaque	0.15	0.67	0.48	0.95	0.80	-0.19	-0.44	-0.39	0.45	1.00	0.79	0.08	0.18	0.58	-0.08
A_total,opaque	0.10	0.74	0.91	0.80	0.98	-0.29	-0.35	-0.46	0.90	0.79	1.00	0.09	0.24	0.60	-0.02
E_avg,n	-0.18	0.31	0.05	0.01	0.03	-0.09	-0.34	-0.28	0.07	0.08	0.09	1.00	0.80	0.45	0.25
E_avg,u,n	0.04	0.29	0.23	0.17	0.23	0.00	-0.22	-0.19	0.23	0.18	0.24	0.80	1.00	0.40	0.30
A'_total,gt500	-0.07	0.85	0.45	0.48	0.53	-0.25	-0.41	-0.40	0.47	0.58	0.60	0.45	0.40	1.00	0.27
El_avg	-0.08	0.23	0.00	-0.13	-0.07	-0.20	0.02	-0.09	0.03	-0.08	-0.02	0.25	0.30	0.27	1.00

- pd
- A_{fp}
- A_{ro}
- A_{fa}
- TR_{ro}
- TR_{total}
- $E_{avg,n}$
- $E_{avg,u,n}$
- El_{avg}
- $A'_{total,gt500}$

4. Selection of measures of distance

Depending on the measurement scale of the attributes, different measures of distance can be employed Bacher et al. (2010). All attributes identified previously possess a metrical measurement scale for which the widely used Minkowski metric can be employed. In the following, the so called squared Euclidian distance (Minkowski metric with r = 2 and q = 1) calculated according to Eq. 6.9 will be used (Backhaus et al. 2008).

$$d_2(x,y) = \sum_{i=1}^{n} (x_i - y_i)^2 \tag{6.9}$$

5. Selection of grouping algorithm

For cluster analysis, a variety of grouping algorithms exists. They can broadly be categorized into hierarchical and partitioning algorithms. Hierarchical algorithms can be further divided into agglomerative and divisive algorithms, depending on whether they start with the number of clusters equaling the number of clustering objects and then aggregate them step-by-step (agglomerative) or alternatively just one cluster exists at the beginning and is then split further and further (divisive).

By contrast, a partitioning algorithm starts with a pre-defined number of clusters and sorts all objects under observation such that the overall heterogeneity measure is minimized. Since in this analysis, it was not yet clear how many clusters will result, a hierarchical clustering algorithm was chosen. Here multiple methodologies exist:

- Single linkage
- Complete linkage
- Average linkage
- Ward algorithm

For a presentation of the algorithms, the interested reader is referred to statistical literature, like Bacher et al. (2010), Backhaus et al. (2008) and Hair (2010), since the focus of this study is not on clustering theory, but on its application. Based on an analysis of Bergs (1980) of 15 different clustering algorithms, the Ward algorithm performs best, with a valid grouping of objects giving a good indication of the correct number of clusters to be formed. It was therefore chosen for the following cluster analysis.[7] According to Hair (2010) also the selected measure of distance, the squared Euclidian distance, is very well suited for usage in combination with the Ward algorithm.

6. Conducting the grouping

Since the measure of distance and therefore cluster analysis is sensitive to different measurement scales, the attributes used have to be standardized. For the standardization, the z-transformation has been chosen, which converts the value of all attributes such that the mean is 0 and the standard deviation is 1 according to Eq. 6.1 (Bacher et al. 2010). Thereby comparability between variables is guaranteed so that the dimensions of the variables do not influence the result of the clustering algorithm.

7. Selection of number of clusters

Since hierarchical cluster algorithms do not result in a definite number for the optimal cluster solution, the number of identified clusters has to be chosen by

[7] The Ward algorithm is an agglomerative hierarchical clustering algorithm. At the beginning, every object forms one cluster. Then clusters are aggregated step-by-step, such that the overall measure of heterogeneity is minimized. This process is repeated until all clusters have been aggregated into a single cluster. Based on the evolution of the overall heterogeneity measure, a decision concerning the optimal number of clusters can be made (Handl 2010).

the researcher. For the assessment in this study, the evolution of the measures of distance, i.e. the sum of squared residues with an increasing number of clusters, was used. As a compromise between homogeneity within clusters and heterogeneity between clusters, a number of clusters after which only slight decreases in the sum of squared residues result can be chosen. This point can be optically identified as a so-called elbow in the curve of the sum of squared residues versus the number of clusters (Hair 2010).

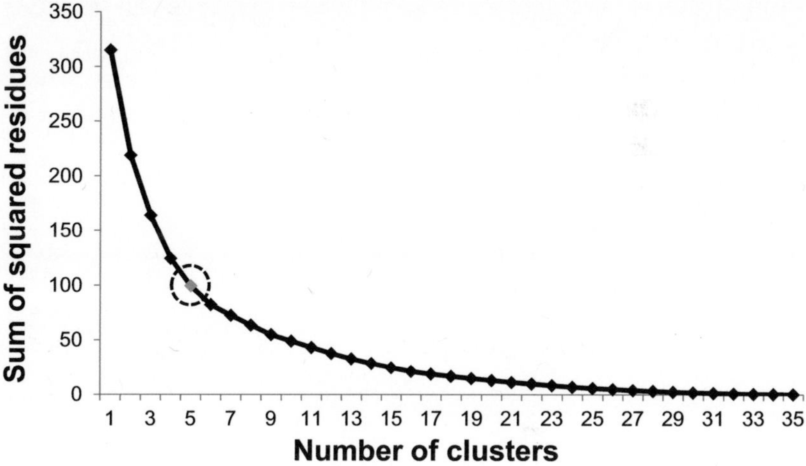

Figure 6.20: Sum of squared residues depending on number of clusters; The so-called elbow of the curve at a number of five clusters is marked.

According to this criterion, five was identified as the number of clusters after which the measure of distance does not decrease greatly with a further increase in the number of clusters. However, conducting the clustering according to the methodology described above resulted in a clustering that always excluded two very large buildings (one logistics and one office building). These buildings have therefore been considered outliers and excluded from the analysis. So the following analysis has only been conducted for 36 buildings. This results in a clustering of objects according to the dendrogram shown in Fig. 6.21. The development of the measure of distance with an increasing number of clusters is shown in Fig. 6.20. The elbow is circled where the number of clusters is five.

8. Analysis and interpretation of results

In Tab. 6.7, an extract of the average attribute values per cluster is depicted. The average of all attribute values are listed in Tab. A.2 in the Annex. To aid interpretation, boxplot diagrams for the attributes used in the cluster analysis and those that were excluded are depicted in the following section. From these statistical attribute distributions, now meaningful interpretations for the five clusters can be derived.

Table 6.7: Average values of selected attributes for the five identified clusters with the number of analyzed buildings *N* assigned to this cluster.

Cluster	**1**	**2**	**3**	**4**	**5**
A_{fp}	2509	1441	2253	9015	2063
A_{ro}	2651	1458	3871	9105	2171
A_{fa}	3742	5645	3169	18300	3592
TR_{total}	27 %	52 %	41 %	26 %	66 %
N	17	6	4	5	4

Starting the interpretation of the clusters by examining the average electricity generation, at first no distinct variation between clusters is visible (Fig. A.9 in the Annex). However, to avoid misinterpretation, one has to consider that only building surfaces with an irradiation above 500 kWh/(m^{2}a) were considered so that the electricity generation on these surfaces is quite similar. Actually, the building surface area receiving more than 500 kWh/(m^{2}a) $A_{total,gt500}$ varies appreciably (Fig. A.10). Naturally, this attribute is directly dependent on the total available building surfacea area A_{total} (Fig. A.4). Therefore, the ratio $s_{gt,500}$ of the building surface area with irradiation above 500 kWh/(m^{2}a) $A_{total,gt500}$ to the total building surface area A_{total} calculated according to Eq. 6.10 is a meaningful indicator (Fig. 6.22).

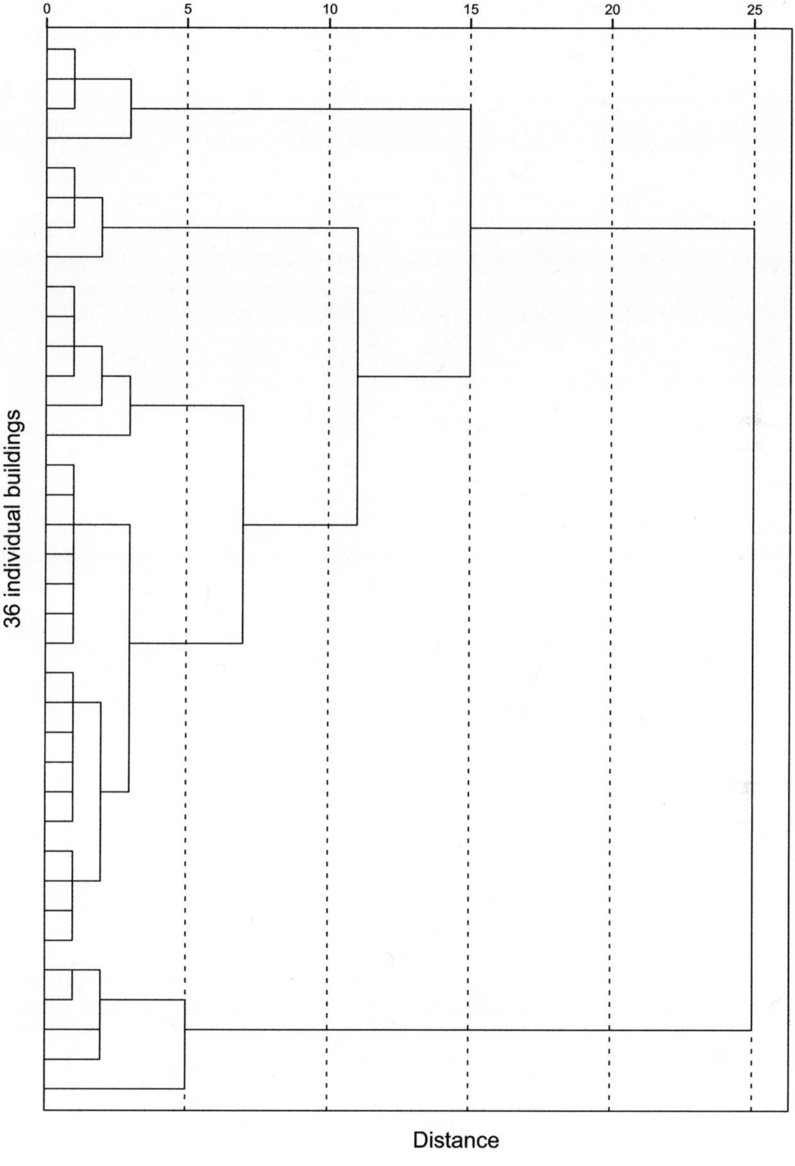

Figure 6.21: Dendrogram of Ward clustering for 36 buildings

$$s_{gt500} = \frac{A_{total,gt500}}{A_{total}} \tag{6.10}$$

From the comparison of s_{gt500} between clusters, the varying availability of suitable surface areas of buildings attributed to these clusters becomes obvious.

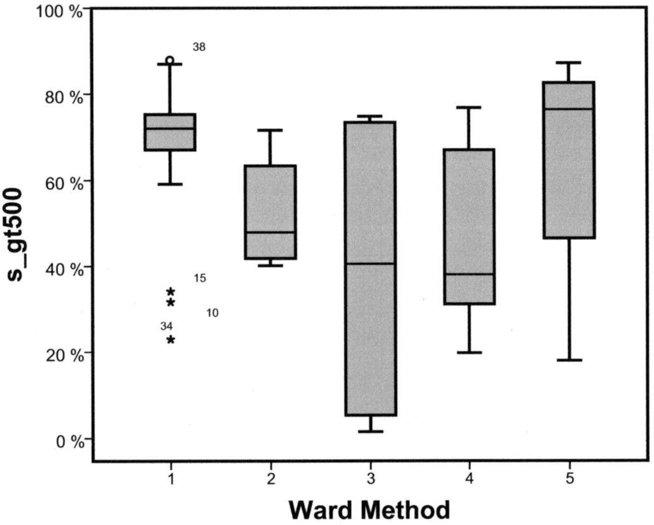

Figure 6.22: Percentage of area with irradiation above 500 kWh/(m^{2}a) relative to total building surface area.

While in cluster 1, the mean s_{gt500} is at 68 %, in cluster 3 the mean is at 39 % but admittedly with a very large spread, i.e. with a standard deviation of 39 %. However, the total available building surface area A_{total} of buildings in cluster 3 and clusters 1 and 2 is actually comparable (Fig. A.4). The large spread in the ratio of suitable surface areas is caused by the fact that the average irradiation, both shaded (E_{avg}) and unshaded ($E_{avg,u}$), is much lower in cluster 3 than in the other clusters (Figs. A.7 and A.8) while the global horizontal irradiation is comparable in all five clusters. So unlike cluster 2, where the average irradiation is lower than in cluster 1 but the average value of $E_{avg,u}$, i.e. the average

irradiation simulated without surrounding buildings (see Section 4.1.2), is quite similar, in cluster 3 another factor contributes to the low average irradiation without surrounding buildings $E_{avg,u}$. The only explanation left, since shading from surrounding buildings can be excluded, is self-shading of the building. This means that cluster 3 comprises buildings that for architectural reasons have non-optimally oriented building surface areas, resulting in a low share of suitable building surface areas for photovoltaic electricity generation.
Cluster 2 features the highest population density *pd* of the building location for all clusters (Fig. 6.23). Assuming that a higher population density translates directly into a higher building density, this leads to the conclusion that the share of shading from surrounding buildings is higher than for cluster 1 where the difference between E_{avg} and $E_{avg,u}$ amounts to only 95 kWh/(m^{2}a) or 16 %, while for cluster 2 it amounts to 143 kWh/(m^{2}a) or 27 %. More buildings strongly affected by shading are those found in cluster 4, which also exhibits a decrease in average irradiation by 174 kWh/(m^{2}a) or 30 % due to shading, being located on average in locations with the second-highest population density, with a mean of more than 2000 citizens per square kilometer. Considering the roof (A_{ro}) (Fig. 6.24), the facade (A_{fa}) (Fig. 6.25) and the building footprint (A_{fp}) areas, these buildings are the largest in terms of area, but not height. Interestingly, in terms of transparency, both the roof (TR_{ro}) and the facade (TR_{fa}) transparency ratio are quite low (Figs. A.5 and A.6). The highest TR_{ro} and TR_{fa}, each with an average of 66 %, characterize buildings in cluster 5. Apart from this, all other attributes are comparable to buildings in cluster 1. These buildings have a high s_{gt500} value but due to the high transparency ratio, actually less of this surface area will be usable for photovoltaic applications.

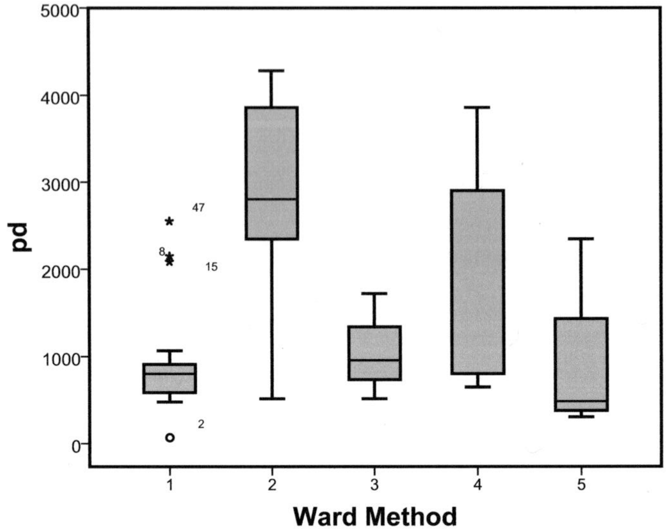

Figure 6.23: Population density *pd* [km^{-2}]

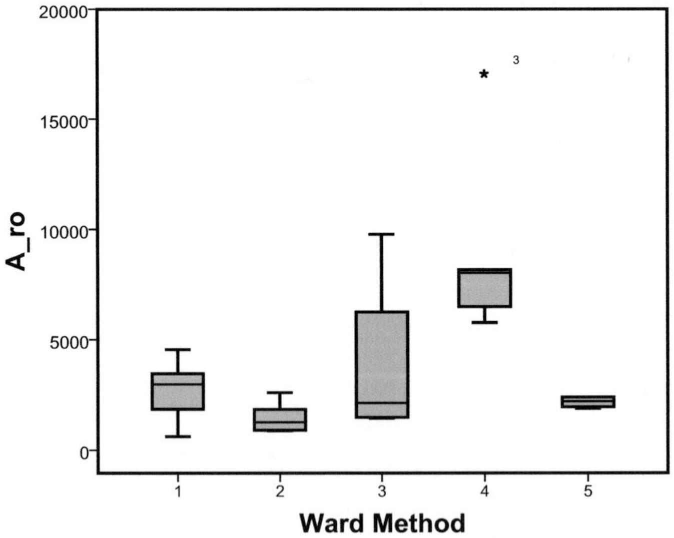

Figure 6.24: Roof area A_{ro} [m^2]

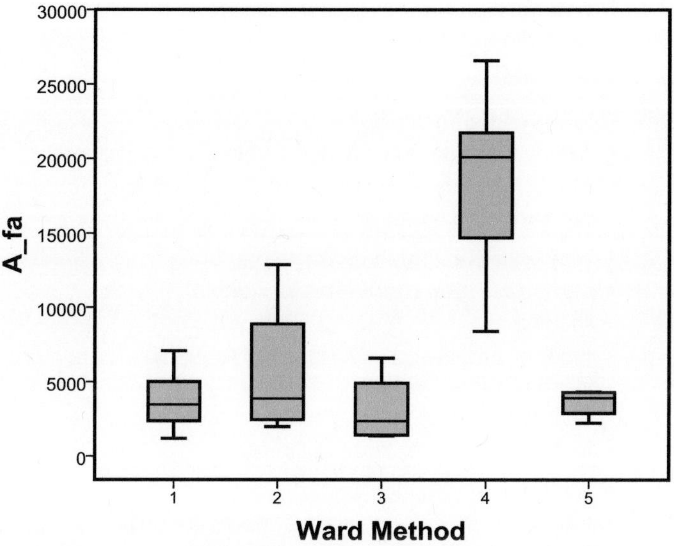

Figure 6.25: Facade area A_{fa} [m^2]

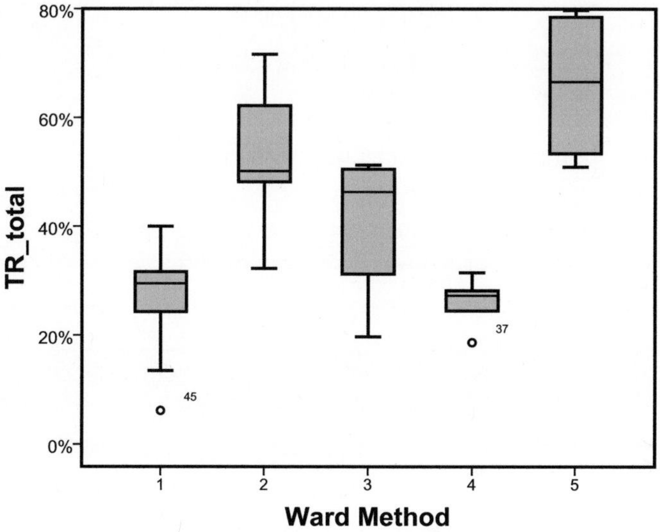

Figure 6.26: Transparency ratio total TR_{total}

Table 6.8: Summary of building attributes for the five clusters

Cluster	Description	Suitability
1	• low population density • high irradiation both shaded and unshaded • low transparency ratio, both roof and facade • not very high building	High
2	• very high population density • high irradiation irradiation loss due to shading • lower irradiation on average due to higher share of facade area • high facade transparency ratio • high building, i. e. large facade area	Medium
3	• small population density • lowest irradiation on average due to architectural reasons • total building surface area comparable to buildings in cluster 1 and 2	Low
4	• high population density • buildings with large building surface areas, but not extremely high • due to large roof area well suited in absolute terms despite shading losses	High
5	• low population density • high irradiation both shaded and unshaded • high transparency ratio, both roof and facade	Medium

The buildings with their characteristic attributes are summarized in Tab. 6.8. In this summary, the suitability for photovoltaic electricity generation is deliberately described qualitatively, with the attributes "high", "medium" and "low" to give the reader a quick overview. This categorization is partly oriented on the s_{gt500} depicted in Fig. 6.22, especially for clusters 1 to 3 which correspondingly exhibit decreasing suitability. However, cluster 4 in comparison to cluster 5 is considered to have a higher suitability, despite the on average lower s_{gt500}, because in absolute terms the available building surface areas of buildings in this cluster are much larger than those in cluster 5. Additionally, building surfaces in cluster 5 have a very high transparency ratio (TR_{fa}, TR_{ro} and TR_{total}), reducing the building surface areas usable for the installation of a photovoltaic plant further. Therefore this cluster only gets a "medium" suitability rating.

Needless to say, the qualitative assessments of the building characteristics in this summary have to be seen in relation to the sample of the 36 analyzed buildings. However, for further calculations in Chapter 8, the mean values of buildings attributed to the five clusters depicted in Tab. 6.7 will be used. The stability of the cluster results has been assessed by repeating the cluster analysis with a random sample of the total sample, which resulted in the same cluster assignment.

Apart from the heterogeneity of results expressed in the measure of distance, also the homogeneity of clusters has been assessed and compared with the homogeneity of the BMVBS (2013) building classification. In Tab. 6.9 the average standard deviation as percentage of the average value of selected attributes for the five clusters is documented. Compared to the BMVBS (2013) building categories (Tab. 6.4), the average standard deviation has decreased. Therefore, the clustering is considered to have resulted in more homogeneous groups than the original classification.

Table 6.9: Standard deviation as percentage of the average for selected attribtues according to the five identified clusters. *N* denotes the number of buildings attributed to this cluster.

Cluster	A_{fp}	A_{ro}	A_{fa}	A_{total}	TR_{total}	N
1	47	45	48	42	32	17
2	50	45	77	69	26	6
3	73	103	77	91	36	4
4	40	50	38	32	18	5
5	8	12	27	18	22	4

6.2.4.3 Economic potential of clusters

As has been stated earlier, the economic potential depends on a large range of influential factors. To illustrate, how the clusters behave in the different economic scenarios, in Figs. 6.27 and 6.28 the percentage of the total building surface area identified to constitute the economic potential is depicted for two economic-investment scenario combinations.

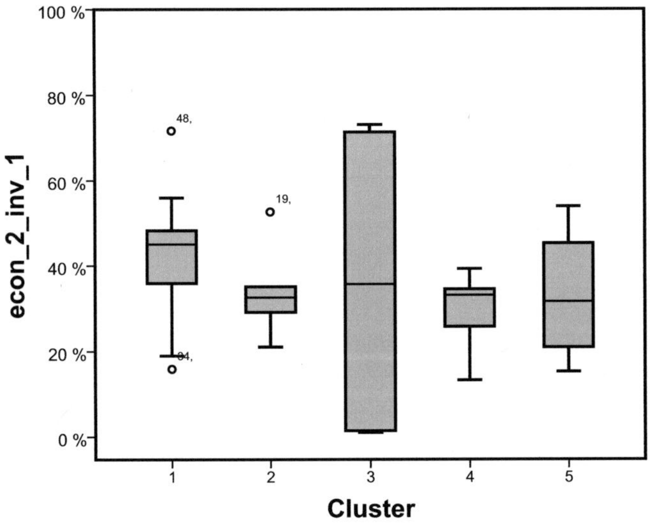

Figure 6.27: Share of economic potential in the theoretical potential (A_{total}) for the economic scenario *Status quo* and the *Conventional investment scenario*

For the other economic-investment scenario combinations, the approximate order of the percentages of the economic potential among the five clusters looks comparable and is therefore not presented here in detail. It should be noted that this order corresponds to the qualitative summary of suitability listed in Tab. 6.8, i.e. buildings in cluster 1 and cluster 4 have on average a higher economic potential with a lower spread compared with the other clusters.

As an additional information, the percentage of the facade (A_{fa}) with respect to the total building surface area (A_{total}) is depicted in Fig. 6.29.

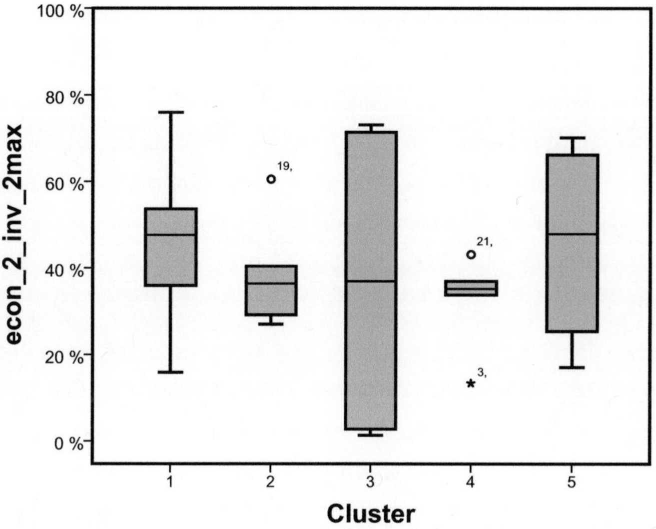

Figure 6.28: Share of economic potential in the theoretical potential (A_{total}) for the economic scenario *Status quo* and the *BIPV investment scenario*

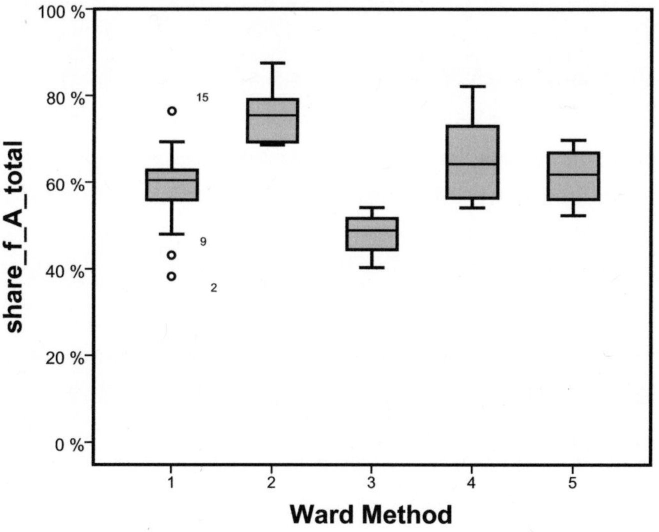

Figure 6.29: Share of facade area in total building surface area

By comparing Fig. 6.29 with Fig. 6.27, clearly the negative influence of the assumed higher investment for facade installations on the economic potential is visible. For example, cluster 2, where the buildings have a large ratio of facade area to total building surface area due to a large building height, the economic potential is lower due to the higher investment combined with the generally lower average irradiation on facades due to the non-optimal tilt angle.

6.2.5 Conclusion on non-residential building analysis

As a general conclusion, the data collection and processing for the individual buildings for the cluster analyis of the non-residential buildings has proven to be very time-consuming. On the one hand, information from a very heterogeneous and sometimes incomplete database had to be gathered. On the other hand, the 3D modeling of the individual buildings based on fragmented documentation has also proven to be very tedious. Unfortunately, building modeling for construction and detailed irradiation simulation are two different disciplines. While in building modeling for construction projects, additional information such as material type, connection with other building elements or cost is stored for each element (therefore also called BIM), for irradiation modeling only surfaces and their material properties are relevant. Therefore by converting a BIM model to the Radiance file format, substantial information is lost, requiring additional effort to attribute irradiation results later to the respective building elements. However, for the analysis conducted here, these efforts were necessary, as demonstrated by the results reaching a level of detail never achieved before.
The detailed cluster analysis of 38 non-residential buildings according to attributes relevant for the solar potential presented in this section led to a final attribution of 36 buildings to 5 clusters with differing suitability for photovoltaic installations, which results from a combination of the absolute available building surface areas, the relative proportion of facade and roof areas, self-shading and shading from surrounding buildings. The core objective of cluster analysis to form clusters that can be meaningfully interpreted was reached. As a result, now

five archetypes of non-residential buildings with detailed quantitative information concerning the afore-mentioned attributes is available, which will be further used in up-scaling the results to a national potential described in Chapter 8. The transparent presentation of the methodology for the identification of the building types and the consequent availability of detailed statistical data constitutes a significant improvement in comparison to previous studies.

6.3 Summary of individual buildings' assessment

In this section, residential and non-residential buildings were analyzed concerning their solar potential. Because the residential building stock is much more homogeneous and statistically much better documented than the non-residential building stock, an existing building typology could be used for residential buildings (Institut Wohnen und Umwelt 2005). For the very heterogeneous non-residential building stock, a database of 38 construction projects was analyzed in detail according to the methodology for assessing the photovoltaic technical potential described in Section 4. The individual building results were analyzed with cluster analysis to form five archetypes of non-residential buildings with detailed statistical information on their building characteristics and photovoltaic potential. From an existing non-residential building typology like from BMVBS (2013), this differentiation regarding the photovoltaic potential and this level of detail for further up-scaling of results was not achievable.

7 Potential for photovoltaic systems in urban districts

In the previous section, individual buildings were assessed concerning their suitability for building-applied or building-integrated photovoltaic electricity generation. From this analysis, it became obvious, that shading from surrounding buildings has a significant effect on the photovoltaic potential. Therefore, buildings were clustered not only according to their architectural characteristics, but also according to their location as characterized by population density. However, this assignment is not yet considered to be sufficient for up-scaling the results to a national potential. Therefore, in this chapter, a medium-scale, i.e. on an urban district level, assessment is performed. First, a literature review of urban fabric structure types in Germany concerning their suitability for usage in a photovoltaic potential assessment is presented. Since the existing specification of urban fabric structure types does not prove to be sufficient for further usage in this study, it was decided to perform an analysis as described in Chapter 4 on an urban district level to arrive at consistent results for further usage in this assessment. Thus, at the end of this analysis, the average losses in the technical potential for photovoltaic installations on buildings in different urban fabric structure types will result.

The building type and its embedding in a certain urban fabric structure, as characterized by the building density in an urban area, directly affects the available surface areas for solar energy usage and shading conditions, and is therefore an important determinant of the potential for solar energy use in buildings as passive and active solar gains, e.g. through windows or from photovoltaic and solar thermal applications.

7.1 Review of urban fabric structure typologies

The German building stock in the past century was shaped by the historic events and conditions already discussed in Section 6.1, which mainly affected building types and materials, but also urban fabric structures. With changing public policies, different developments were propagated, changing from suburbanization trends in the 1960s to inner city redevelopments in the 1970s and nowadays an increasing focus on sustainable urban development responding to social, economic and demographic challenges (Breuer 2010).
In the 1980s, a typology for urban fabric structures in German municipalities was established for energy system planning (Volwahsen 1980). The following nine urban fabric structure types (German: Siedlungstypen - ST) were identified:

- ST1 - Single- and multi-family dwellings with low building density
- ST2 - Villages
- ST3 - Terraced housing
- ST4 - Ribbon development with medium building density
- ST5 - Ribbon development with high building density
- ST6 - Urban frontage development
- ST7 - Cities starting from the mid 19th century
- ST8 - Medieval historic city center
- ST9 - Industrial and commerical zone

For each of these urban fabric structure types, attributes like building floor area, building density, building age and roof shapes are specified with a certain range. Concerning the photovoltaic potential, indicators like shading from plants, window-to-wall ratio and surface area-to-volume ratio are given and could be used in further analysis. However, in this publication, no information on the assessment method is given. Additionally, the information on shading only relates to plants and is only classified qualitatively into the categories "none", "partly" and "strong". The identified urban fabric structure types were

used by Roth (1980) in an assessment of the interdependence with the heat supply system, which was applied for energy system planning in the city of Frankfurt/Main (Winkens and Günter-Dioszeghy 1985).
Subsequently, in a large-scale study on the potential for combined heat and power (CHP) (Schulz et al. 1994) and supplemented by renewable energy (Lutsch et al. 2004) based on a detailed analysis of nine exemplary cities, a distribution of residential units for these urban fabric structure types was determined. For this purpose, three out of the nine urban fabric structure types were further differentiated (ST3, ST5 and ST7) and extended by four additional categories:

- ST0 - Free-standing single buildings
- ST10 - Public special buildings
- ST11 - Industrial special buildings / service buildings
- ST12 - Other buildings

Urban fabric structure types ST10 and ST11 were also further differentiated. The focus of this study was on the potential for a district heating network in the urban fabric structure types, such that the attributes specified in this study were the distances between streets and buildings rather than solar irradiation conditions. However, this study actually gives an estimate of the distribution of building type and age combinations per urban fabric structure type. This study was later refined by laser-scanning measurements (Blesl et al. 2010) and an up-scaling to communities according to the distribution of the urban fabric structure types in 8 community type categories.
In Buchert et al. (2004), a distribution of residential units on the three broad urban fabric structure categories "city center", "suburban" and "rural" is given for a sustainability analysis of the German construction and residential sector, which mainly focuses on mass flows.
In Everding and Kloos (2007), an analysis of the solar potential of 20 urban fabric structure types is performed. For the buildings in the urban fabric structure types, a solar quality index was calculated based on solar irradiation simulations

on generic building designs. Additionally, Everding and Kloos (2007) consider architectural constraints. For an estimate of the national solar potential, results are up-scaled according to the 20 urban fabric structure types, based on statistical information on the net building land use in the German federal states. However, Everding and Kloos (2007) mainly consider the usage of solar energy for heat supply, such that the solar quality indices can not be easily transferred for the purposes of this study focusing on the photovoltaic potential.
In Blum (2010), based on an analysis of the utility infrastructure, eight urban fabric structure types are differentiated for an estimate of the future cost of utility infrastructure development. For the urban fabric structure types, an average ratio of the building footprint area to total building gross floor area is specified, but no information on the solar irradiation availability is given.
Even though automatic procedures for building type classification exist now, employing powerful GIS capabilities, no large-scale database on the distribution of urban fabric structure types in German cities is available (Meinel et al. (2009); Hecht (2014)).
Also, all authors classify urban fabric structures according to the purposes of their investigations. The purpose of this study is approximately comparable to the analysis performed by Everding and Kloos (2007). However, since here solar thermal energy generation was the focus, the specified solar quality index and the up-scaling of results according to the urban fabric structure type distribution cannot be immediately transferred to the present photovoltaic study. Therefore, the author performed her own analysis of the solar irradiation potential per urban fabric structure type and applied it for up-scaling the results to a national potential in Chapter 8 according to a consistent database.

7.2 Irradiation simulation on urban fabric structures

An irradiation analysis for a whole urban district according to the methodology described in Chapter 4 was performed by Fath et al. (2015) for the city of

Karlsruhe. Then, an extract of the 3D city model with an area of approximately 2 km^2 with 1,750 buildings, i.e. approximately 2 % of the city area and the building stock of Karlsruhe (Liegenschaftsamt Stadt Karlsruhe 2012), was analyzed in greater detail. The 3D city model contains buildings modeled in LOD2 (Fig. 7.1).

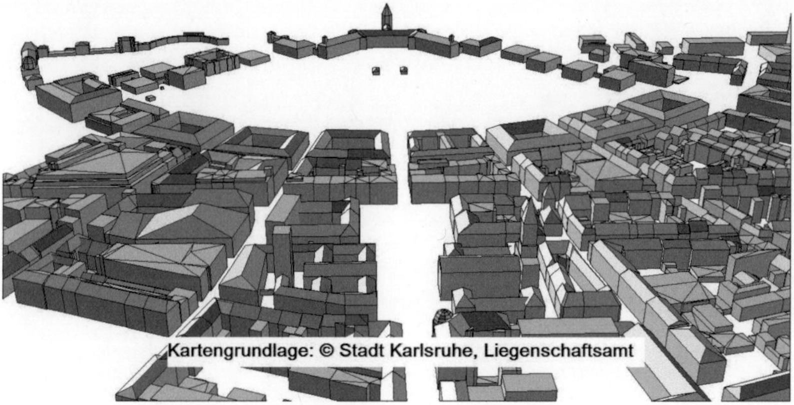

Figure 7.1: View towards the palace of Karlsruhe in the 3D city model; Data source: Stadt Karlsruhe, Liegenschaftsamt

Due to shading and non-optimal inclination and orientation, the area-weighted average irradiation on building surfaces in the analyzed extract of the 3D city model is only 369 kWh/(m^2a). Roof surfaces receive an area-weighted average irradiation of 846 kWh/(m^2a) while facades receive an area-weighted average irradiation of 191 kWh/(m^2a). Fig. 7.2 shows the distribution of surface areas according to the different levels of irradiation for roofs and facades. 5 % of the facade area (81,000 m^2) receive the highest annual irradiation on facades of 700 to 800 kWh/(m^2a), 55 % (947,000 m^2) receive less than 100 kWh/(m^2a). In the irradiation class of 1000 to 1100 kWh/(m^2a) a peak for the roof surfaces is noticeable since 46 % of all roof areas (300,000 m^2) receiving the annual horizontal irradiation in Karlsruhe of 1084 kWh/(m^2a) fall into this category.

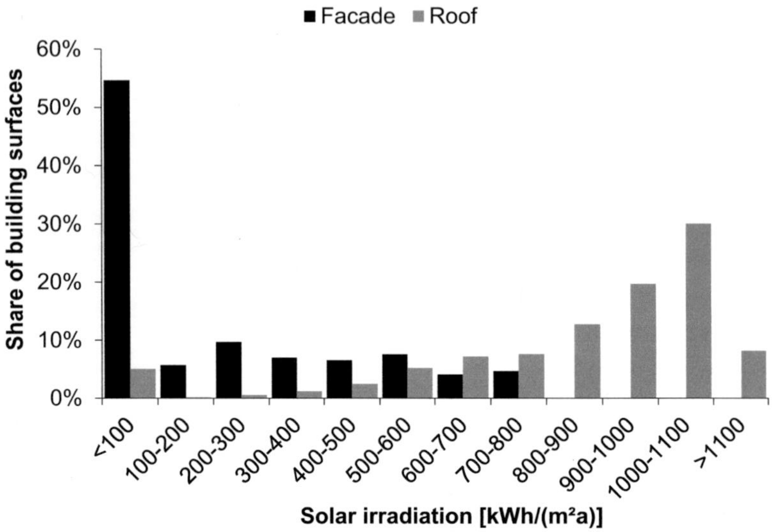

Figure 7.2: Distribution of surface areas according to irradiation class

Since in the provided extract of the Karlsruhe 3D city model, only one urban fabric structure type was present, for the analysis presented in this thesis, 3D models of other urban structure types were sought. In contrast to Everding and Kloos (2007), where generic building models were used, a database reflecting real world conditions as closely as possible was preferred. From the analysis of non-residential buildings performed in Section 6.2 it was clear, that it is not realistic to build multiple urban district models in the required quality only for this study in a reasonable timeframe. Fortunately, in recent years faster internet connections and the wide-spread use of Google Earth have encouraged cities to develop 3D models of their cities. They can be used for marketing purposes but also for a wide range of scientific applications. For example, the 3D city model of Neubrandenburg in LOD2, i.e. with standard roof shapes (see Section 2.1.2), was available to the author. The medium-scale solar irradiation analysis performed on this model is presented in detail in the following sections.

3D city model of Neubrandenburg

An approximately 28 km^2 area with different urban fabric structure types in Neubrandenburg has been analyzed. Neubrandenburg is a medium-sized city located in the State of Mecklenburg-Vorpommern in Northern Germany with approximately 65,000 inhabitants. The 3D city model of Neubrandenburg was provided in a SketchUp format. For the purposes of this study, the total model has been divided into areas where the following urban fabric structure types were mainly present as identified from visual inspection:

- Single and multi-family dwellings with low building density
- Small multi-family dwellings
- Large multi-family dwellings
- Industrial and commercial zone
- City center

The SketchUp models were transformed to the Radiance file format for irradiation analysis as described in Chapter 4.

7.3 Shading analysis

For the analysis of the shading situation in the different urban fabric structures, a solar irradiation simulation as described in Chapter 4 has been performed. To the knowledge of the author, at present no study with a comparable area-scale and equally detailed irradiation simulation exists, apart from Fath et al. (2015). When the geometrical information for the buildings in the urban districts was exported to the Radiance file format, information on the attribution of the building surfaces to the buildings was lost, since in Radiance only the geometrical information is stored in the form of coordinates in a text file. However, in order to be able to eventually attribute the solar irradiation simulation results to individual buildings, a recursive script was programed that assigns the building surfaces to buildings by matching the building surfaces' geometrical coordinates. Surfaces with a subset of identical coordinates are adjacent and are therefore considered to belong to one building. However, one has to be aware that in the case of terraced houses, this procedure leads to distortions in the results. Therefore, results on total building surfaces have to be carefully examined with respect to this aspect. Solar irradiation simulation results for individual building surfaces are not affected by these circumstances.

7.3.1 Single and multi-family dwellings with low building density

The first analyzed urban area consists mainly of single, terraced and multi-family dwellings. From visual inspection, the urban fabric structure was identified as single- and multi-family dwellings with low building density. An extract of the analyzed model is depicted in Fig. 7.3. With the recursive algorithm described in Section 7.2, 281 distinct buildings with a total building surface area of 200,424 m^2 (59 % facades, 41 % roofs) were identified.

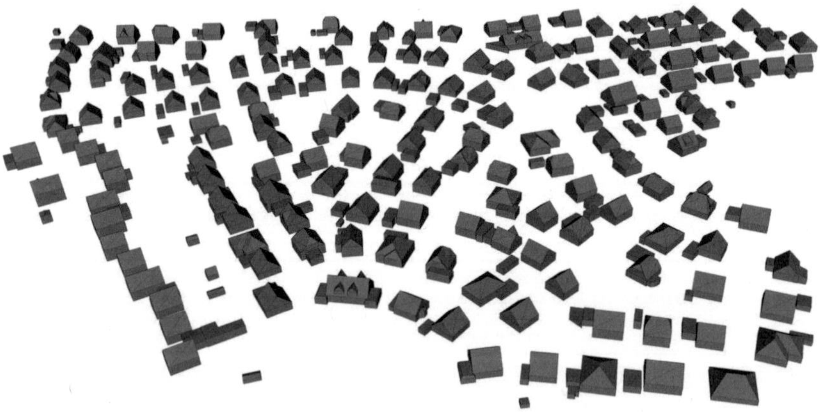

Figure 7.3: SFH and MFH with low building density

In Fig. 7.4 the accumulated size of the building surface areas is depicted. In addition, marked as individual points, the percentage of facade area relative to the total building surface area is depicted for each building. In Fig. 7.5, in addition to the building surface areas in the analyzed urban district, the range of building surface area sizes for the residential building types identified in Section 6.1 is marked, since the total building surface area is the only item of building information available from the 3D model that can be assessed in an automated fashion. From this, it can be concluded that multiple building types are present and an indication of the number of buildings per building type could be derived. However, the number of analyzed urban districts and the number of buildings cannot be considered to be representative. Therefore, this information will not be used in further analysis since the purpose of this analysis is to assess the shading conditions on building surfaces. Therefore, the actual building type is not relevant in this case. As a consequence, also the 35 identified buildings with a building surface area of less than 87 m^2, which is below the minimum building surface area of the residential building type with the smallest building surface area, i.e. terraced houses, and can therefore be assumed not to represent a residential building but an auxiliary building like a garage or a shed, will not be excluded from further analysis. Instead, it is noted that in Lutsch et al. (2004), a detailed analysis of the number of building types per urban structure is provided which can be used in further analysis.

In Fig. 7.6, the annual solar irradiation is shown for the shaded and unshaded cases (see Section 4.1.2) for every building surface in the analyzed urban district marked as an individual point. The distinction between roof and facade surfaces was made based on the tilt angle. I.e. surfaces with a tilt angle greater than 85° were considered facades and the remaining surfaces roofs. Roof surfaces generally have a higher solar irradiation due to their more favorable tilt angle. On the y-axis at an orientation angle of 0°, i.e. north, an accumulation of roof surfaces with a large range of solar irradiation value is visible for both the shaded and unshaded case. This is due to the fact that all the horizontal roof surfaces, i.e. with a tilt angle of 0° which do not actually have a specific compass orientation, are shown here. To illustrate this fact better, in Fig. 7.7 the roof surfaces are marked as individual points according to orientation.

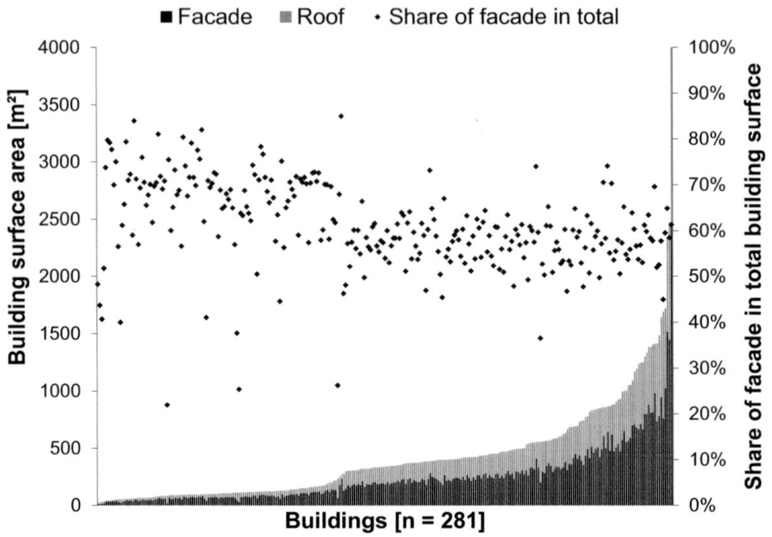

Figure 7.4: Size of building surface areas and share of the facade in the total building surface area for an urban district in Neubrandenburg with low building density with mainly SFH and MFH

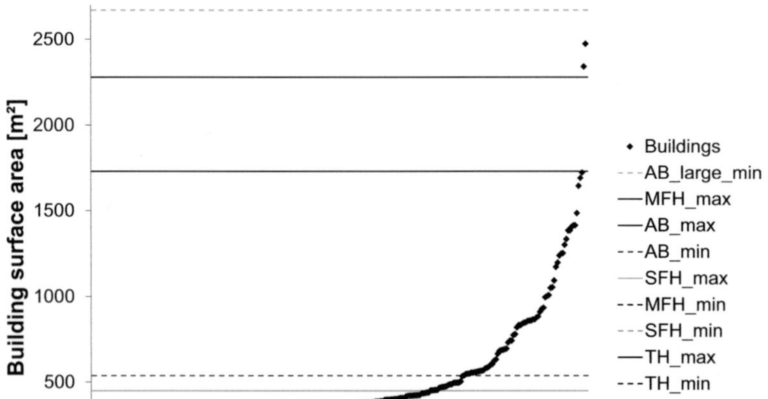

Figure 7.5: Building sizes in urban district with low building density with mainly SFH and MFH

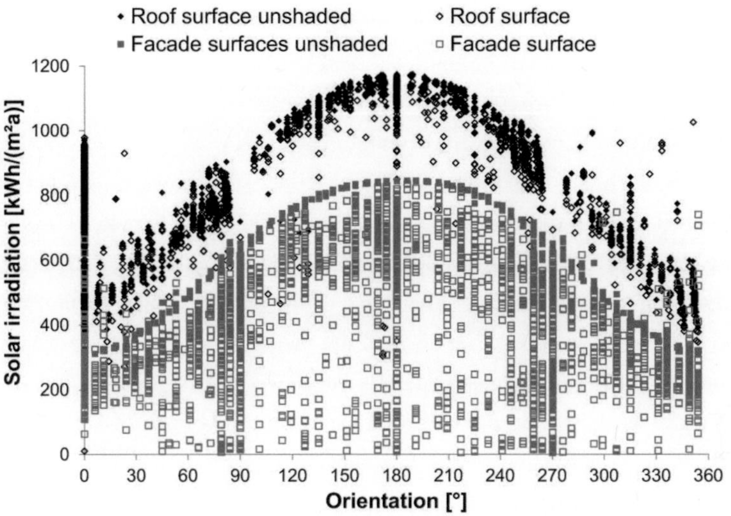

Figure 7.6: Solar irradiation on building surfaces with and without shading sorted by surface orientation (0° = north, 90° = east, 180° = south, 270° = west) in an urban district with low building density with mainly SFH and MFH

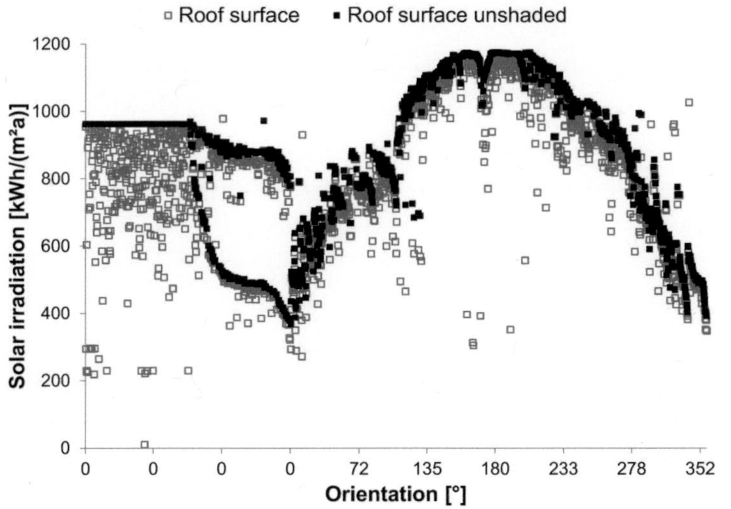

Figure 7.7: Solar irradiation on roof surfaces sorted consecutively by orientation in urban district with low building density with mainly SFH and MFH

At the beginning, the solar irradiation for the unshaded case is constant due to the considered surfaces being horizontal while for the shaded case the solar irradiation varies. From the point where the solar irradiation for the unshaded case drops, these are truly north-oriented tilted surfaces.
In Fig. 7.8, the share of building surface area per shading class, i.e. defined by the share of annual solar irradiation lost due to shading, is depicted. It is clearly visible that roof surfaces are generally less shaded, i.e. on more than 90 % of the total roof surface area less than 10 % of the annual solar irradiation is lost due to shading. By contrast, on 88 % of the facade area, shading losses amount to more than 10 % (e.g. losses of 10 % to 20 % on 29 % of total facade area, losses of 20 % to 30 % on 25 % of total facade area). On 4 % of the facade area, more than 90 % of the annual solar irradiation is lost due to shading. It has also been analyzed whether the facade orientation has an influence on shading losses. However, no general correlation could be observed for this parameter.
In addition to the first urban district with low building density and mainly single and multi-family dwellings, a second urban district of Neubrandenburg with a similar building structure was available to the author of this study. It has been analyzed to allow a comparison of results of the two districts. In this urban district, 311 buildings could be distinguished with a total building surface area of 358,756 m^2 (68 % facades, 32 % roofs).
In Fig. 7.9 the accumulated size of the building surface areas is depicted with the share of the facade in the total building surface area marked as an individual point for each building.
Fig. 7.10 illustrates the distribution of building surface area per shading class. In this urban district, 82 % of the total roof surface area is shaded by less than 10 % while 85 % of the facade area is shaded by more than 10 %, with 35 % being shaded even more than 50 %.
The numerical values for both analyzed urban districts are given in Tab. 7.1. While the percentages per shading class for the two analyzed urban districts differ in absolute values, the course is similar. This range shows the uncertainty connected with transferring flat irradiation factors from urban fabric structures

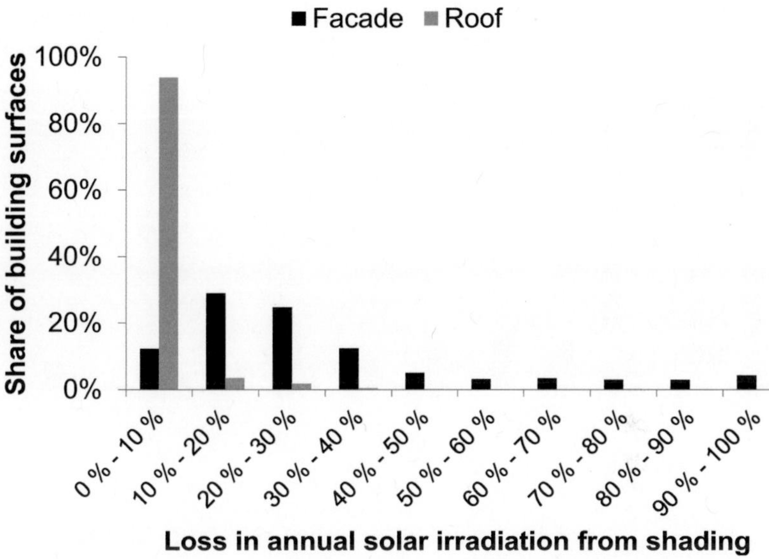

Figure 7.8: Loss in solar irradiation from shading in urban district with low building density with mainly SFH and MFH

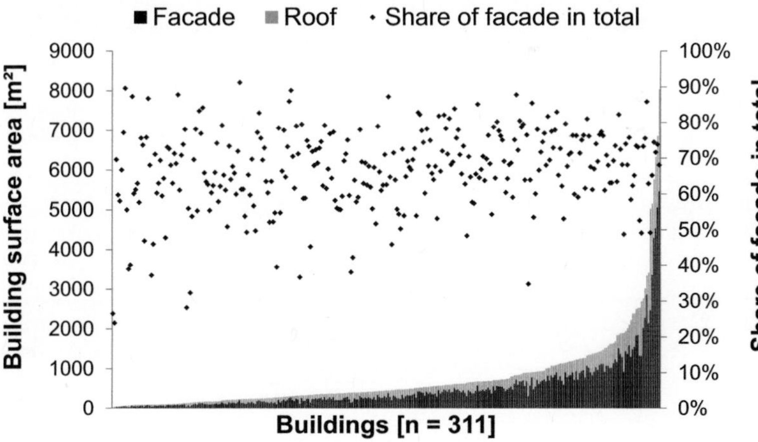

Figure 7.9: Size of building surface areas and share of the facade in total building surface area for the second urban district with low building density with mainly SFH and MFH

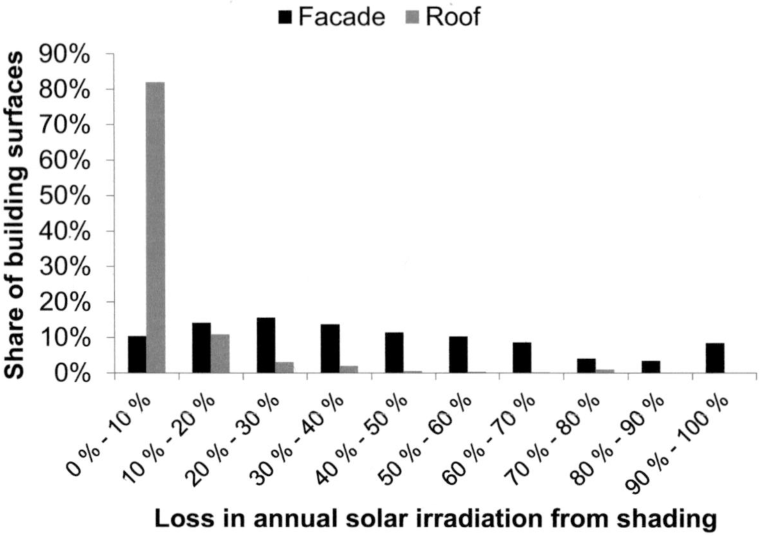

Figure 7.10: Loss in solar irradiation from shading for the second urban district with low building density with mainly SFH and MFH

Table 7.1: Percentage of building surface area per shading class and area-weighted average values for analyzed urban districts with mainly SFH and MFH with low building density

	SFH1		**SFH2**		**Average SFH**	
Shading class	Facade	Roof	Facade	Roof	Average facade	Average roof
0 % - 10 %	12 %	94 %	10 %	82 %	11 %	87 %
10 % - 20 %	29 %	4 %	14 %	11 %	19 %	8 %
20 % - 30 %	25 %	2 %	16 %	3 %	19 %	3 %
30 % - 40 %	12 %	0 %	14 %	2 %	13 %	1 %
40 % - 50 %	5 %	0 %	11 %	1 %	9 %	0 %
50 % - 60 %	3 %	0 %	10 %	0 %	8 %	0 %
60 % - 70 %	3 %	0 %	9 %	0 %	7 %	0 %
70 % - 80 %	3 %	0 %	4 %	1 %	4 %	1 %
80 % - 90 %	3 %	0 %	3 %	0 %	3 %	0 %
90 % - 100 %	4 %	0 %	8 %	0 %	7 %	0 %
Sum	100 %	100 %	100 %	100 %	100 %	100 %

to other areas. However, for the national-scale objective of this study, this uncertainty is considered neglegible in comparison with the uncertainty induced by estimating the total number of buildings, presented in Chapter 8. The area-weighted average values listed in the last column will be used in further analysis.

7.3.2 Small multi-family dwellings

In the second analyzed urban fabric structure type, an extract of which is depicted in Fig. 7.11, mainly small multi-family dwellings are present. Here, 122 buildings were distinguished with a total surface area of 326,363 m^2 (69 % facades, 31 % roofs). In Fig. 7.12, the accumulated size of the building surface areas is depicted with the percentage of the facade relative to the total building surface area marked as an individual point for each building. Fig. 7.13 illustrates the solar irradiation for the shaded and unshaded cases for every building surface in the analyzed urban district with an individual point. Again, also the horizontal roof surface areas without a specific orientation are plotted at an orientation angle of 0°.

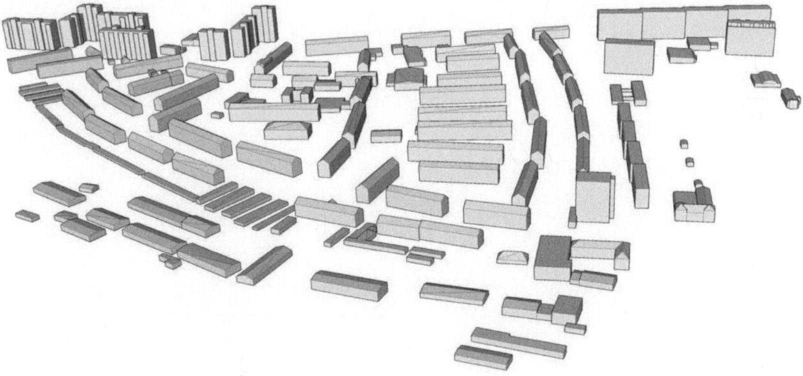

Figure 7.11: View of urban district with mainly small MFH

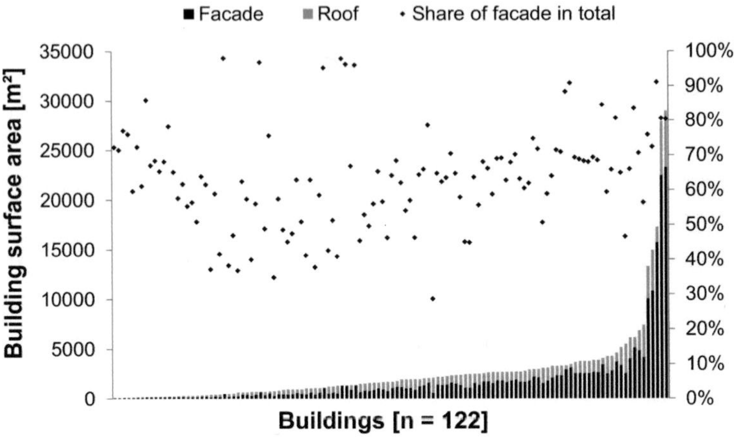

Figure 7.12: Building sizes in urban district with mainly small MFH

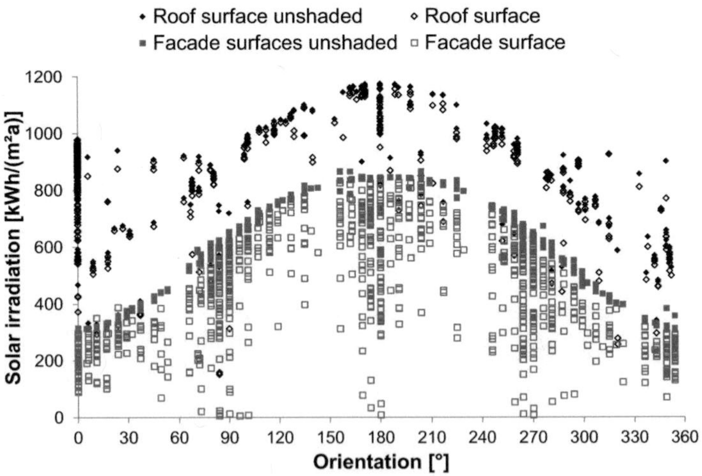

Figure 7.13: Solar irradiation on building surfaces with and without shading sorted by surface orientation (0° = north, 90° = east, 180° = south, 270° = west) in urban district with mainly small MFH

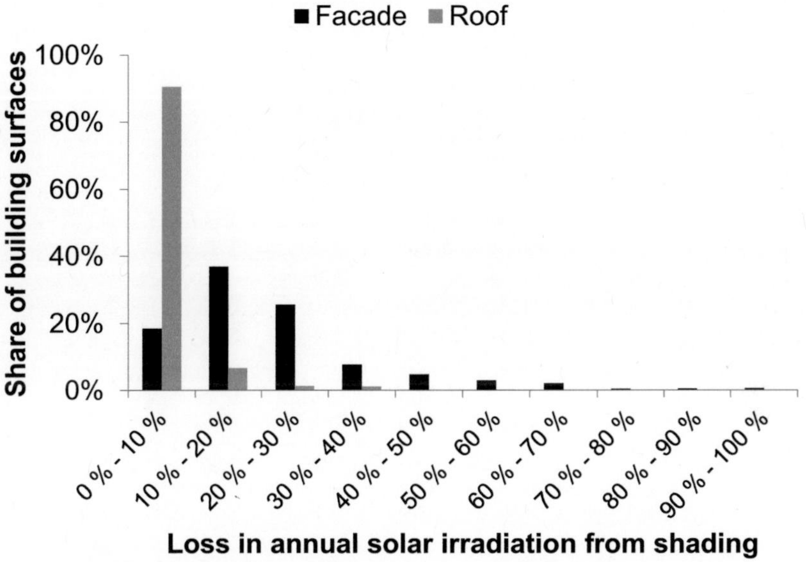

Figure 7.14: Loss in solar irradiation from shading in urban district with mainly small MFH

In Fig. 7.14 the share of building surface area per shading class in this urban area is depicted. Again, roof surfaces are generally less shaded, i.e. on more than 90 % of the total roof surface area less than 10 % of the annual solar irradiation is lost due to shading. By contrast, on 82 % of the facade area, shading losses amount to more than 10 % (e.g. losses of 10 % to 20 % on 37 % of total facade area, losses of 20 % to 30 % on 26 % of total facade area). On only 1% of total facade area, shading losses amount to more than 90 %. The numerical values which will be used in further analysis are given in Tab. 7.2.

7.3.3 Large multi-family dwellings

In the next analyzed urban district, an extract of which is depicted in Fig. 7.15, mainly large multi-family dwellings were present. Here, a total building surface area of 663,633 m^2 was analyzed (70 % facades, 30 % roofs).

Table 7.2: Share of building surface area per shading class for analyzed urban district with mainly small MFH

Shading class	Small MFH	
	Facade	Roof
0 % - 10 %	18 %	91 %
10 % - 20 %	37 %	7 %
20 % - 30 %	26 %	1 %
30 % - 40 %	8 %	1 %
40 % - 50 %	5 %	0 %
50 % - 60 %	3 %	0 %
60 % - 70 %	2 %	0 %
70 % - 80 %	0 %	0 %
80 % - 90 %	0 %	0 %
90 % - 100 %	1 %	0 %
Sum	100 %	100 %

In Fig. 7.16, the accumulated size of the building surface areas is depicted, including the percentage of the facade relative to the total building surface area.

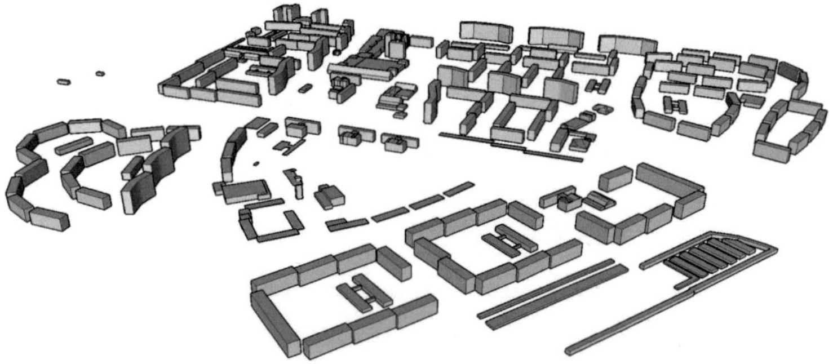

Figure 7.15: View of urban district with mainly large MFH

In Fig. 7.17, the solar irradiation is illustrated for the shaded and unshaded case for every building surface in the analyzed urban district marked as an individual point. Again, also the horizontal roof surface areas without a specific orientation are plotted at an orientation angle of 0°.

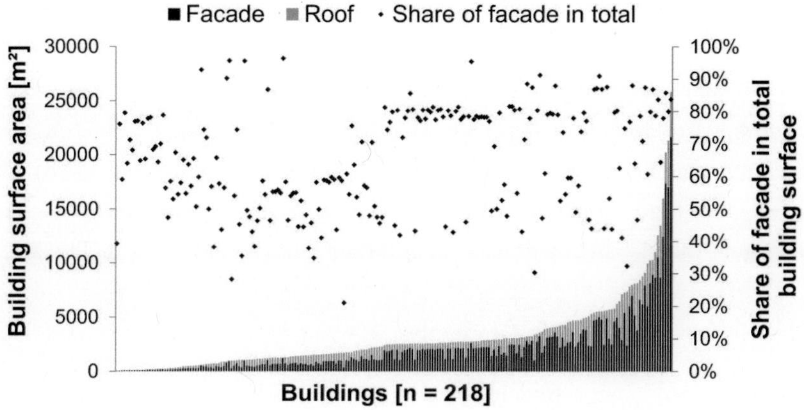

Figure 7.16: Building sizes in urban district with mainly large MFH with the percentage of the facade relative to the total building surface area marked as individual points

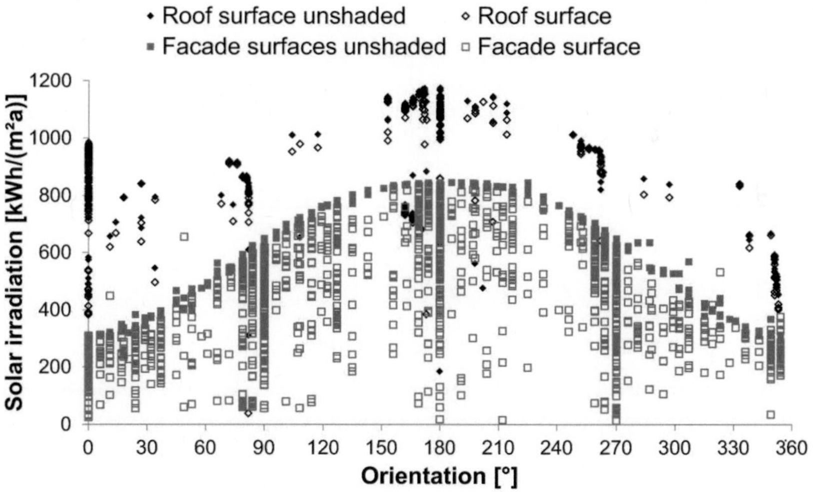

Figure 7.17: Solar irradiation on building surfaces with and without shading sorted by surface orientation (0° = North, 90° = East, 180° = South, 270° = West) in urban district with mainly large MFH

In Fig. 7.18, the share of building surface area per shading class in this urban area is depicted. On 94 % of the total roof surface area, less than 10 % of the annual solar irradiation is lost due to shading. On 79 % of the facade area shading losses amount to less than 40 % (e.g. losses of 10 % to 20 % on 30 % of total facade area, losses of 20 % to 30 % on 18 % of total facade area). On only 1 % of total facade area shading losses amount to more than 90 %. The numerical values which will be used in further analysis are given in Tab. 7.3.

Table 7.3: Share of building surface area per shading class for analyzed urban area with large MFH

Shading class	**Large MFH**	
	Facade	Roof
0 % - 10 %	21 %	94 %
10 % - 20 %	30 %	4 %
20 % - 30 %	18 %	2 %
30 % - 40 %	10 %	0 %
40 % - 50 %	5 %	0 %
50 % - 60 %	11 %	0 %
60 % - 70 %	2 %	0 %
70 % - 80 %	1 %	0 %
80 % - 90 %	2 %	0 %
90 % - 100 %	1 %	0 %
Sum	100 %	100 %

7.3.4 Industrial buildings

One urban district, an extract of which is depicted in Fig. 7.19, consisted mainly of commercial and industrial buildings. Here, a building surface area of 1,257,445 m^2 was analyzed (53 % facades, 47 % roofs). In Fig. 7.20, the accumulated size of the building surface areas is depicted with the share of the facade relative to the total building surface area marked as an individual point.

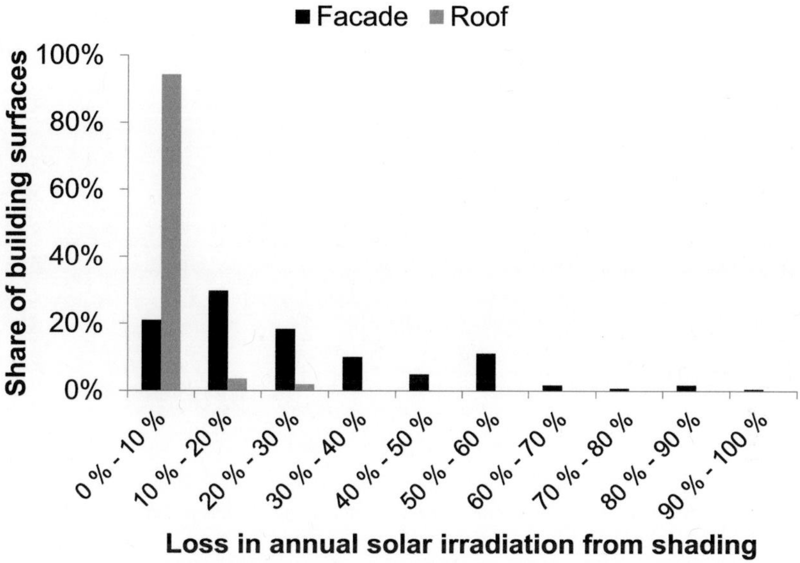

Figure 7.18: Loss in solar irradiation from shading in urban district with mainly large MFH

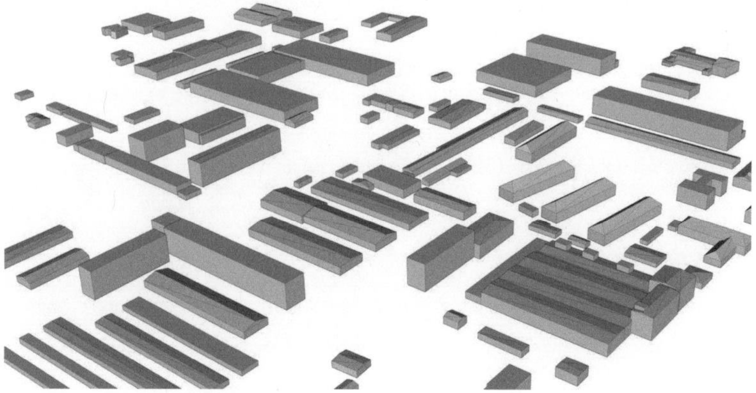

Figure 7.19: View on extract of urban district with mainly industrial and commercial buildings

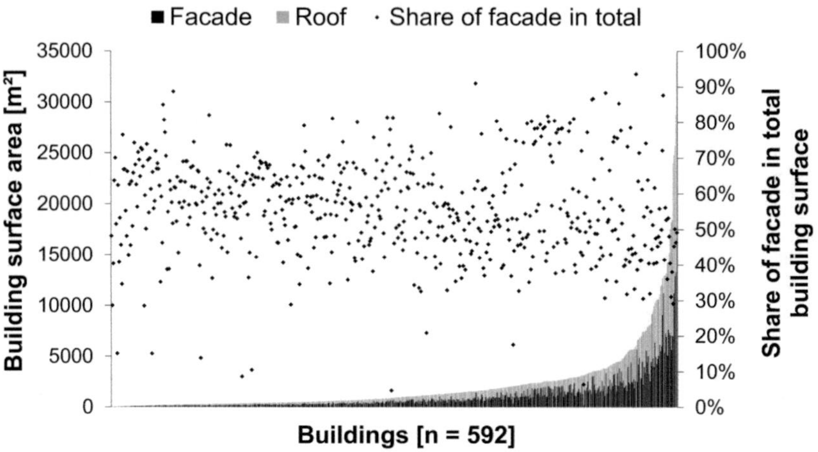

Figure 7.20: Building sizes in urban district with mainly industrial and commercial buildings

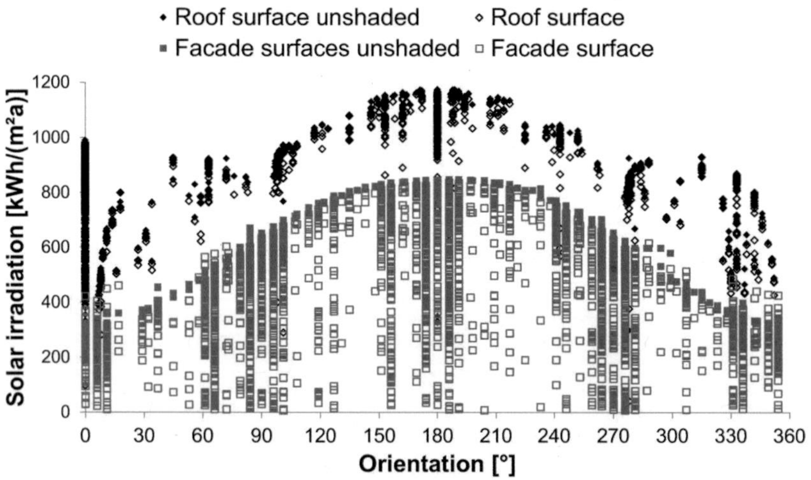

Figure 7.21: Solar irradiation on building surfaces with and without shading sorted by surface orientation (0° = North, 90° = East, 180° = South, 270° = West) in urban district with mainly industrial and commercial buildings

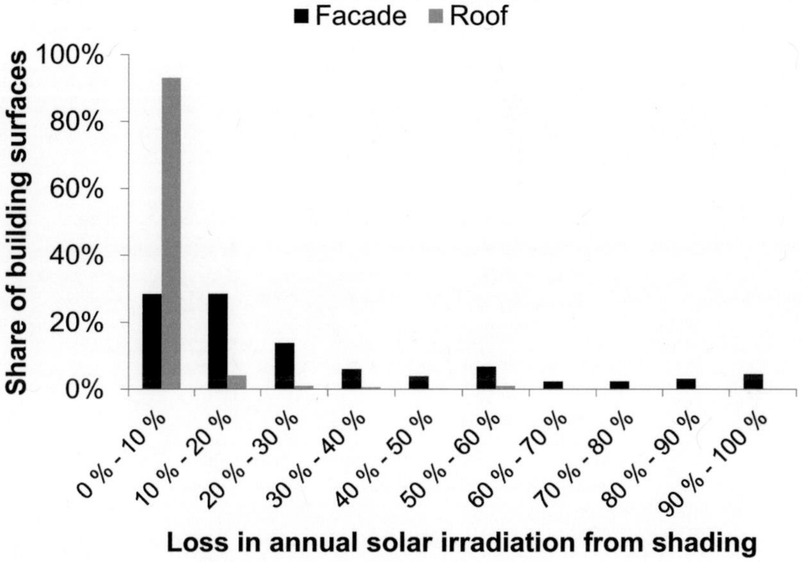

Figure 7.22: Loss in solar irradiation from shading in urban district with mainly industrial and commercial buildings

Fig. 7.21 illustrates the solar irradiation for the shaded and unshaded case for every building surface in the analyzed urban district marked as an individual point. Again, at an orientation angle of 0°, also the horizontal roof surface areas without a specific orientation are plotted, which account for more than 50 % of the total roof surface area in this urban area. 72 % have a tilt angle below 10 %. In Fig. 7.22, the share of building surface area per shading class in this urban area is depicted. On 93 % of the total roof surface area, less than 10 % of the annual solar irradiation are lost due to shading. On 71 % of the facade area shading losses amount to less than 30 % (e.g. losses of 0 % to 10 % and of 10 % to 20 % on 28 % of total facade area each). On 5 % of the total facade area, shading losses amount to more than 90 %. The numerical values which will be used in further analysis are given in Tab. 7.4.

Table 7.4: Share of building surfaces per shading class for analyzed urban district with mainly industrial and commercial buildings

Shading class	**Industrial**	
	Facade	Roof
0 % - 10 %	28 %	93 %
10 % - 20 %	28 %	4 %
20 % - 30 %	14 %	1 %
30 % - 40 %	6 %	1 %
40 % - 50 %	4 %	0 %
50 % - 60 %	7 %	1 %
60 % - 70 %	2 %	0 %
70 % - 80 %	2 %	0 %
80 % - 90 %	3 %	0 %
90 % - 100 %	5 %	0 %
Sum	100 %	100 %

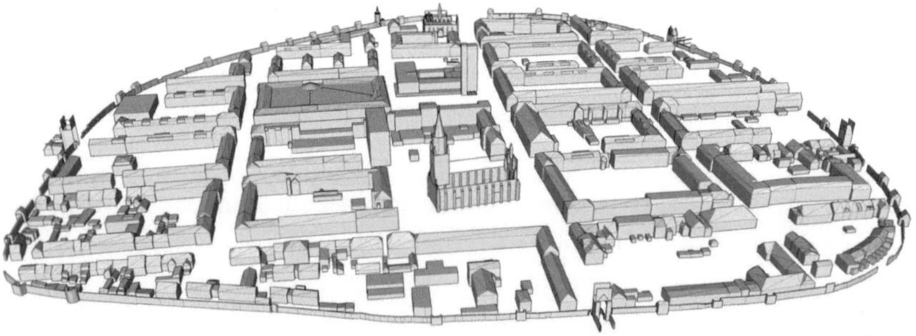

Figure 7.23: View of city center

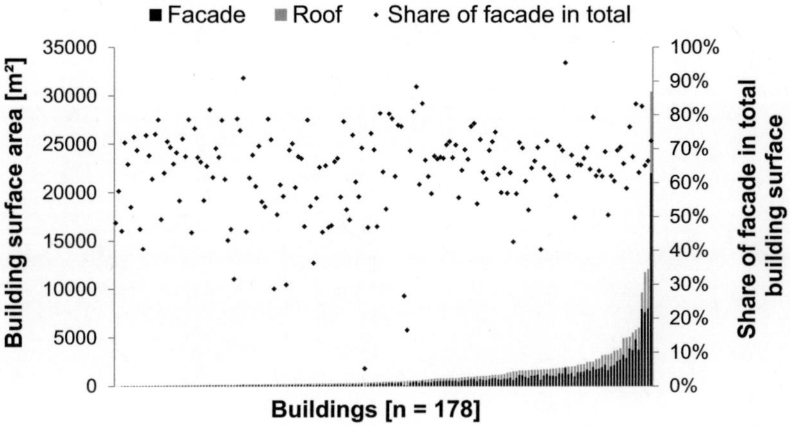

Figure 7.24: Building sizes in city center

7.3.5 City center

A view of the city center of Neubrandenburg is depicted in Fig. 7.23. In this urban area, 177 buildings could be distinguished with a total surface area of 230,491 m^2 (67 % facades, 33 % roofs). The surrounding city wall has been excluded from the solar irradiation analysis. In Fig. 7.24, the accumulated size of the building surface areas is depicted with the share of the facade relative to the total building surface area marked as an individual point for each building. Fig. 7.25 illustrates the solar irradiation for the shaded and unshaded case for every building surface in the analyzed urban district marked as an individual point. Interestingly, an accumulation of building surfaces with north, east, south and west orientations can be observed which can be attributed to the streeted grid visible in Fig. 7.23.

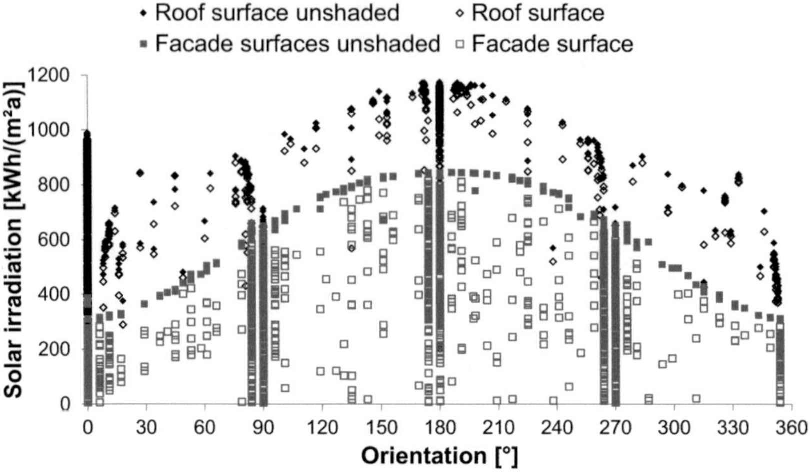

Figure 7.25: Solar irradiation on building surfaces with and without shading sorted by surface orientation (0° = North, 90° = East, 180° = South, 270° = West) in city center

In Fig. 7.26, the share of building surface area per shading class in this urban district is depicted. On 76 % of the total roof surface area, less than 10 % of the annual solar irradiation is lost due to shading. On 11 % of the roof area, 20 % to 30 % of solar irradiation is lost due to shading. Only 2 % of the facade area experiences less than 10 % shading. 78 % of the facade area experiences between 10 % and 50% shading. On 4 % of the total facade area, shading losses amount to more than 90 %. The numerical values which will be used in further analysis are listed in Tab. 7.5.

7.3.6 Summary of shading analysis for urban districts

Fig 7.27 summarizes the share of facade surfaces per shading class in the analyzed urban districts. Generally, facade surfaces in the city center experience most shading due to the higher building density. In the urban district with mainly small multi-family houses most facade surfaces are shaded by 10 % to 20 %.

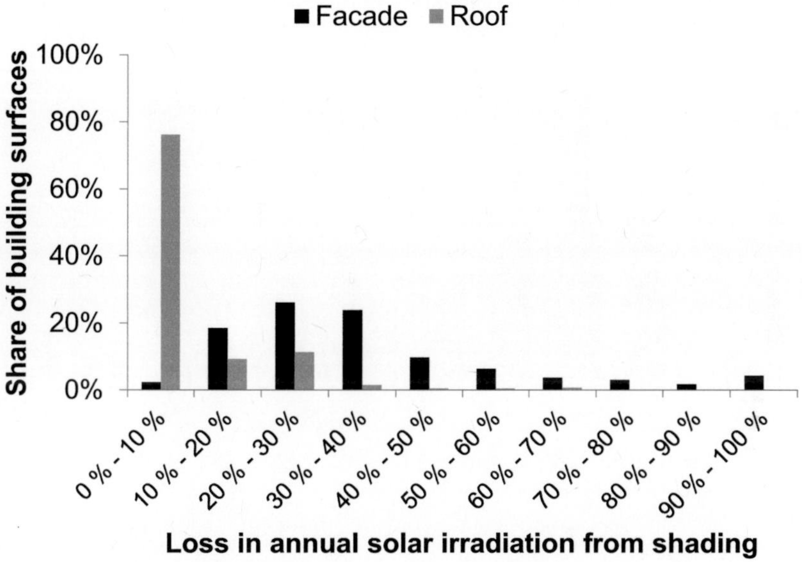

Figure 7.26: Loss in solar irradiation from shading in city center

Table 7.5: Share of building surfaces per shading class for city center

Shading class	City center Facade	City center Roof
0 % - 10 %	2 %	76 %
10 % - 20 %	18 %	9 %
20 % - 30 %	26 %	11 %
30 % - 40 %	24 %	1 %
40 % - 50 %	10 %	0 %
50 % - 60 %	6 %	0 %
60 % - 70 %	4 %	1 %
70 % - 80 %	3 %	0 %
80 % - 90 %	2 %	0 %
90 % - 100 %	4 %	0 %
Sum	100 %	100 %

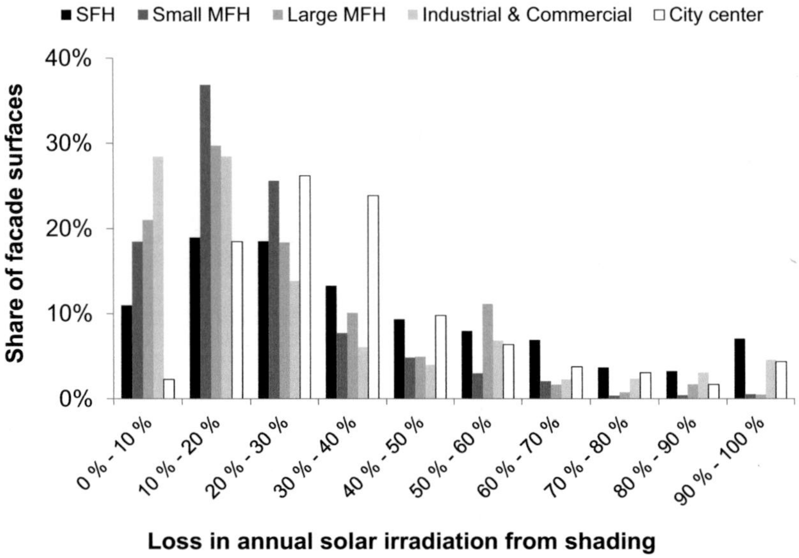

Figure 7.27: Share of facade surfaces per shading class for all analyzed urban districts

In the urban district with mainly single-family houses the share of facade surfaces per shading class is most evenly distributed. In Fig. 7.28, the share of roof areas per shading class in the analyzed urban districts is summarized. Generally, roof areas are less shaded than facade areas. More than 85 % of all roof areas are shaded less than 10 % in all analyzed urban districts except for the city center where only 76 % of roof surfaces correspond to this shading class. In addition, roof areas generally have a higher irradition due to the tilt angle. This has been clearly illustrated in the figures with the solar irradiation on building surfaces with and without shading sorted by surface orientation. There, the solar irradiation level on roof surfaces was generally above the facade areas. However, it should be noted that in this analysis, a 3D city model in LOD2 has been used such that shading from dormer windows and chimneys and additional roof structures like those for heating, ventilation and air conditioning (HVAC) equipment could not be taken into account.

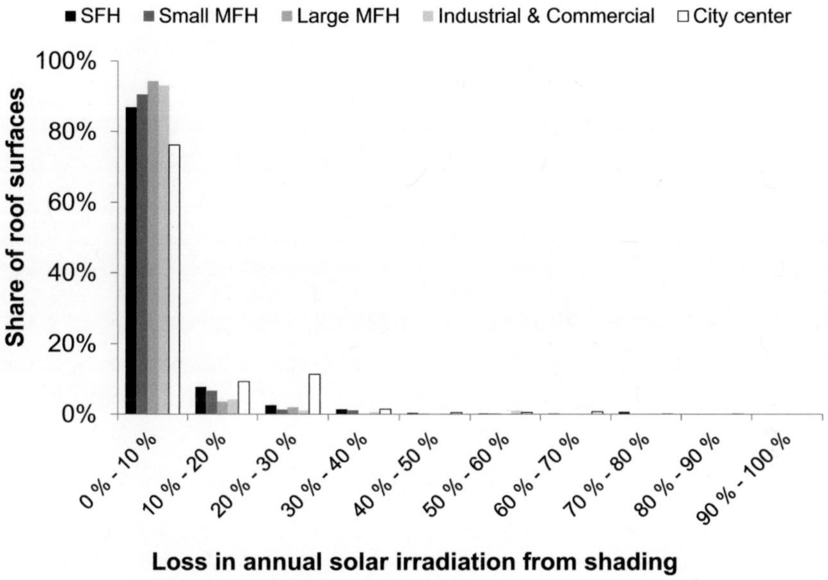

Figure 7.28: Share of roof surfaces per shading class for all analyzed urban districts

7.4 Irradiation analysis

Unlike the non-residential buildings, an irradiation analysis for residential buildings was not presented in Section 6.1. Therefore it is not clear, which share of the residential building surface area receives which level of solar irradiation. For this purpose, the results of the shading analysis reported earlier in this chapter have been additionally assessed concerning the average irradiation on building surface areas both for the shaded and the unshaded case. As previously, the "shaded case" refers to results where the effects of obstruction and reflection by the building and its surroundings have been included in the radiation simulation, whereas the "unshaded" case refers to the radiation that would be incident on each building surface if it were free-standing and completely independent of any surroundings (see Section 4.1.2).

7.4.1 Single and multi-family dwellings with low building density

Depending on the average incident irradiation, the building surface areas of the urban district in Neubrandenburg with mainly single and multi-family dwellings and low building density have been sorted into the irradiation classes depicted in Fig. 7.29. Using these values in conjunction with the shading values calculated in Section 7.3.1 shading would be taken doubly into account. Therefore, in Fig. 7.30 the frequency distribution of building surfaces per irradiation class is also presented for the unshaded case. These values, in combination with the shading values from Section 7.3.1 can be used in further potential estimates.

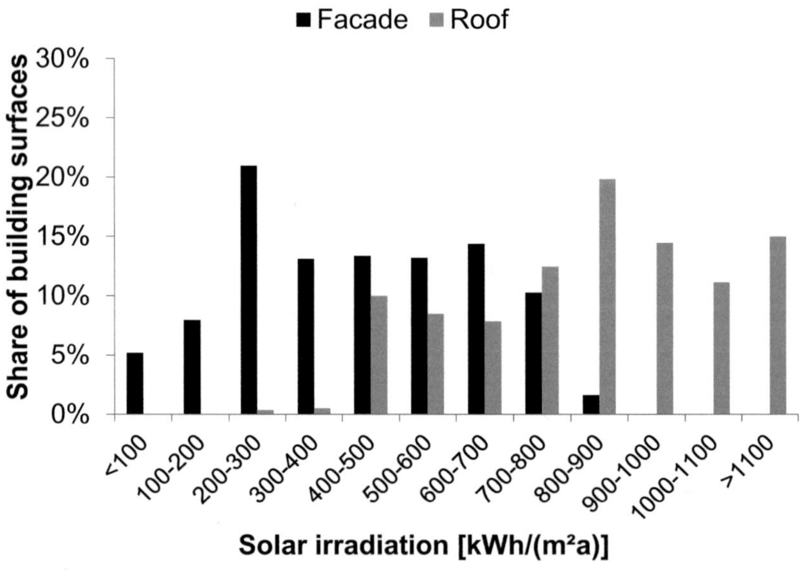

Figure 7.29: Share of building surfaces per irradiation class in the urban district with mainly SFH and MFH and low building density for the shaded case

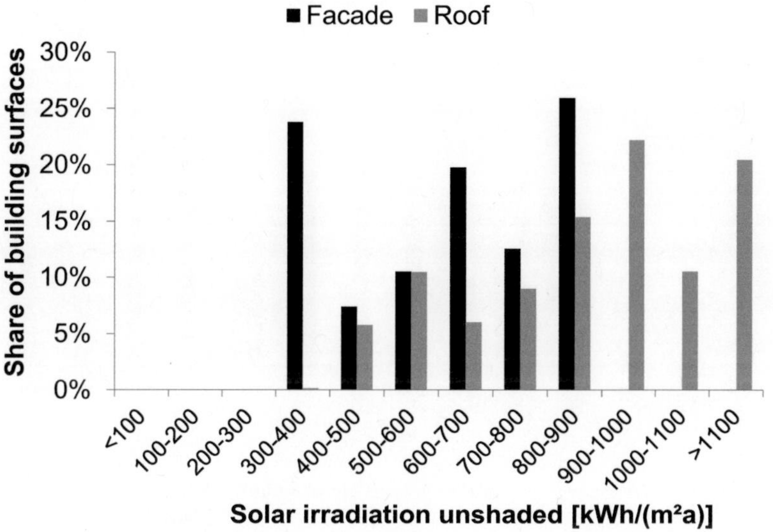

Figure 7.30: Share of building surfaces per irradiation class in the urban district with mainly SFH and MFH and low building density for the unshaded case

7.4.2 Small multi-family dwellings

Also for small-multi family dwellings, the results of the performed shading analysis have additionally been assessed with respect to the average irradiation on the building surfaces. In Fig. 7.31 the share of building surfaces per irradiation class is depicted for the shaded case.

Fig. 7.32 shows the share of building surfaces for the unshaded case. For the facade surfaces, the distribution over the irradiation classes is almost symmetric, with an intermediate share of the surfaces in the irradiation classes 800 to 900 kWh/(m^2a) and 300 to 400 kWh/(m^2a), i.e. south and north-oriented respectively, and the largest share in irradiation class 600 to 700 kWh/(m^2a), i.e. east and west-oriented. For single-family houses, this distribution was different, i.e. with the largest shares north and south-oriented.

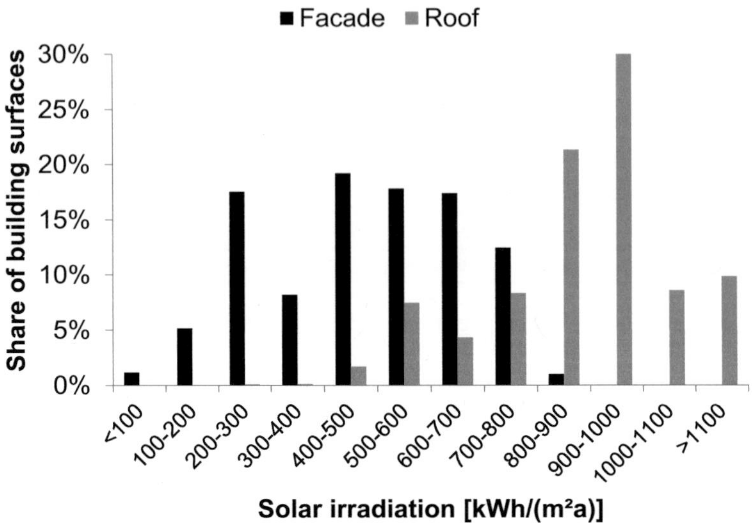

Figure 7.31: Share of building surfaces per irradiation class for the urban district with mainly small MFH for the shaded case

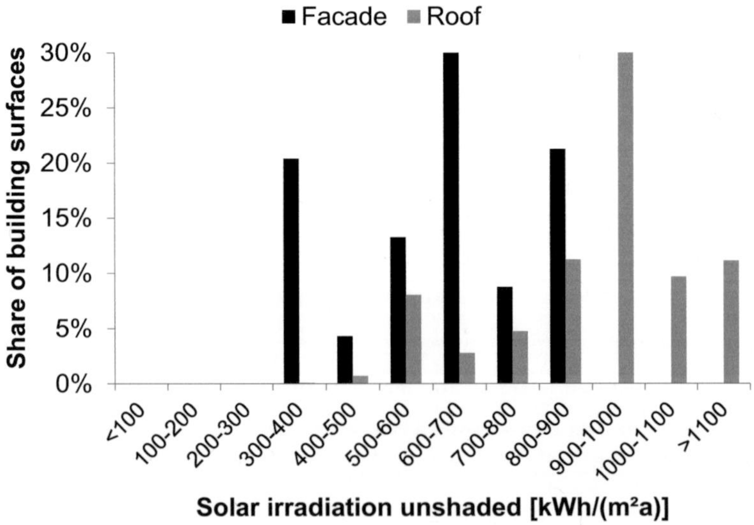

Figure 7.32: Share of building surfaces per irradiation class in the urban district with mainly small MFH for the unshaded case

7.4.3 Large multi-family dwellings

For large multi-family dwellings, the results of the performed shading analysis have also been assessed additionally with respect to the average irradiation on the building surfaces. In Fig. 7.33, the share of building surfaces per irradiation class is depicted for the shaded case.

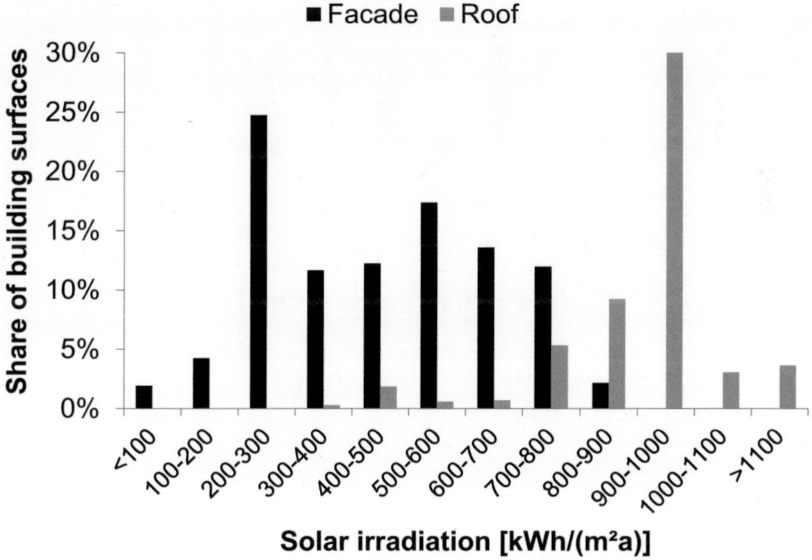

Figure 7.33: Share of building surfaces per irradiation class for the urban district featuring large MFH for the shaded case

In Fig. 7.34, again the share of building surfaces for the unshaded case is given. For the facade surfaces, the distribution over the irradiation classes is almost symmetric, with the second-largest share of the surfaces in irradiation classes 800 to 900 kWh/(m^2a) and 300 to 400 kWh/(m^2a), i.e. south and north-oriented respectively, and the largest share in irradiation class 600 to 700 kWh/(m^2a), i.e. east and west-oriented.

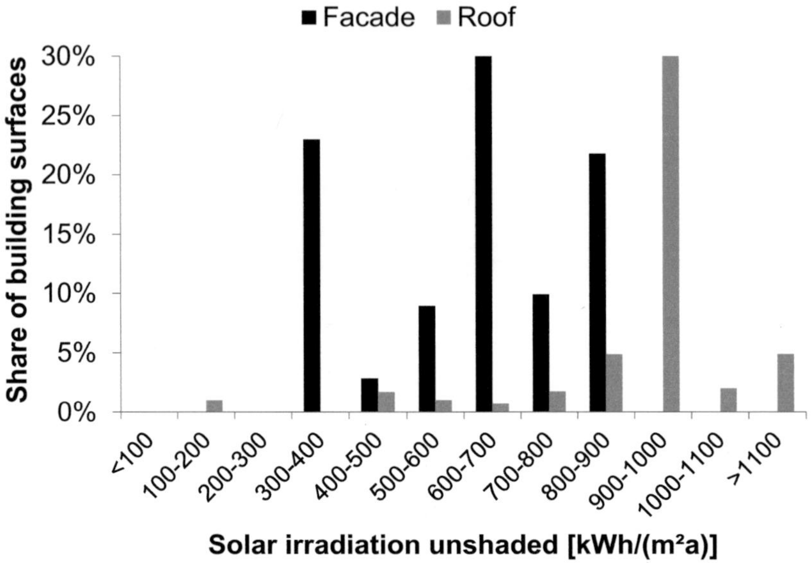

Figure 7.34: Share of building surfaces per irradiation class for the urban district featuring large MFH for the unshaded case

7.4.4 Industrial buildings

To complete the analysis, in Fig. 7.35 and Fig. 7.36, also the shares of building surfaces per irradiation class are illustrated for the industrial urban district for the shaded and unshaded cases, respectively.

7.4.5 City center

Finally, in Fig. 7.37 also the share of building surfaces per irradiation class for buildings in the city center is depicted for the shaded case. In Fig. 7.38 the same is depicted for the unshaded case.

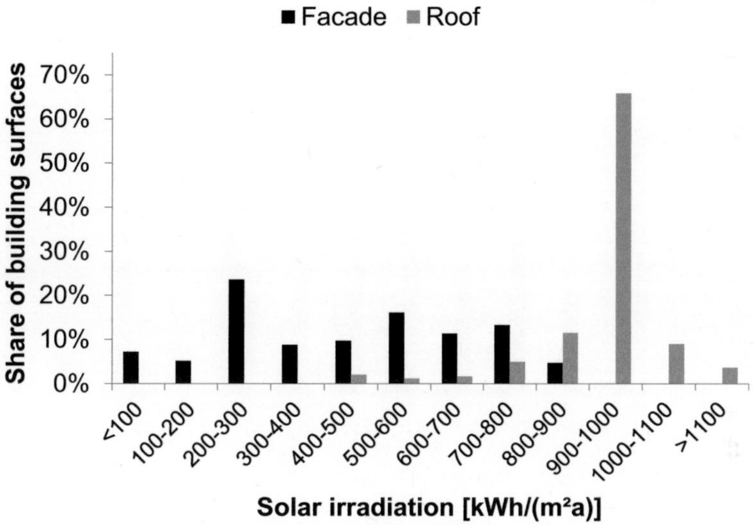

Figure 7.35: Share of building surfaces per irradiation class for the industrial urban district for the shaded case

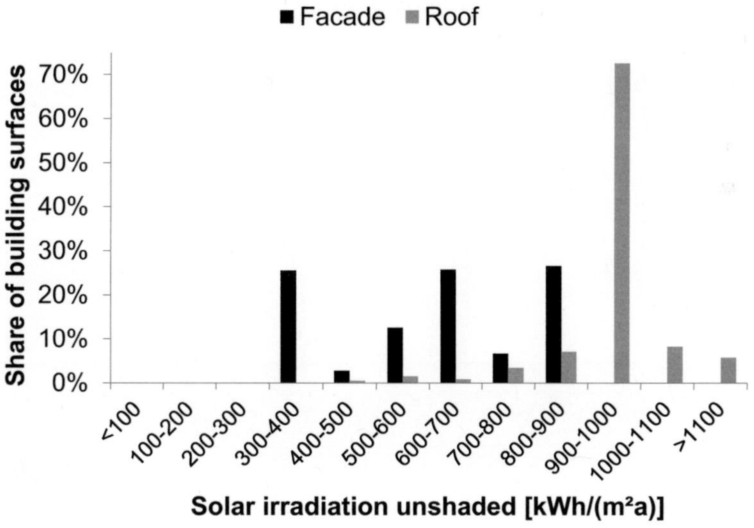

Figure 7.36: Share of building surfaces per irradiation class for the industrial urban district for the unshaded case

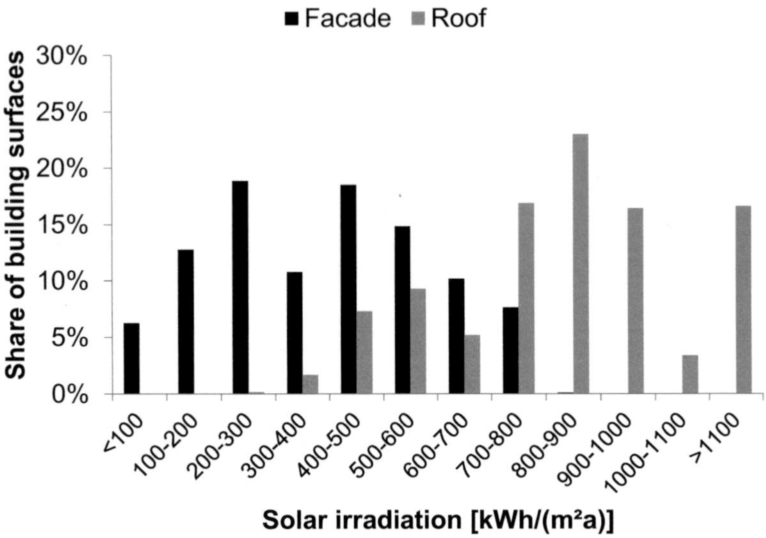

Figure 7.37: Share of building surfaces per irradiation class for the city center and the shaded case

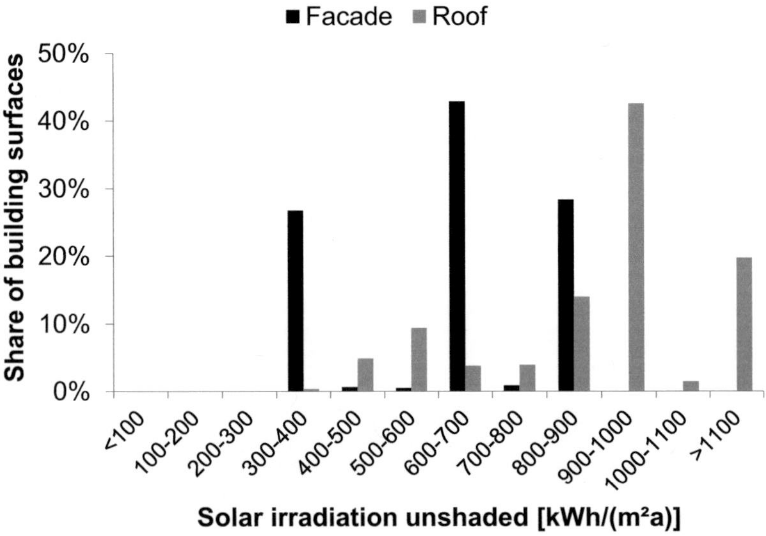

Figure 7.38: Share of building surfaces per irradiation class for the city center and the unshaded case

7.4.6 Summary of irradiation analysis for urban districts

Figs. 7.39 to 7.42 summarize the distribution of roof and facade surface area over the irradiation classes both for the shaded and the unshaded case. Buildings located in the urban districts with mainly large multi-family buildings and industrial buildings have the highest share of roof surface area in the irradiation class 900 to 1000 kWh/(m^2a) in both the shaded and the unshaded cases, since these roofs are mainly flat and unobstructed.

Facade surface areas experience a high loss in irradiation due to shading in all considered urban districts, as is evident when Fig. 7.40 and Fig. 7.42 are compared. From Fig. 7.42, a clear north-south orientation of building facades in the urban district with mainly large multi-family houses and in the city center, as was discussed in Sections 7.4.3 and 7.3.5.

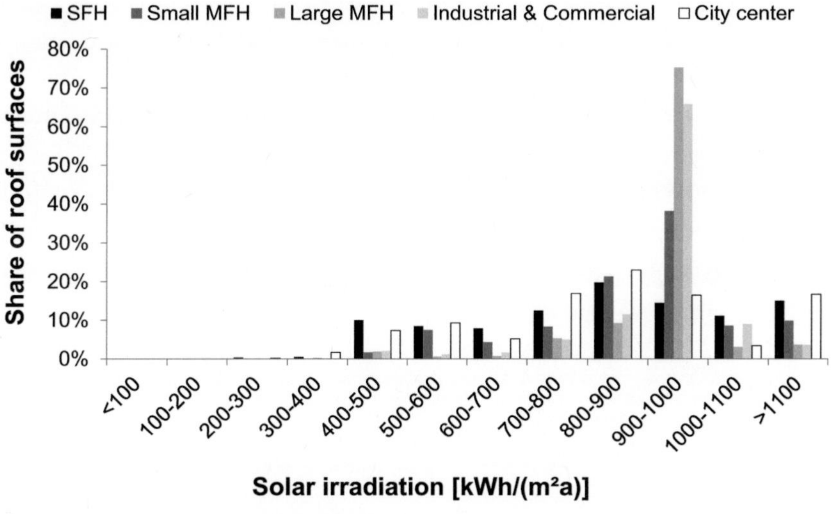

Figure 7.39: Share of roof surfaces per irradiation class for the analyzed urban districts and the shaded case

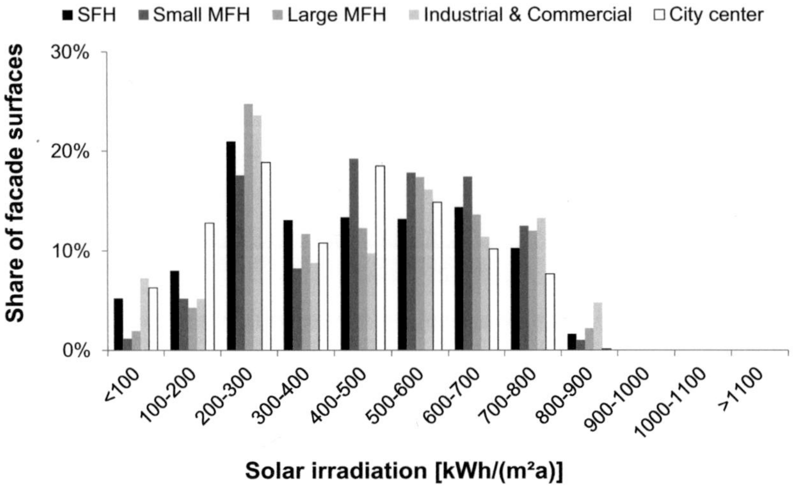

Figure 7.40: Share of facade surfaces per irradiation class for the analyzed urban districts and the shaded case

The highest shares of facade surfaces of the large multi-family houses and in the city center correspond to the irradiation classes 800 to 900 kWh/(m^{2}a) (south), 600 to 700 kWh/(m^{2}a) (east and west) and 300 to 400 kWh/(m^{2}a) (north). This distribution can no longer be observed for the shaded case as depicted in Fig. 7.40. In the other analyzed urban districts, such a pronounced general building orientation cannot be identified.

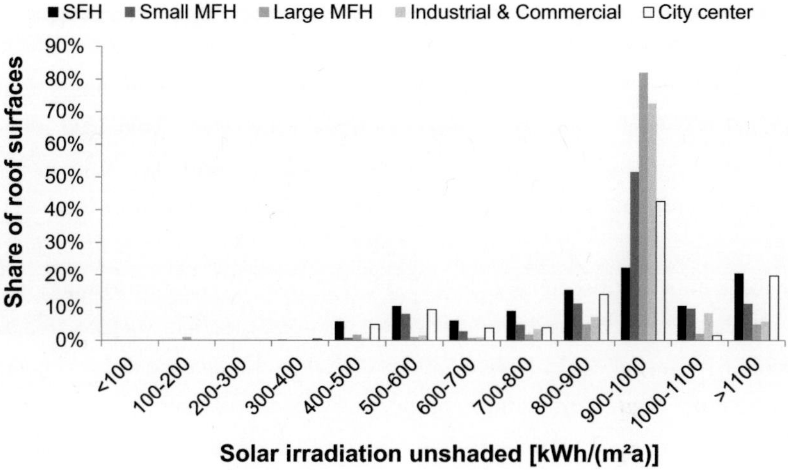

Figure 7.41: Share of roof surfaces per irradiation class for the analyzed urban districts and the unshaded case

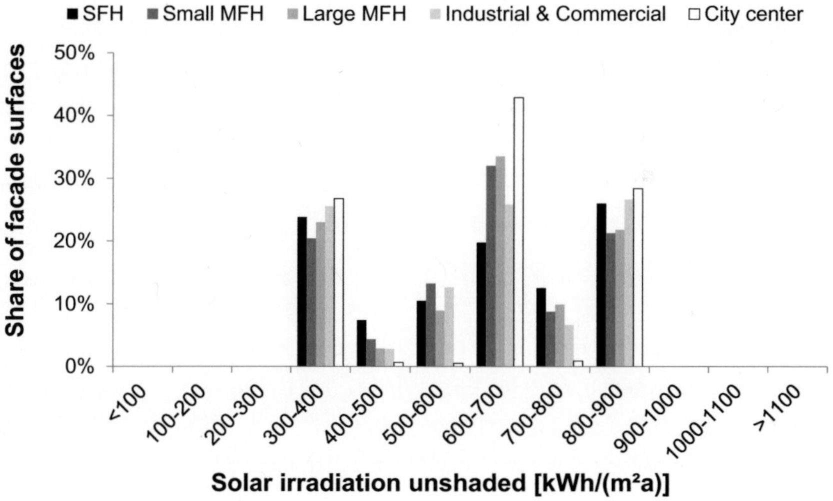

Figure 7.42: Share of facade surfaces per irradiation class for the analyzed urban districts and the unshaded case

7.5 Conclusion on urban district assessment

Redweik et al. (2013) have assessed roof and facade areas of buildings on the campus of Lisbon university employing a shadow algorithm. They have plotted the location potential, i.e. the cumulative annual irradiation, with respect to the share of the area used respectively for roofs, facades and in total. This type of diagram is depicted for the analysis of the Karlsruhe 3D city model by the author of this thesis in Fig. 7.43. For this, the annual irradiation on roofs and facades has been multiplied by the corresponding surface area and ordered from highest to lowest. Even though roofs again exhibit a greater potential (i.e. higher irradiation), in this case facades also show a considerable contribution to the total potential, in contrast to the findings of Redweik et al. (2013) where the 25 % best positions are located solely on roofs. This can be attributed to the different latitudes of the considered cities (Karlsruhe - 49°; Lisbon - 38°), resulting in proportionally higher irradiation values on vertical surfaces in comparison to horizontal surfaces in Karlsruhe than in Lisbon.
In the analyzed extract of the Karlsruhe 3D city model, the location potential on building roofs and facades totals 930 GWh/a (59 % on roofs; 41 % on facades). Thus, the irradiation on facades should not be neglected in solar potential studies since they can constitute more than 70 % of the available building surfaces in urban areas (Redweik et al. (2013); Fath et al. (2015)). For more densely populated cities featuring even skyscrapers, the share of facade areas in total building surfaces can be expected to increase further.
In Fig. 7.44, the same type of graph is shown for the analyzed urban structure with mainly small multi-family dwellings in the Neubrandenburg 3D city model introduced in Section 7.2 of this thesis. Here, due to less shading, facades and roofs contribute an approximately equal share to the location potential, i.e. in Germany, even for urban structures with a smaller share of facade surfaces than a city center, facades provide a significant share of the location potential due to the latitude-induced smaller solar altitude angles in fall and winter.

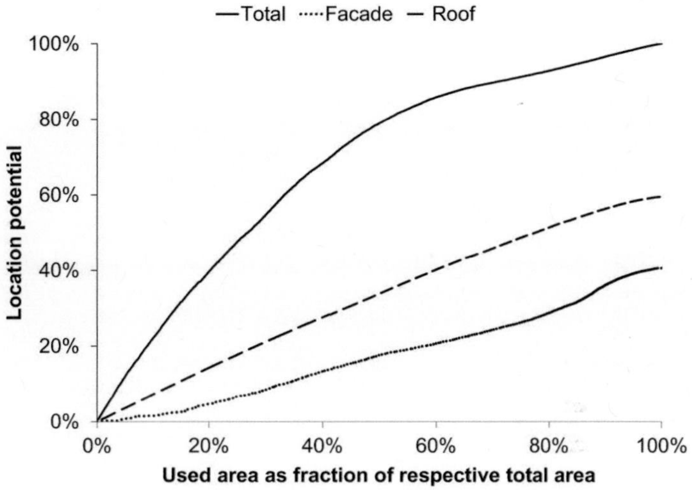

Figure 7.43: Cumulative location potential, i.e. annual irradiation on suitable building surfaces versus the share of area used respectively in total, for roofs and facades in the analyzed extract of the Karlsruhe 3D city model

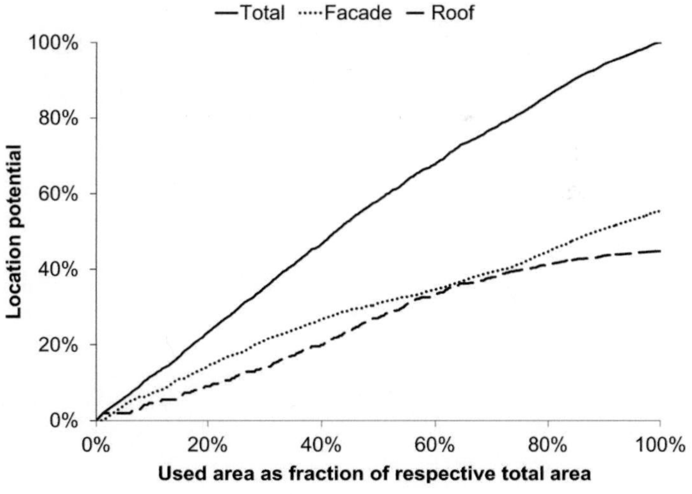

Figure 7.44: Cumulative location potential, i.e. annual irradiation on building surfaces, versus the share of total surface area used respectively in total, for roofs and for facades for the analyzed low-density urban structure with mainly small multi-family dwellings in the Neubrandenburg 3D city model

8 Methodology for national potential assessment

The objective of this study is the calculation of a national potential for building-applied or building-integrated photovoltaic installations. For this purpose, the potential on individual buildings (Chapter 6) and of urban districts (Chapter 7) has been assessed such that, based on these results, a national potential can be calculated in Chapter 9. For this purpose, first in Section 8.1, data sources with a national coverage will be reviewed. Then, in Section 8.2, a large-scale analysis of German municipalities according to typical characteristics influencing the building stock and the urban structure is carried out. Detailed building stock information for a German State and data from a national census of the residential building stock and the population have been used as training and validation data for exploring and describing typical characteristics and identifying municipalities with similar building and urban fabric structures. Finally, the results will be used in the calculation of a national potential for building-associated photovoltaic installations.

All analyses are based on publicly available geographical and statistical data. Statistical measures and methods coupled with GIS were used. In this way, the statistical building data is enhanced with geographical information, thereby adding a new dimension to the data that allows conclusions on the embedding of the buildings in the urban context to be drawn. Additionally, for non-residential buildings, for which only geographical information are available at present, for the first time a thorough statistical analysis is performed and presented.

8.1 Review of national building stock and databases of urban fabric structures

With 64 % of the German residential building stock having been constructed before 1979 (Statistisches Bundesamt 2013) and the responsibility for cadastral data split up between different Federal and State institutions (Meinel et al. 2013), existing data on building stock and urban structure was highly fragmented, often incomplete and/or inconsistent. Therefore, for large-scale building and urban structure analysis, typologies were used instead of data sets obtained from individual buildings (see also Chapter 7). In the following, the development and current status of these typologies is presented.

In the past, studies estimating the total number of buildings in Germany had to rely on readily available statistical data. While the German residential building stock was recently statistically assessed and documented (Statistisches Bundesamt 2013), little reliable official information exists on the number and distribution of the non-residential building stock. From the AdV (2014b), a database with 50.5 million geographically referenced building footprints for all German buildings (i.e. residential and non-residential) has recently become available but without information on the building type. Therefore, non-residential buildings will be a special focus of this section.

With increasing amounts of spatial information being supplied by governmental organizations (INSPIRE 2014) and also becoming publicly available (GODI 2014), research possibilities have increased tremendously. Coupling statistical information with spatial information by employing a GIS provides additional insights not only for researchers but also for public authorities, companies and interested individuals. Analyses of urban fabric structures and patterns by coupling statistical analysis with the powerful capabilities of a Geographic Information System (GIS) have already been performed by Behnisch (2008) and Behnisch and Ultsch (2008), who employed a regression function after identifying a high correlation between the total number of buildings and population in different locations. A review of data-mining techniques can be found in Liao et al. (2012). Behnisch and Ultsch (2010) have comprehensively treated the use of geographical data for knowledge generation.

In the following sections, the data sources available and used in the analysis as well as necessary adaptations are presented. The data can be divided into statistical data and geographically referenced data, which was processed using the GIS software package ArcGIS, version 10.2. Additionally, the statistical software package IBM SPSS 20.0.0, has been used. This study focuses on the German building stock and urban fabric structure. However, with similar databases available, the employed methodology and approach can easily be transferred to other countries.

For the analysis and identification of building stock and urban fabric structure characteristics in municipalities, the following 3-step procedure was applied:

1. Analysis of building stock and its embedding in the urban context (number, size and distribution over urban fabric structures)
2. Combined analysis of building stock and urban fabric structures
3. Large-scale analysis of municipalities according to building stock and urban fabric structure

8.1.1 Statistical data

8.1.1.1 Number of buildings

The most recent analysis of the German residential building stock is the "Zensus 2011" which also encompassed a census of the German population (Statistisches Bundesamt 2013). The results of the Zensus 2011 have been published online at `https://www.zensus2011.de`, offering both pre-defined reports and dynamic search queries. National analyses for an individual selection of attributes are available on request. For this thesis, an analysis of the distribution of residential units according to building type (Attributes: free-standing, twin-house, terraced house, other) number of residential units in the building (Attributes: 1, 2, 3-6, 7-12, $\geq$ 13) and building age (10 building age categories) was supplied to the author by the German Federal Statistical Office. These classifications result in 200 building classes per municipalities which had to be reduced to be manageable in the following calculations. Therefore 30 building categories were formed aggregating the provided data as documented in Tab. 8.1. Unlike the definition employed in Section 6.1, building types are defined in this chapter as follows (Statistisches Bundesamt 2013):

- Free-standing house: No adjacent buildings
- Twin-house: Building adjacent to exactly one building
- Terraced house: Building adjacent to more than building
- Other: All other types of buildings

8.1.1.2 Population data

From the Zensus 2011, also current, high-resolution (i.e. at municipality level) population data as of May 9th, 2011 were available for all German municipalities. Then, the German population amounted to 80.2 million people (Statistisches Bundesamt 2013). This data was used in this analysis for the calculation of population densities per municipality.

8.1.2 Geographically referenced data

8.1.2.1 Administrative Boundaries of German municipalities

From the German Federal Agency for Cartography and Geodesy (BKG), geographically referenced boundaries for the various administrative levels (National, State, municipality) as of December 31st, 2013 were downloaded as shapefiles in a 1:250,000 resolution (BKG 2014).

8.1.2.2 Official cadastral data for the State of Baden-Württemberg

The data from the Zensus 2011 only encompasses statistical data on residential buildings. Therefore, the only available source to the author of this study for non-residential buildings, including detailed building type information, were

Table 8.1: Formation of 30 residential building classes from originally 200 in Zensus 2011; Further reduction to 15 classes for cluster analysis (Section 8.3); N_{res} = number of residential units

Building type	N_{res}	Building age	Building classes	Reduced building classes for cluster analysis	Solar typology
Free-standing, twin-houses	1, 2	Before 1919	1	1	SFH/TH
		1919 - 1948	2	2	SFH/TH
		1949 - 1978	3	3	SFH/TH
		1979 - 1990	4	4	SFH/TH
		After 1990	5	5	SFH/TH
	3 - 12	Before 1919	6	6	MFH
		1919 - 1948	7	7	MFH
		1949 - 1978	8	8	MFH_{large}
		1979 - 1990	9	9	MFH
		After 1990	10	10	MFH
	>12	Before 1919	11	-	-
		1919 - 1948	12	-	-
		1949 - 1978	13	11	AB_{large}
		1979 - 1990	14	12	AB
		After 1990	15	13	AB
Terraced houses, Other	1, 2	Before 1919	16	1	SFH/TH
		1919 - 1948	17	2	SFH/TH
		1949 - 1978	18	3	SFH/TH
		1979 - 1990	19	4	SFH/TH
		After 1990	20	5	SFH/TH
	3 - 12	Before 1919	21	6	MFH
		1919 - 1948	22	7	MFH
		1949 - 1978	23	8	MFH_{large}
		1979 - 1990	24	9	MFH
		After 1990	25	10	MFH
	>12	Before 1919	26	-	-
		1919 - 1948	27	-	-
		1949 - 1978	28	11	AB_{large}
		1979 - 1990	29	12	AB
		After 1990	30	13	AB

5.7 million building footprints, i.e. geographically referenced 2D outlines of the building ground floor plan, including building type, of all registered buildings in the Federal State of Baden-Württemberg in 2012 (GeoBasis ©LGL, `www.lgl-bw.de`) (LGL 2012). The Federal State of Baden-Württemberg is located in Southern Germany and is the third-largest German Federal State (approximately 10 % of the German land area) with 13 % of the German population (Statistisches Bundesamt 2013).

8.1.2.3 Urban Atlas from the European Environment Agency (EEA)

As an indicator of urban fabric structure, data from the Urban Atlas of the European Environment Agency (EEA) was used in the following sections (European Environment Agency 2014). In this database, 20 urban fabric structure categories for 34 urban areas in Germany are defined (European Environment Agency 2014). The geographically referenced data sets can be downloaded free of charge. With this high level of detail, the very recent point of assessment and the good availability this data was considered suitable for the purposes of this study. Developing a methodology based on this data, which is also available for other countries, allows easy transfer of the results.

In the complete EEA data set for Europe at the time of completion of this study in 2015, 305 urban areas with more than 100,000 inhabitants in 20 urban fabric structure categories are distinguished, based on satellite imagery provided by the European Space Agency's Copernicus program on Earth Observation. With a resolution of 2.5 m, the EEA data constitute a significant improvement in comparison to the previously available data on European land cover, the Corine Land Cover database (GMES 2014). Applications of the EEA data so far encompass the analysis of urban climate (D-GMES (2014); Larondelle et al. (2014)) and accessibility to green spaces (La Rosa 2014). Rehrl et al. (2012) discuss the utilization of the EEA data in international traffic accessibility analysis. However, in Rehrl's publication, due to the limited coverage of the EEA data, finally OpenStreetMap data are used.

In Fig. 8.1, part of the urban fabric structure of the German city Karlsruhe is depicted, showing the high level of detail of the EEA data. From this, even the characteristic fan-shaped street layout of Karlsruhe is recognizable.

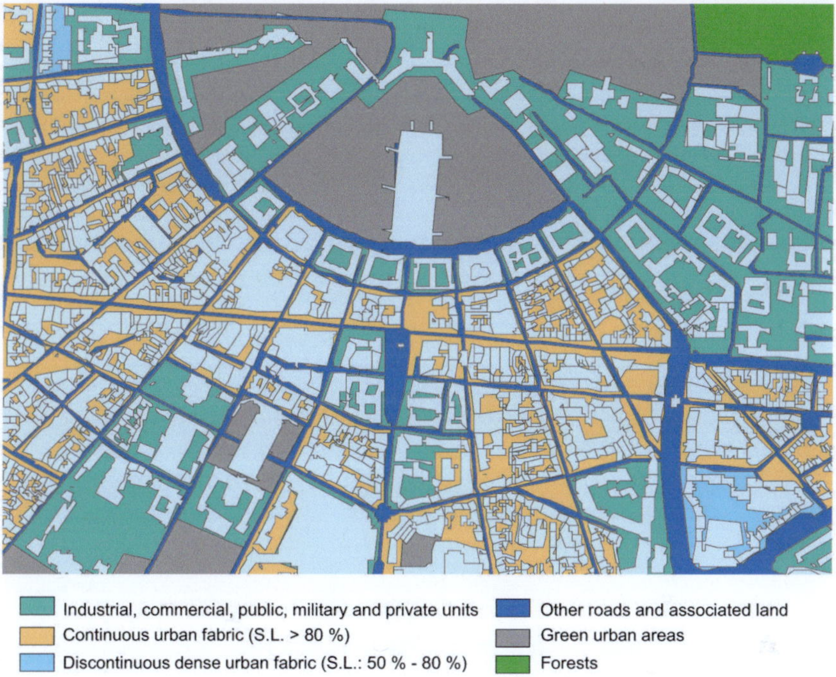

Figure 8.1: Urban fabric structures of Karlsruhe with buildings; Map prepared by the author of this thesis, based on geographical base data from EEA 2014 and © LGL

For the analysis presented here, the detailed urban fabric structure data (resolution 1:10,000) for the 34 urban areas located in Germany were used as of May 28th, 2010. The urban areas considered are depicted in Fig. 8.2.

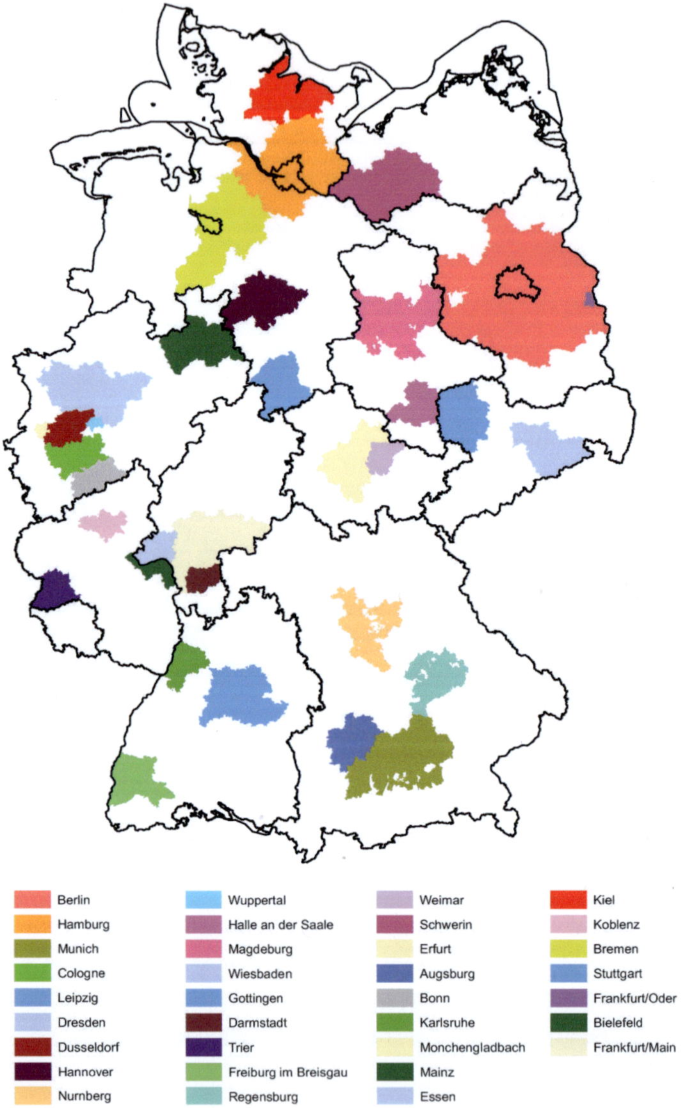

Figure 8.2: Considered urban areas; Source: Map prepared by the author of this thesis, based on EEA and administrative boundaries © GeoBasis-DE/BKG 2013

8.2 Analysis of building stock and urban fabric structures

8.2.1 Analysis of building number and size

Starting at the individual building level, first the distribution of buildings according to building type was analyzed for the different urban fabric structure categories. Only data for the three metropolitan areas of Stuttgart, Karlsruhe and Freiburg, located in the Federal State of Baden-Württemberg, for which both cadastral data and data from the EEA were available, could be used. With population densities of analyzed municipalities ranging from 34 inhabitants/km^2 (Schluchsee municipality in the Breisgau-Hochschwarzwald district, which is attributed to Freiburg in Fig. 8.2) to 2791 inhabitants/km^2 (metropolitan area of Stuttgart), the characteristics of this sample can be considered to be valid also for the 2867 municipalities under analysis on the whole.

To reduce complexity and to focus on the relevant building types, only buildings with a footprint area greater than 10 m^2 were considered. This results in 1,706,325 considered buildings in the urban areas of Freiburg (17 % of buildings), Karlsruhe (21 % of buildings) and Stuttgart (63 % of buildings). Their distribution according to the BMVBS (2013) building categories can be found in Fig. 8.3 ordered according to the sum of their building footprint area's share of the total building area.

As has been described already in Section 6.2, the 78 building types distinguished in the cadastral data are often quite similar, such that the reduced non-residential building typology according to BMVBS (2013) with 8 building categories supplemented by the three additional building categories 'Agricultural', 'Other' and 'Residential' were used (see Tab. 6.2 for the assignment of ALK building categories to BMVBS (2013) categories). With 'Agricultural' (15 %), 'Commercial & Industrial' (14 %), 'Education' (3 %), 'Offices & Administration' (4 %), 'Trade & Service' (7 %) and 'Residential' (37 %) buildings together accounting for 80 % of the total building footprint area (58 % of the total number of buildings), only these building categories are considered in further analysis. The building category 'other' is too heterogeneous to be considered here further, since 28 different building types are aggregated there. It accounts for 17 % of the total building footprint area.

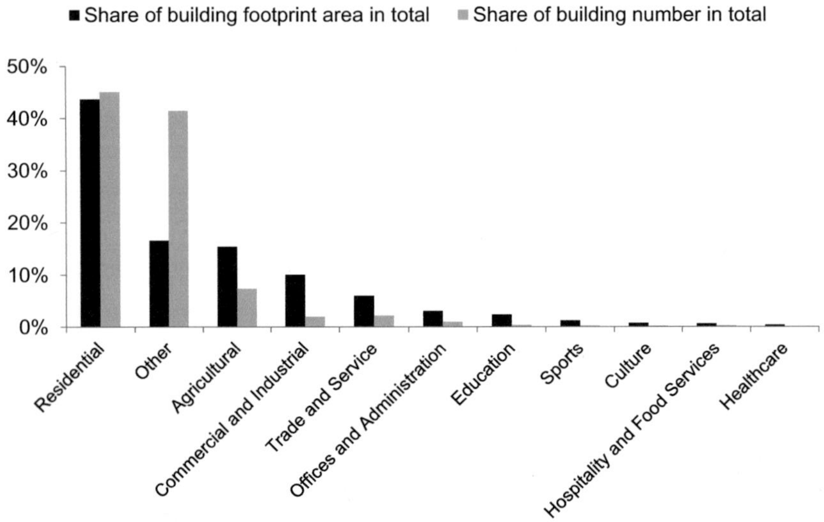

Figure 8.3: Distribution of the number of buildings and sum of building areas according to building types for the metropolitan areas of Freiburg, Karlsruhe and Stuttgart (GeoBasis ©LGL)

8.2.2 Building distribution in urban fabric structures

For the analysis of the building stock distribution according to urban structures, only the six urban fabric structure categories marked in Tab. 8.2 were chosen out of the 20 categories differentiated in the EEA data as typically containing buildings (European Environment Agency 2014).[1]

[1] The codes assigned to the urban fabric structure categories follow the EEA notation.

Table 8.2: EEA urban fabric structure categories with the EEA notation; Categories considered in further analysis are marked.

EEA-Code	Description	Sealing level	Considered further
11100	Continuous urban fabric	$> 80\%$	x
11210	Discontinuous dense urban fabric	50% - 80%	x
11220	Discontinuous medium density urban fabric	30% - 50%	x
11230	Discontinuous low density urban fabric	10% - 30%	x
11240	Discontinuous very low density urban fabric	$< 10\%$	x
11300	Isolated structures	-	
12100	Industrial, commercial, public, military and private units	-	x
12200	Road and rail network and associated land	-	
12210	Fast transit roads and associated land	-	
12220	Other roads and associated land	-	
12230	Railways and associated land	-	
12300	Port areas	-	
12400	Airports	-	
13100	Mineral extraction and dump sites	-	
13300	Construction sites	-	
13400	Land without current use	-	
14100	Green urban areas	-	
14200	Sports and leisure facilities	-	
20000	Agrictultural areas, semi-natural areas and wetlands	-	
30000	Forests	-	
50000	Water	-	

Employing the GIS software ArcGIS, the cadastral and the EEA data, i.e. building footprints and urban fabric structures, were intersected geographically, resulting in the type, number, average size and area coverage ratio of buildings per urban structure for 279 municipalities.

Buildings attributed in the combination of cadastral and EEA data to other urban fabric structures than the six types of Tab. 8.2 were not considered, thereby reducing the number of considered buildings to 952,656 (56 % of original data set). In Fig. 8.4, the normalized percentage of the total building footprint area and the total number of buildings is distributed according to the considered building categores. For normalization, the total area of each specific building type in the considered urban fabric structure categories was used.

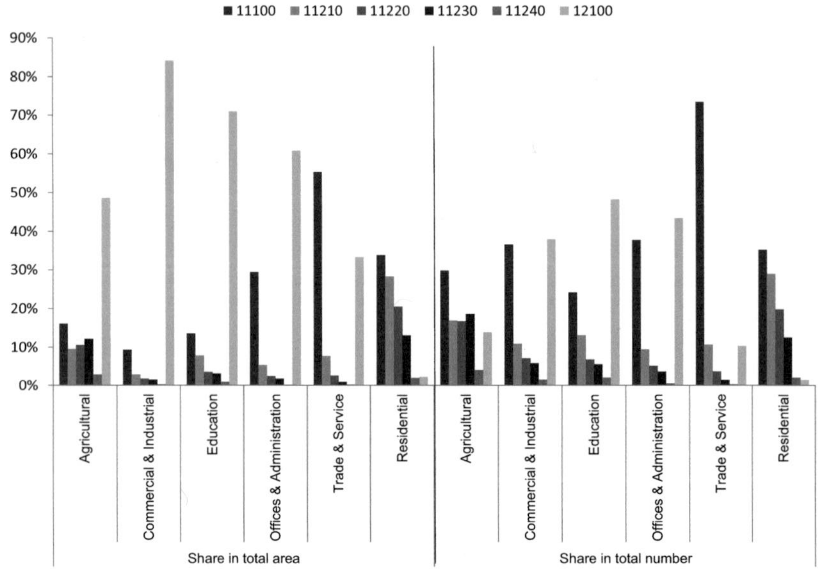

Figure 8.4: Distribution of share of number of buildings and sum of building footprint area of considered building types according to EEA urban fabric structure categories, using the codes listed in Tab. 8.2 for identification

From this analysis, the large building footprint area of non-residential buildings in urban structure category 12100 is clearly visible. While for 'Commercial & Industrial' buildings, the shares of number of buildings in the urban fabric structure categories 11100 and 12100 are similar, for 'Trade & Service' buildings the number of buildings allocated to urban fabric structure category 12100 is much lower. For 'Agricultural' buildings, the discrepancy in average building footprint area between urban fabric structure categories 11100 and 12100 is obvious from the comparison of shares in total area and shares in total number between these two categories. 'Offices & Administration' and 'Education' buildings are mainly located in urban fabric structure categories 11100 and 12100. Logically, the number and area of 'Residential' buildings show a trend proportional to the sealing level indicated in Tab. 8.2 with almost no buildings located in urban fabric structure category 12100.

8.2.3 Average building sizes in urban fabric structures

For the analysis of typical building sizes per building type in an urban fabric structure for the six non-residential building types in the six considered urban fabric structure categories, the mean and median building footprint areas were investigated. Since statistical measures, especially the mean, can be affected by outliers, for valid results outliers have to be deleted from the data set (Glantz 1997). Therefore, initially outliers were deleted from the data on the individual buildings. For their identification, standardized z-scores are calculated with mean and standard deviation with respect to building type and urban structure category according to Eq. 6.1. Buildings with a z-score above 4 (i.e. differing from the sample average by more than 4 standard deviations) are considered outliers (Hair 2010).[2] Without outliers, the data set contains a total number of 945,761 buildings.

The mean and median building footprints are plotted in Fig. 8.5. For 'Education', 'Offices & Administration', 'Trade & Service' and 'Commercial & Industrial' buildings, the urban fabric structure category 11240 - 'Discontinuous very low density urban fabric (S.L.: $< 10\,\%$)' was not considered, because it contained fewer than 20 buildings in each building category. For the urban fabric structure category 12100 - 'Industrial, commercial, public, military and private units' a clear peak in the mean and median of the building footprint area for all considered building categories is recognizable, which is due to the definition of the urban fabric structure category as containing large buildings. Since for

[2] The selection criterion of a z-score above 4 for outliers can be considered a liberal approach that is justified by the large sample size. For smaller sample sizes, data with z-scores above 2.5 are considered outliers in the literature (Hair 2010). This value was used as the normative criterion in Section 6.2.

the other urban fabric structure categories, also differences in the mean and median of the building footprint area are recognizable visually, the statistical significance of these differences was tested and reported in the following section.

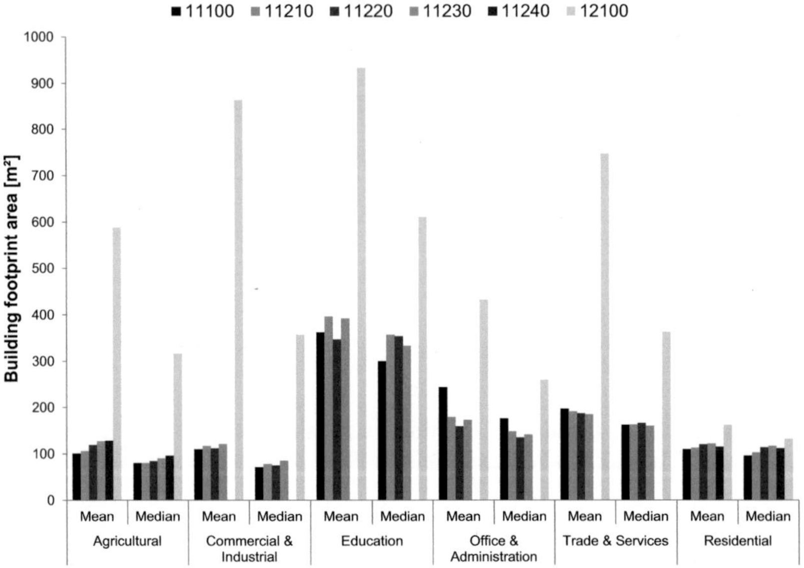

Figure 8.5: Mean and median of building footprint area for building types in urban fabric structure categories (GeoBasis ©LGL)

8.2.3.1 Statistical tests

Since for very heterogeneous data sets, often no conclusion on significant differences can be drawn solely from inspection of the distribution mean and median, statistical tests can be employed. For a detailed description of the employed statistical tests, the interested reader is referred to the cited literature and the IBM SPSS 20.0.0 documentation.

Since here different buildings are considered to belong solely to one of the considered urban structure categories, tests for independent samples must be applied. For the comparison of differences between samples, in statistics parametric and non-parametric tests can be applied. Parametric tests require a normal distribution of variables while non-parametric tests do not (Mittag 2014). The normal distribution of building footprint area for the 36 considered categories (combinations of building type and urban fabric structures) was tested on a 95 % significance level employing the Kolmogorov-Smirnoff-test with SPSS[3] (Glantz 1997). Since this test proved to be highly significant for each considered category, i.e. no normal distribution can be assumed, non-parametric tests are used in the further analysis.

The *Kruskal-Wallis* test is a non-parametric statistical test that does not analyze absolute values but ranks of attributes in independent distributions (Hollander 2014). It has been performed for the urban fabric structure categories in each building category separately. This test also proved highly significant, signifying that there were significant differences between urban fabric structure categories within building categories. However, this does not yet give information on the significantly different urban fabric structure categories since tests designed for multiple samples just give an indication of whether there is a difference between samples. A test designed for pairwise comparison will lead to erroneous results when applied multiple times without any adaptations. In non-parametric testing, the *Kruskal-Wallis* test can be adapted for testing significant differences between only two independent samples (Schaich and Hamerle 1984).

Therefore, in the next step, pairwise comparisons were performed employing the *Mann-Whitney-U* test (Hollander 2014) and the adapted *Kruskal-Wallis* test for two samples (Schaich and Hamerle 1984). Both tests are non-parametric tests and employ the rank of the sample elements instead of actual values, making them much more resistant to distortion by outliers (Glantz 1997).

Pairwise comparisons of the building footprint area according to *Mann-Whitney-U* and *Kruskal-Wallis* between all urban fabric structure categories in each building category were performed on a 95 % significance level, resulting in the

[3] For the definition of the null hypothesis and test statistic for this and the following tests, the interested reader is referred to the cited literature.

mean and median building footprint areas displayed in Tab. 8.3 as numerical values for usage in further analysis. For urban structure categories, where no significant difference was found, the mean and median were calculated for the combined number of buildings, as indicated by the grouping in Tab. 8.3.
The comparison of *Mann-Whitney-U* and *Kruskal-Wallis* test results at a 95 % significance level shows that the *Kruskal-Wallis* test adapted to only two samples is more conservative than the *Mann-Whitney-U* test, i.e. a larger difference in building footprint area between urban fabric structure categories is necessary for the null hypothesis of similar distribution types between samples to be rejected. The *Kruskal-Wallis* test results were taken as binding here.
As mentioned before, in urban fabric structure category 12100, building footprint areas are significantly larger than in the remaining categories due to its definition, which is the only significant difference for 'Education', 'Commercial & Industrial' and 'Trade & Service' buildings. 'Offices & Administration' buildings in high-density urban fabric structure category 11100 are significantly larger than in categories 11210, 11220 and 11230. For 'Agricultural' buildings, the building footprint area increases with decreasing urban density. For 'Residential' buildings, which accounted for 45 % of the analyzed buildings, significant differences between all urban fabric structure categories were found.

8.2.3.2 Discussion of results

However, from this analysis, information on total building floor area cannot yet be derived, since information on the building height is missing. Information on the average number of storeys per building is given e.g. in BMVBS (2013), based on an analysis of cadastral data and estimates of the authors.

Table 8.3: Significantly different mean and median building footprint areas per building and urban fabric structure category

Building category	Urban fabric structure category	Building footprint area [m^2] Mean	Median	Number of buildings
Education	11100 11210 11220 11230	380	337	2,343
	12100	933	611	3,814
Office & Administration	11100	244	176	3,751
	11210 11220 11230	176	146	2,929
	12100	433	259	9,417
Trade & Service	11100 11210 11220 11230	113	74	14,848
	12100	864	357	17,206
Commercial & Industrial	11100 11210 11220 11230	196	162	29,822
	12100	747	363	6,423
Agricultural	11100 11210	104	80	67,716
	11220	119	84	11,691
	11230 11240	127	90	2,880
	12100	589	316	27,660
Residential	11100	110	96	198,595
	11210	113	103	430,566
	11220	120	114	85,956
	11230	122	117	11,214
	11240	115	112	621
	12100	163	132	18,281

8.3 Classification of municipalities by urban fabric structures

No national database on the total distribution of the urban fabric structures in all German municipalities exists, which could immediately be used for the large-scale analysis of the building-associated photovoltaic potential. As depicted in Fig. 8.2, the EEA data cover only 27 % of the German land area, but account for 50 % of the German population. In the following, now a classification of municipalities according to urban fabric structures will be performed, again employing the multivariate analysis methodology cluster analysis (Section 6.2.4) following the 8-step procedure according to Backhaus et al. (2008).

1. Specifying the problem and objective of the cluster analysis

In this cluster analysis, municipalities shall be classified according to similarities in their building stock and urban fabric structure characteristics.

2. Defining the objects to be classified

In order to reach the objective of the cluster analysis, only municipalities for which detailed information on building stock and urban fabric structure distribution are available can be classified. This requirement leaves only the 281 municipalities in the metropolitan areas of Freiburg, Karlsruhe and Stuttgart, for which information on residential (Statistisches Bundesamt 2013) and non-residential (LGL 2012) building stock, urban fabric structure (European Environment Agency 2014) and population (Statistisches Bundesamt 2013) is available.

3. Selection of attributes

For the analysis, the following attributes are available for the considered municipalities:

- Share of number of buildings in six building categories (see Section 8.2.2) in total number of buildings (6 attributes)
- Total number of buildings in the municipality (1 attribute)
- Proportion of total building footprint area in municipality area (1 attribute)

- Share of five urban fabric structures (see Section 8.2.3, without category 11240) in total municipality area (5 attributes)
- Population density (1 attribute)
- Share of 30 residential building classes (see Tab. 8.1) in total number of residential units per municipality (30 attributes)

In order to delete highly correlated attributes before the cluster analysis (Backhaus et al. 2008), a correlation analysis employing Pearson's correlation coefficient according to Eq. 6.8 was performed for all of the attributes mentioned above, choosing a threshold value for the correlation coefficient of 0.80, which is more strict than in Section 6.2.4 due to the large number of attributes. Since the 'share of total building footprint area in municipality area' and the 'population density' were strongly correlated with each other and with other attributes, they were excluded from the analysis. For the 30 residential building classes, the two considered building types (i.e. free-standing/twin-houses and terraced-houses/other) are strongly correlated since they are complementary, such that the building types were combined, resulting in excluding this distinction from the analysis. In addition, the building classes '>12' residential units in building age categories 'Before 1919' and '1919-1948' were found not to differ much between groups and therefore not considered further in the analysis. The reduced set of building classes (15 attributes) is documented in Tab. 8.1.
For the 25 remaining attributes, standardized z-scores were calculated according to Eq. 6.1 and used in the cluster algorithm so that results would not be distorted by use of different measurement units (Hair 2010).

4. Selection of measures of distance

As in Section 6.2.4, the squared Euclidian distance has been used as the measure of distance (Hair 2010).

5. Selection of grouping algorithm

As in Section 6.2.4, the Ward clustering algorithm has been used for grouping (Hair 2010).

6. Conducting the grouping

The grouping was conducted for 278 municipalities within the three previously defined metropolitan areas of Baden-Württemberg, excluding the urban municipalities of Freiburg, Karlsruhe and Stuttgart from the analysis. The highly concentrated urban fabric structure and population density were considered to make them outliers in comparison to the other considered municipalities, which would distort clustering results.

7. Selection of number of clusters

Applying the visual elbow criterion, i.e. the number of clusters after which the measure of distance is only slightly increased further, 5 clusters were chosen as suitable for grouping the considered objects.

8. Analysis and interpretation of results

In Fig. 8.6, the analyzed municipalities are colour-coded according to the cluster assignment, with the omitted urban municipalities of Freiburg, Karlsruhe and Stuttgart marked in red. The identified clusters demonstrate different sizes, with 6, 45, 145, 69 and 13 municipalities attributed to the clusters 1 to 5, respectively (see also Fig. 8.10).

For the attributes used in the cluster analysis, the statistical distribution of selected attributes for the 5 identified clusters is depicted in Fig. 8.7 to Fig. 8.9. The total number of buildings in the identified clusters decreases from cluster 1 to cluster 5. The population density follows the same trend. However, since it was highly correlated, it was not used in the clustering and is therefore also not depicted here.

The 6 municipalities assigned to cluster 1 exhibit the largest share of densely populated urban fabric structure category 11100 (see Fig. 8.7) and the industrial urban fabric structure category 12100. Therefore, this cluster can be called the ‘urban’ cluster. Here, small (3-12 residential units in a building) and large ($\geq$13 residential units in a building) MFH dominate, while the share of SFH (Fig. 8.9) is smaller than in the other clusters. Geographically, 4 out of these 6 municipalities are located in the direct vicinity of the urban district of Stuttgart.

However, the geographic location was not considered in the cluster analysis. The 69 municipalities assigned to cluster 4 are located mainly in the Freiburg region. In these municipalities, the share of newly constructed (since 1991) one-or-two family houses is highest (Fig. 8.9), indicating an economically prospering region resulting in a population increase.

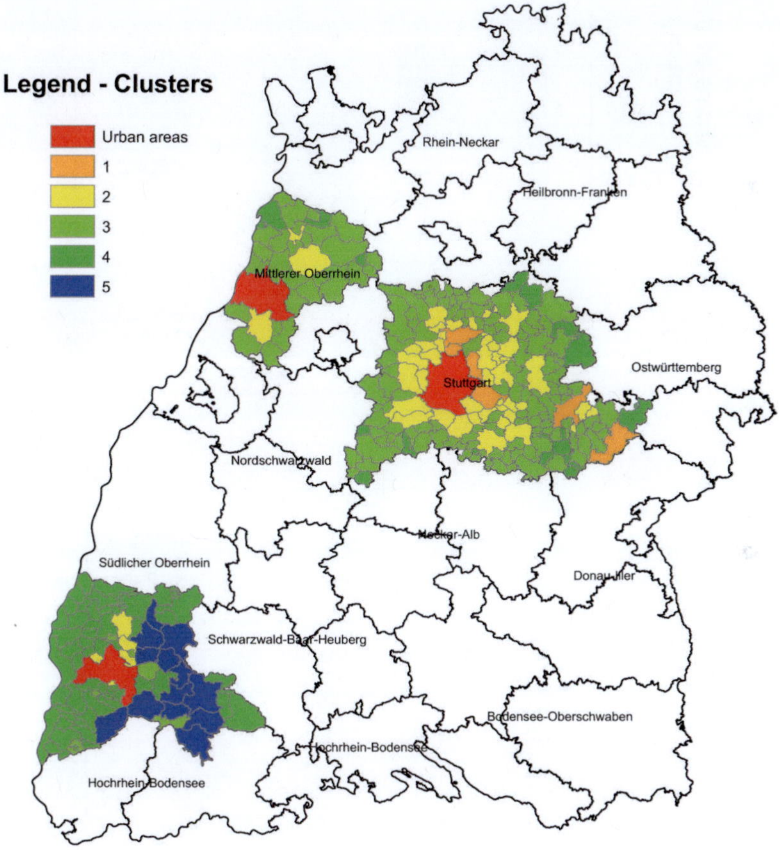

Figure 8.6: Result of cluster analysis of the municipalities in the German State of Baden-Württemberg

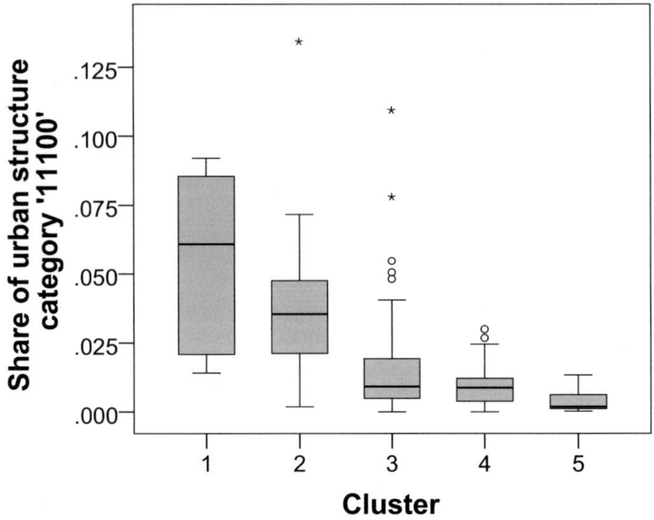

Figure 8.7: Share of continuous urban fabric structure (category 11100) in clusters

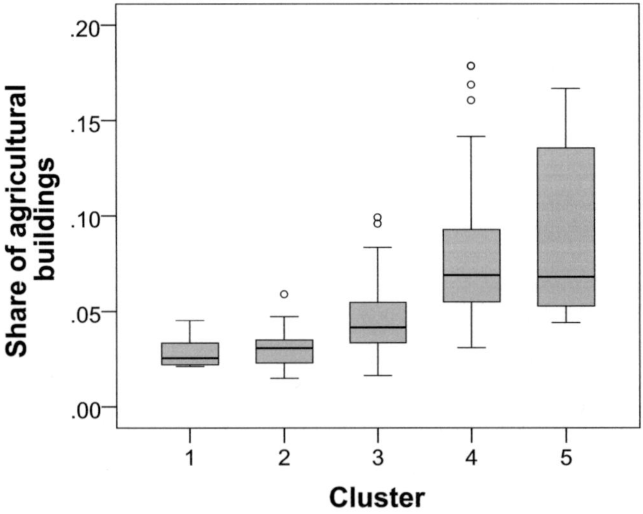

Figure 8.8: Share of agricultural buildings in clusters

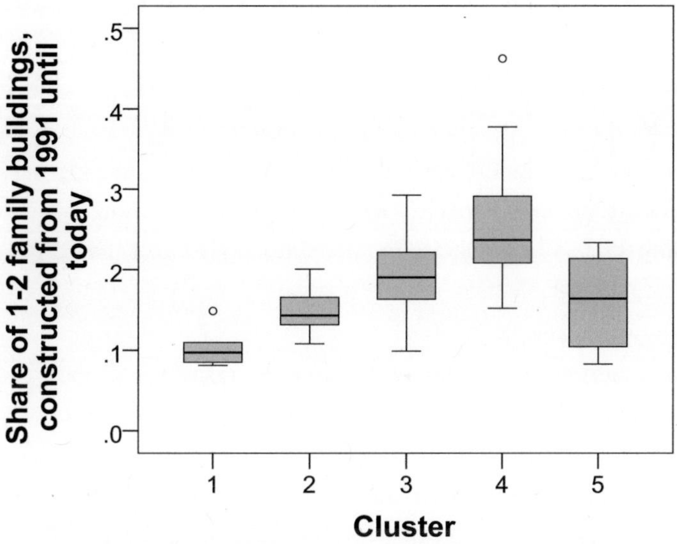

Figure 8.9: Share of 1-2 family buildings in clusters constructed after 1991

13 municipalities in the Freiburg region with the smallest population density on average were assigned to cluster 5, exhibiting the largest share of agricultural buildings in total building number (Fig. 8.8) and a large share of small MFH (Fig. 8.9). These municipalities have the largest and the second largest share of old one-or-two-family houses (built before 1919) and MFH (built before 1948). The share of the number of 'Trade & Service' buildings decreases from cluster 1 to cluster 4 with cluster 5 being in between clusters 2 and 3. Contrary to that, the share of number of 'Agricultural' buildings increases from clusters 1 to 5. Interestingly, for the share of number of 'Commercial & Industrial' buildings, no large differences between clusters are evident (not depicted). However, as has been discussed already earlier, these buildings exhibit significantly larger building footprint sizes in the industrial urban fabric structure category 12100, the average share of which decreases from clusters 1 to 5.

For sensitivity analysis of the cluster result, the grouping has been additionally performed with the same variables, transformed logarithmically and then z-standardized, resulting in a reallocation of 10 municipalities in total to different clusters. Furthermore, the clustering was performed with the k-means algorithm instead of the Ward-algorithm, both for only z-standardized and log-transformed and then z-standardized variables, with both approaches resulting in one cluster containing 95 % of the analyzed municipalities. Therefore, this approach was not considered suitable here.

Discussion of results

According to Behnisch (2008) and Behnisch and Ultsch (2009), geospatial data often violate the fundamental assumptions of hierarchical clustering algorithms such as independence of samples and identical distributions. Therefore, according to them, hierarchical clustering algorithms are not appropriate for geospatial analysis. Thus, Behnisch (2008) and Behnisch and Ultsch (2009) employ (Emergent) Self-Organizing Maps ((E)SOM) (Kohonen 2001) for a classification of growing and shrinking municipalities in Germany according to different attributes. Even though, as foreseen by Behnisch (2008) and Behnisch and Ultsch (2009), and shown in this cluster analysis, the analyzed data violate especially the condition of a similar statistical distribution, the basic objective of a cluster analysis, to identify similar groups maximizing the heterogeneity between them is considered to have been achieved here. Since the results of the cluster analysis are meaningful and the clusters can be interpreted, the chosen clustering algorithm is considered appropriate. Also, the sensitivity analysis has demonstrated a stable assignment of municipalities to clusters. The condition of achieving meaningful cluster results is therefore considered here to over-rule the recommendations for employing hierarchical clustering methods to normally distributed samples only.

Regional planning in Germany is based on the central places theory (German: Raumordnungsgesetz (ROG)) (Blotevogel 1996). Municipalities in Germany are categorized into the following broad functions resulting in different economic, social and infrastructural development plants (Burgdorf 2012)[4]:

- Regional center
- Medium-sized center
- Subcenter
- Small center
- No function according to the central places theory

However, a statistical analysis of the municipalities from the cluster analysis according to the aforementioned attributes according to the BBSR classification resulted in no significant differences between different centers, since the BBSR classification is not focused on urban fabric structure and building stock. In Tab. 8.4, the categorization of municipalities according to this classification in the 5 identified clusters is documented.

Table 8.4: Municipality classification according to central places categorization in the identified clusters where N denotes the total number of municipalities assigned to each cluster

	Central places category				
Cluster	Medium-sized center	Sub-center	Small center	No function	N
1	100 %	-	-	-	6
2	27%	20 %	16 %	38 %	45
3	3 %	6 %	21 %	70 %	145
4	6 %	10 %	12 %	72 %	69
5	15 %	-	23 %	62 %	13

[4] Intermediate categories were left out for readability reasons.

From this, a certain analogy between the found clusters and this classification is recognizable. However, since the 5 identified clusters are based on attributes specific to urban fabric structure and building stock, this classification can be assumed to better reflect the municipalities' characteristics, therefore making it more suitable for the application fields discussed in Section 8.2.
Also, according to Siedentop et al. (2003), due to the different municipality classification procedures in different German States, this classification does not form a uniform database for large-scale assessments.
Additionally, from the BBSR, a categorization of municipalities according to the population and the central places classification exists (BBSR 2011):

- Large city with population $>$ 100,000 functioning as a regional center
- Medium-sized town with 20,000 to 100,000 residents functioning as a medium-sized center
- Small town with population $>$ 10,000 functioning as a small center
- Small town with population $\leq$ 10,000 functioning as a small center
- Rural municipality without central function

In Tab. 8.5 the distribution within the identified clusters according to the BBSR city categorization is depicted. Again similarities are visible, but the two classification schemes are not completely congruent.

Table 8.5: Municipality classification according to BBSR city categorization in the identified clusters, where *N* denotes the total number of municipalities assigned to each cluster

Cluster	**Central places and population category**				*N*
	Medium-sized town	Small town ($>$ 10,000 residents)	Small town ($\leq$ 10,000 residents)	Rural community	
1	100 %	-	-	-	6
2	49 %	42 %	7 %	2 %	45
3	26 %	36 %	36 %	2 %	145
4	7 %	23 %	57 %	13 %	69
5	23 %	8 %	23 %	46 %	13

8.4 Large-scale analysis of municipalities

For the large-scale analysis of German municipalities according to building stock and urban fabric structure, now methodologies from urban data mining are used. Based on the EEA data and the administrative boundaries for 2867 municipalities throughout Germany, the detailed distribution of urban fabric structures in relation to the total municipality area was available. With a total area of 97,308 km^2, these municipalities account for 27 % of the area of Germany but with 39.5 million inhabitants, for almost 50 % of the German population. For these municipalities, also the share of the 13 reduced residential building classes (Tab. 8.1) in the total number of residential units per municipality is available. Following the approach of Behnisch and Ultsch (2010), a classification established for elements of a sample with known attributes can be transferred to similar elements of a sample for which some of the attributes used in clustering are unknown. For this, the *k-Nearest-Neighbor (KNN)* algorithm is a simple algorithm employing the assignment of a specified number (*k*) of neighbors of an element to a group in the assignment of the respective element. The *cluster-center analysis* belonging to the partitioning clustering algorithms can also be conducted when an assumption concerning the number of clusters already exists. Since these algorithms are quite sensitive to changes in data, sensitivity analysis is crucial (Hair 2010).

For the assignment of sample elements to groups, first for validation purposes, the *k-Nearest-Neighbor* algorithm was applied to the 281 municipalities already analyzed and the 5 identified clusters. This procedure resulted in 100 % congruence with the three urban municipalities of Freiburg, Karlsruhe and Stuttgart assigned to cluster 1.

In the next step, using 2007 municipalities (70 % of total) as the training data set, the *k-Nearest-Neighbor* algorithm was used to classify all 2867 municipalities according to their urban structure and residential building stock characteristics into the 5 previously identified clusters (*KNN_70%_1* in Fig. 8.11 (a)). For *k*, a range of 3 to 5 neighboring elements to be used in the classification procedure was specified. The assignment to clusters and the geographical distribution of all considered municipalities is depicted in Fig. 8.11. This procedure was conducted a second time to check for sensitivity (*KNN_70%_2* in Fig. 8.11 (b)). Additionally, the assignment was performed using 100 % of the municipalities (*KNN_100%* in Fig. 8.11 (c)). Also, the *cluster-center analysis* was applied to the 2867 municipalities for partitioning the data set into the pre-defined number of 5 clusters (*cluster-center analysis* in Fig. 8.11 (d)). From visual inspection of the municipality assignment to clusters depicted in Figs. 8.10 and 8.11, the strongly differing outcomes of these approaches are obvious.

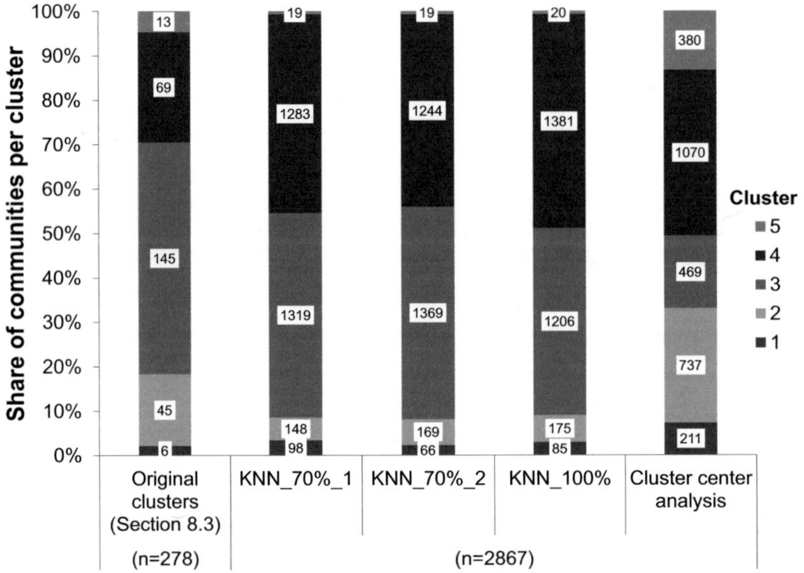

Figure 8.10: Comparison of number of municipalities per cluster according to the *k-Nearest-Neighbor*-algorithm with 70 % (KNN_ 70%_1 and KNN_70%_2) and 100 % (KNN_100%) of municipalities used as the training data set and according to the *cluster-center analysis*. The absolute numbers of municipalities are given as numerical values.

In Fig. 8.10, the distribution of number of municipalities in clusters 1 to 5 is depicted both as relative (bar diagram) and absolute values (numerical values) for the original data set (i.e. 278 municipalities) and the nationwide data set of 2867 municipalities is depicted. Compared to the other algorithms, the *cluster-center* algorithm resulted in a more even distribution of municipalities over clusters. However, considering the heterogeneous nature of the analyzed municipalities, the author of this thesis does not consider this distribution to be meaningful. Therefore in the following, scenario *c) KNN_100%* will be used further. In Tab. A.3, the descriptive statistical values for the municipalities assigned to the five clusters are documented.

The municipalities assigned to cluster 1 still exhibit the highest population density and the highest share of densely populated (11100 and 11210) and industrial (12100) urban areas. The municipalities in the other clusters show a decreasing population density as before.

In Figs. 8.12 to Fig. 8.14, the change of shares of the share of residential building types from the clustering of the 278 and the 2780 municipalities is depicted. In other words, the average share of residential building type of the 2780 municipalities assigned to the clusters has been deducted from the average share of residential building types in the 270 municipalities assigned to the clusters. From this, it is clear that the share of older buildings, i.e. constructed before 1948 is greater in all building type categories (SFH, TH, MFH, AB) when much of Germany rather than just Baden-Württemberg is analyzed. By contrast, the share of SFH, TH and MFH constructed between 1949 and 1990 has decreased in almost all clusters compared to the original data set. However, whereas the share of residential units has also decreased for MFH buildings constructed after 1991, for SFH and TH this share has increased in all clusters. The share of AB is almost unchanged. The change in shares is depicted in absolute values.

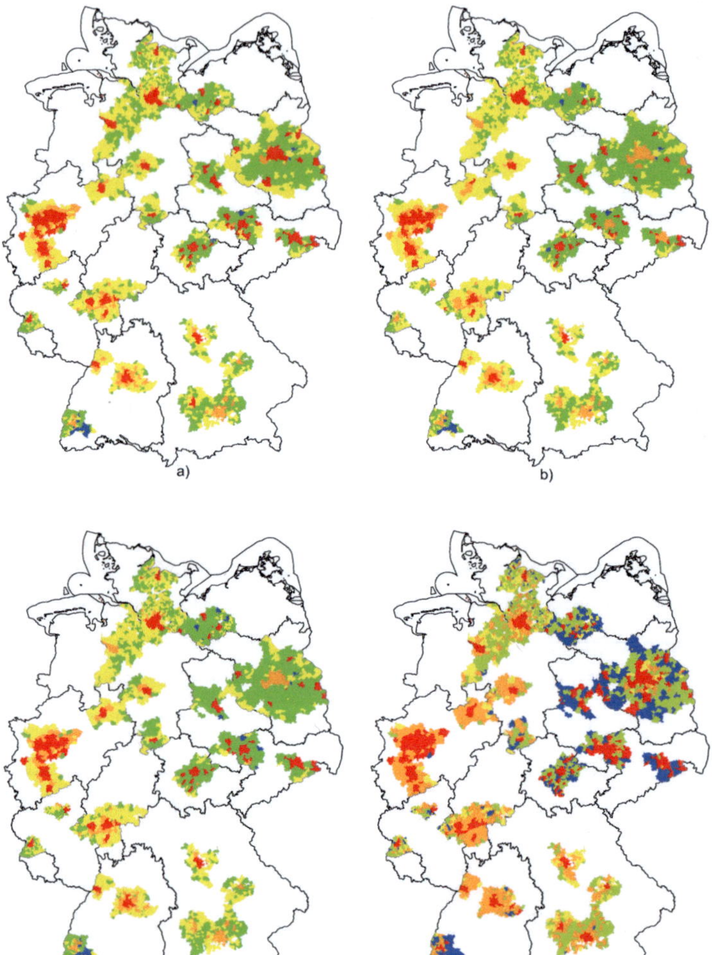

Figure 8.11: Municipalities assigned to clusters 1 (red), 2 (orange), 3 (yellow), 4 (green) and 5 (blue): a) / b) *k-Nearest-Neighbor*-algorithm with two different selections representing 70 % of municipalities used as training data set (KNN_70%_1 / KNN_70%_2); c) *k-Nearest-Neighbor*-algorithm with 100 % of municipalities used as the training data set (KNN_100%); d) *cluster-center analysis*; Clusters 1, 2, 3, 4, 5 marked in Map source: ©GeoBasis-DE/BKG 2013

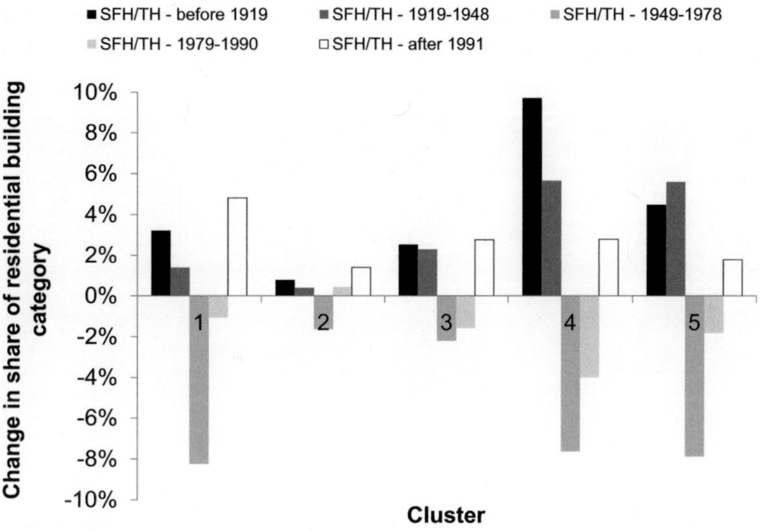

Figure 8.12: Change of shares of building categories for SFH and TH from the clustering of the 278 communities in Baden-Württemberg and the 2780 municipalities throughout Germany

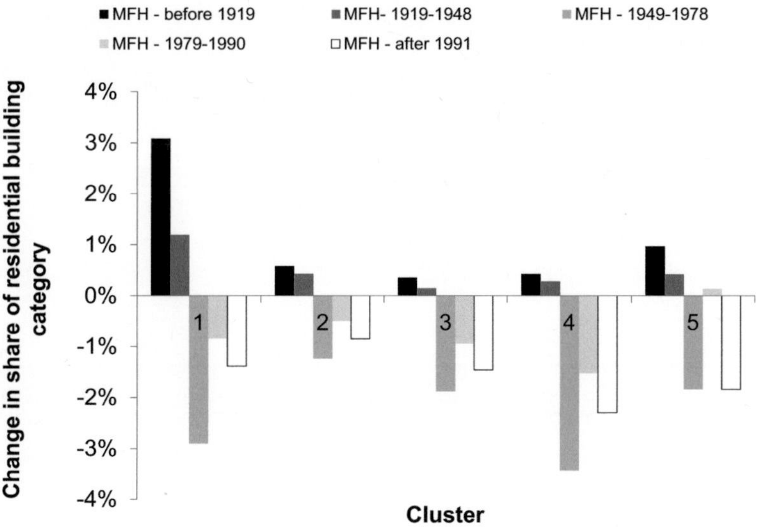

Figure 8.13: Change of shares of building categories for MFH from the clustering of the 278 communities in Baden-Württemberg and the 2780 communities throughout Germany

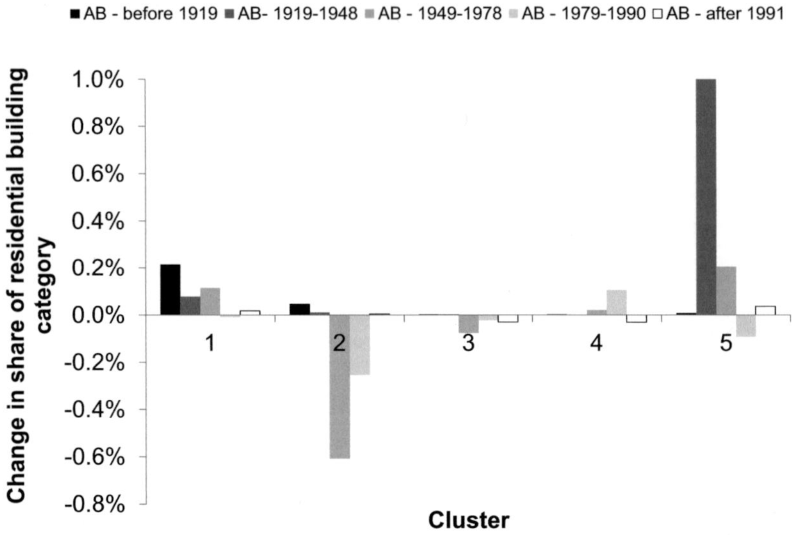

Figure 8.14: Change of shares of building categories for AB from the clustering of the 278 communities in Baden-Württemberg and the 2780 communities throughout Germany

9 Potential for building-associated photovoltaic systems in Germany

In this chapter, based on the analysis performed and the methodology developed in the previous chapter, the national potential for building-associated photovoltaic installations in Germany is calculated. The analysis is structured according to the potential definition presented in Section 2.1, i.e. the theoretical potential (Section 9.1), the technical potential (Section 9.2) and different scenarios for the economic potential (Section 9.3). Based on these results in section 9.4, a prognosis is made for the potential development until 2050, again structured according to the different potentials.

9.1 National theoretical potential

No database for the total German building stock exists, which would provide a direct route to derive a national potential for photovoltaic installations on buildings. The only data source on buildings with national coverage is from the census taken in 2011 that included residential buildings (Section 8.1.1.1) and the German population. This information has been used in the following to classify municipalities according to the classification scheme developed in Section 8.4.

In Section 6.1.2, a solar residential building typology based on an existing building typology for residential buildings (Institut Wohnen und Umwelt 2005) was defined that focuses on the attributes relevant for the photovoltaic potential, resulting in the six residential building types SFH, TH, MFH, MFH_{large}, AB and AB_{large} with the attributes listed in Tab. 6.1. For the cluster analysis, the 30 building classes were reduced to 13 due to high correlation between the eliminated sub-classes. However, the distribution of buildings over the building classes must be known for further calculations. Fig. 9.1 shows the average share of SFH and TH in the different building age categories as average over all German municipalities. From this, an average share of SFH in single- and two-family houses of 67 % and terraced and other houses of 33 % can be derived. For the other building categories, this distinction is not necessary, since here no distinction was made in the solar residential building typology. As depicted in Tab. 8.1, the building types MFH_{large} and AB_{large} were attributed to the respective building age category.

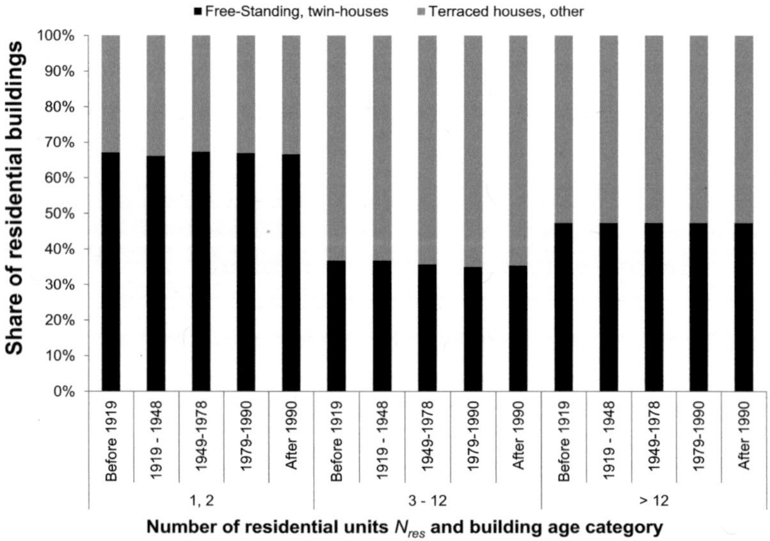

Figure 9.1: Share of building types in building age categories in residential units

To allow up-scaling the results to a national potential, also the remaining muncipalities should be classified. Since there is no geographically-referenced information available for these communities, the only available data, which has also been used in the cluster analysis in Section 8.4, consists of the following 16 attributes taken from the census:

- Population density (1 attribute)
- Share of 15 reduced residential building classes (Tab. 8.1) in total number of residential units per municipality (15 attributes)

As has been stated earlier, although the municipalities analyzed in detail account for only 27 % of the area of Germany, approximately 39.5 million inhabitants live in them, i.e. almost 50 % of the German population. Since the EEA data cover the densely populated areas, the remaining municipalities have an average population density of only 168 people/km^2, in contrast to 319 people/km^2 for the municipalities already analyzed.

Again for training purposes, first the *k-Nearest-Neighbor* algorithm has been applied to the original data set to check whether results are comparable. As in Section 8.4, it was first performed with 70 % of the data set for training resulting in 85 % of municipalities being attributed to the same cluster as previously. This deviation is partly attributable to the fact that for the clustering, again standardized values have been used, however this time standardized for all 11,343 municipalities under analysis.

In the next step, using 70 % as the training data set, the *k-Nearest-Neighbor* algorithm was used to classify all 11,343 municipalities according to their residential building stock characteristics into the 5 previously identified clusters (*KNN_70%_1* in Fig. 9.2 (a)). For *k*, a range of 3 to 5 neighboring elements to be used in the classification procedure was specified. This procedure was conducted a second time to check for sensitivity (*KNN_70%_2* in Fig. 9.2 (b)) and resulted in a very similar distribution to KNN_70%_1. Additionally, the assignment was performed using 100 % of the municipalities in the training of the algorithm (*KNN_100%* in Fig. 9.2 (c)). Additionally, the *cluster-center analysis* was applied to the 11,343 municipalities for partitioning the data set into the pre-defined number of 5 clusters (*cluster-center analysis* (d)). From visual inspection of the municipality assignment to clusters, the strongly differing outcome of this last approach is obvious. In Fig. 9.2, the distribution of number of municipalities over clusters 1 to 5 is depicted both in relative (bar diagram) and absolute values (numerical values) for the original data set (i.e. 2867 municipalities) and the large-scale data set of 11,343 municipalities. Compared to the other algorithms, the *cluster-center* algorithm resulted in a more even distribution of municipalities on clusters. However, considering the heterogeneous nature of analyzed municipalities, the author of this thesis does not consider this distribution to be meaningful.

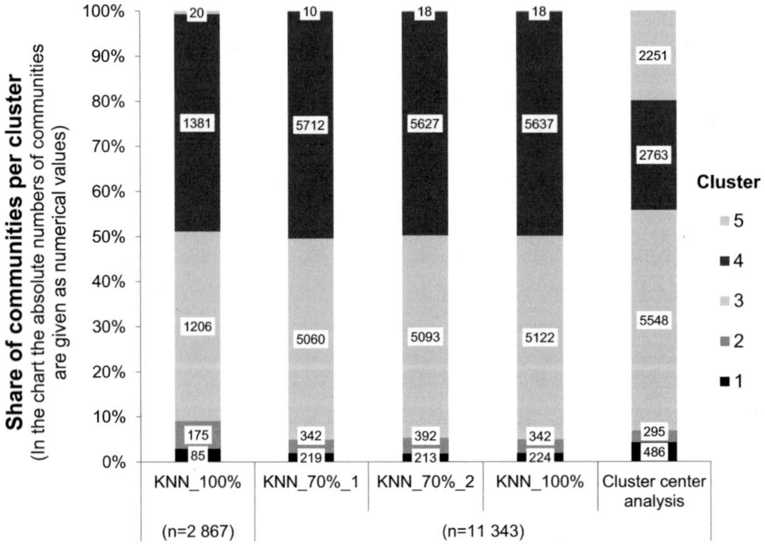

Figure 9.2: Comparison of number of municipalities per cluster for the 11,343 municipalities of Germany.

Fig. 9.3 shows the distribution of number of buildings in the total residential building stock according to building size and age category in each of the five clusters for the 2876 municipalities (in Baden-Württemberg previously analyzed in Section 8.4) resulting from *c) KNN_100%*. For comparison, in Fig. 9.4 the same type of distribution is depicted for the clustering of the 11,343 municipalities according to the same algorithm, i.e. also *c) KNN_100%*. The maximum difference in shares of buildings between the clustering of the 2876 municipalities in Baden-Württemberg and the 11,343 municipalities in all of Germany amounts to 4 percentage-points.

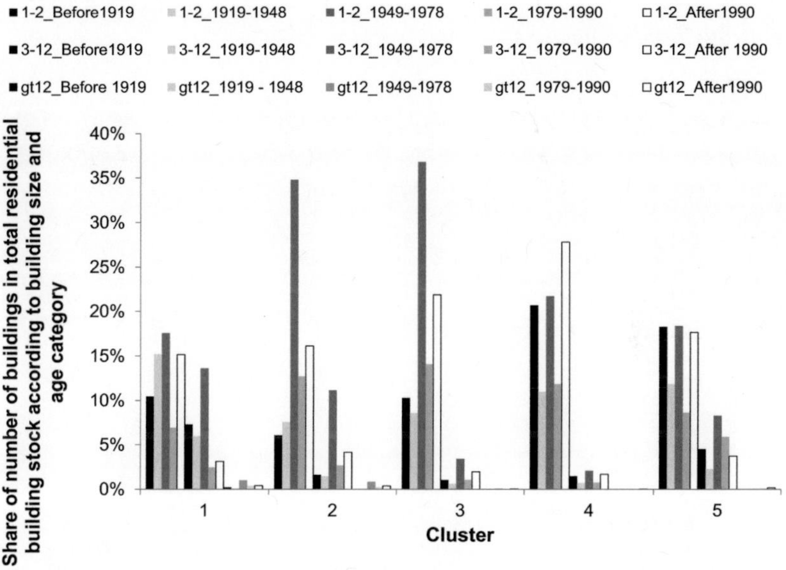

Figure 9.3: Distribution of building stock in the previously analyzed 2876 municipalities of Baden-Württemberg according to building size and age for each of the five clusters.

In the original interpretation of municipalities assigned to clusters in Section 8.3, all available information, i.e. urban structure, non-residential and residential building stock could be used. However, since the clustering has been used successively, municipalities assigned to cluster 1 in this section can be assumed to be similar to municipalities assigned to cluster 1 in Section 8.3. In this cluster, large urban districts are summarized, exhibiting with 34 % the largest share of MFH (sum of share of buildings with 3 to 12 and more than 12 residential units for all age categories) of all clusters and the smallest share of SFH (sum for all building age categories). They can therefore be further assumed to represent the densely populated urban areas.

Municipalities in cluster 2 are located mainly in the vicinity of municipalities assigned to cluster 1. They have the second-smallest share of SFH and a lower share of MFH and AB. Only 15 % of SFH were constructed before 1949 in contrast to 28 % in cluster 1.

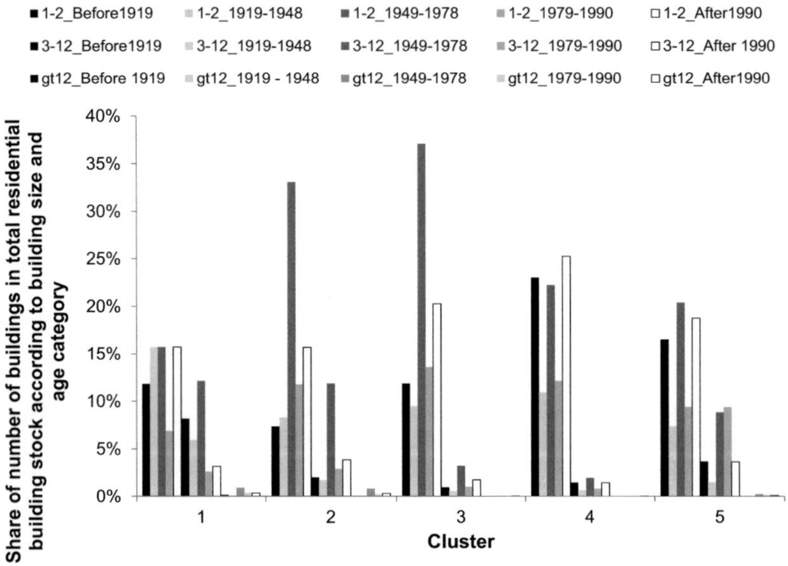

Figure 9.4: Distribution of building stock in the 11,343 municipalities of Germany according to building size and age for each of the five clusters.

In municipalities in cluster 3, 92 % of the buildings are SFH, 40 % of which were constructed between 1949 and 1978. By contrast, the share of newly constructed SFH is highest in municipalities in cluster 4.

The few municipalities assigned to cluster 5 in all analyses employing the *KNN* algorithm have the highest share of MFH constructed between 1949 and 1990 and the second-lowest share of SFH.

In Fig. 9.5, the geographic distribution of the 11,343 municipalities assigned to the clusters is depicted for the four algorithms applied on a national scale. Municipalities that were not included in the assessment are marked in white. They

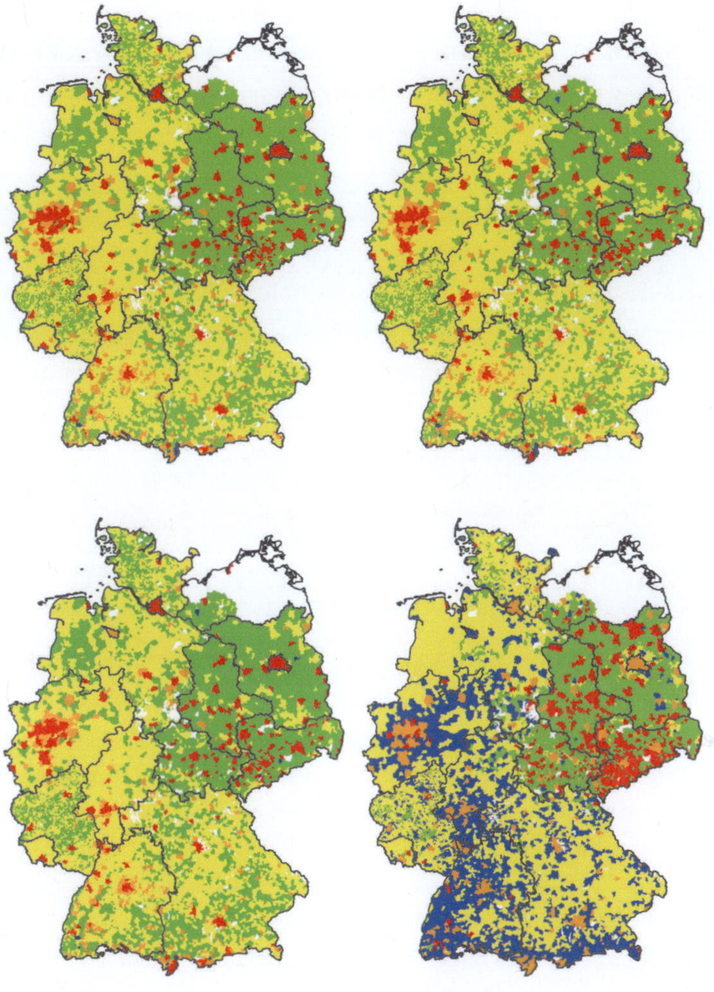

Figure 9.5: Geographic distribution of German municipalities according to clusters 1 (red), 2 (orange), 3 (yellow), 4 (green) and 5 (blue) by the following methods: a) / b) *k-Nearest-Neighbor*-algorithm with 70 % of municipalities used as the training data set (KNN_70%_1 / KNN_70%_2); c) *k-Nearest-Neighbor*-algorithm with 100 % of municipalities used as the training data set (KNN_100%); d) *cluster-center analysis*; Map source: ©GeoBasis-DE/BKG 2013

are mainly located in the Northern German State of Mecklenburg-Vorpommern, where no detailed information on the residential building stock has been published due to the low population density and the small number of buildings. Therefore, they were not considered in this analysis. Again, from this graphical presentation, the strongly deviating result of the *cluster-center analysis* from the others is clear.

In the next step, for the calculation of a national theoretical potential, the average of the larger set of attributes available for the clustering of the 2786 municipalities of Baden-Württemberg (Section 8.4) is taken as the average of all municipalities assigned to the respective cluster and transferred to the municipalities of the respective clustering of the 11,343 municipalitiesof Germany. In this way, for the five considered urban fabric structures (Section 8.3) an estimate is obtained for the national distribution (Fig. 9.7).

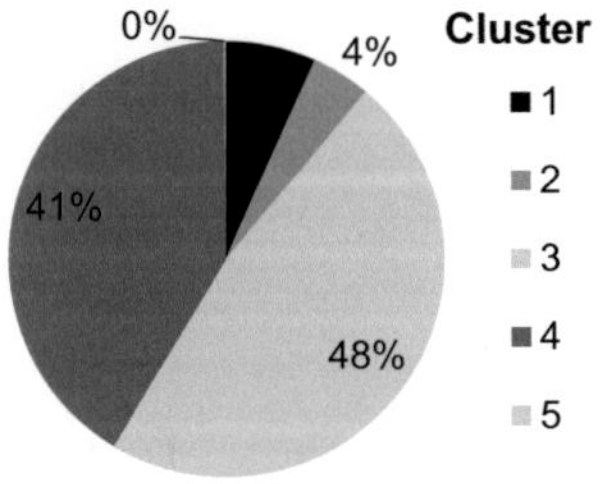

Figure 9.6: National German distribution of municipality area among clusters

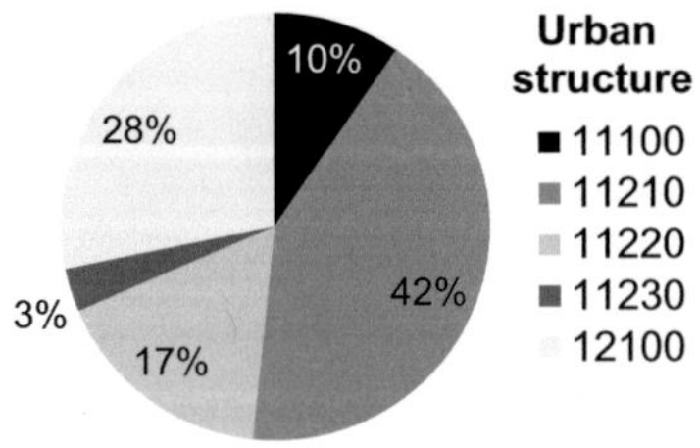

Figure 9.7: National German distribution of municipality area among urban fabric structure area

Based on this distribution of urban fabric structures, in the next step the area-weighted average number of non-residential buildings for the 2876 municipalities analyzed in Section 8.2.2 for each of the five considered building usage types has been calculated.

The average number of buildings per km^{2}displayed in Tab. 9.1 has then been multiplied with the available area per urban fabric structure. As identified in Section 8.2.2, the average non-residential buildings' building footprint differs between non-residential building categories and urban fabric structures. Therefore, the average building footprint area from Tab. 8.5 has been multiplied by the number of buildings in the respective urban fabric structure category.

Table 9.1: Area-weighted average number of non-residential buildings in urban fabric structures based on municipalities of Baden-Württemberg analyzed in Section 8.4.

	[Number of buildings / km^2_{EEA}]				
Building usage type	**11100**	**11210**	**11220**	**11230**	**12100**
Education	5	7	2	0	24
Office & Administration	53	33	8	2	135
Trade & Service	403	131	18	2	144
Commercial & Industrial	51	34	9	2	134
Agricultural	115	172	74	21	127

Now, in order to arrive at the roof and facade area relevant for the technical potential, the results from Section 6.2.4 were used. As documented in Tab. 9.2, the five identified building clusters have been assigned to the urban fabric structures on the basis of the average population density. Then, for the calculation of the building surface areas, the proportion of roof and facade surface area to building footprint area was used for all the non-residential buildings in the respective urban fabric structure category. From this, the building surface area available on roofs and facades according to urban fabric structures is available for the municipalities assigned to the five settlement structure clusters (Fig. 9.8).

Table 9.2: Building attributes in clusters (see Tab. 6.7 in Section 6.2.4.2)

Population density *pd* [km^{-2}]	2769	2223	1037	973	905
Building cluster	2	4	3	1	5
EEA Code	11100	11210	11220	11230	12100
A_{fa} [m^2]	5645	18300	3169	3742	3592
A_{ro} [m^2]	1458	9105	3871	2651	2171
A_{fa}/A_{fp}	3.79	1.85	1.41	1.49	1.59
A_{ro}/A_{fp}	0.98	0.92	1.72	1.06	0.96

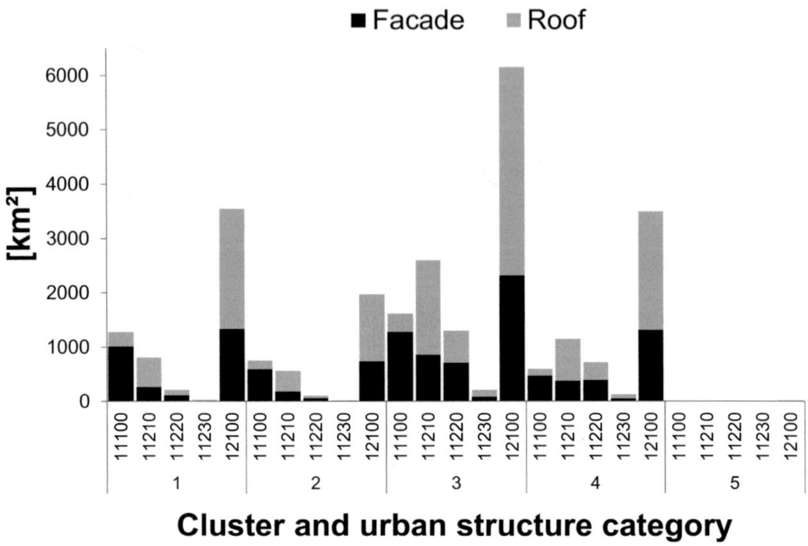

Figure 9.8: Roof and facade areas in settlement structure clusters and urban fabric structure categories for non-residential buildings

Since only 18 municipalities have been assigned to cluster 5 (Fig. 9.2), the total calculated theoretical potential for this cluster amounts to only 26 km^2 as the total for all urban fabric structure categories, which in comparison to more than 11,873 km^2 of available surface area on buildings in urban fabric structures in municipalities assigned to cluster 3 is not visible. For municipalities assigned to clusters 1 and 2, the large share of surfaces on building facades is evident, while for municipalities assigned to cluster 3, surfaces on building roofs also contribute a significant share. This can be attributed to the fact that municipalities in clusters 1 and 2 were more densely populated such that the ratio of building facades to building footprint was higher than for buildings in less densely populated areas. For up-scaling the potential on residential buildings, the distribution of each residential building type among the urban fabric structure codes was determined, as shown in Fig. 9.9.

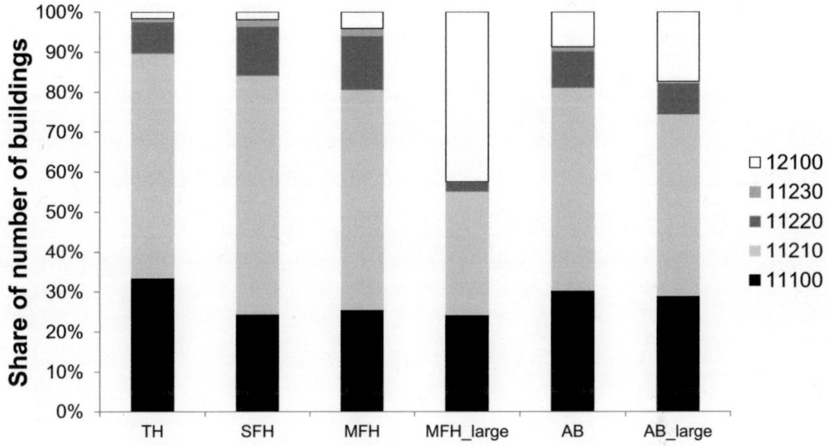

Figure 9.9: Distribution of number of each residential building type according to urban fabric structure categories in the cities of Freiburg, Karlsruhe and Stuttgart

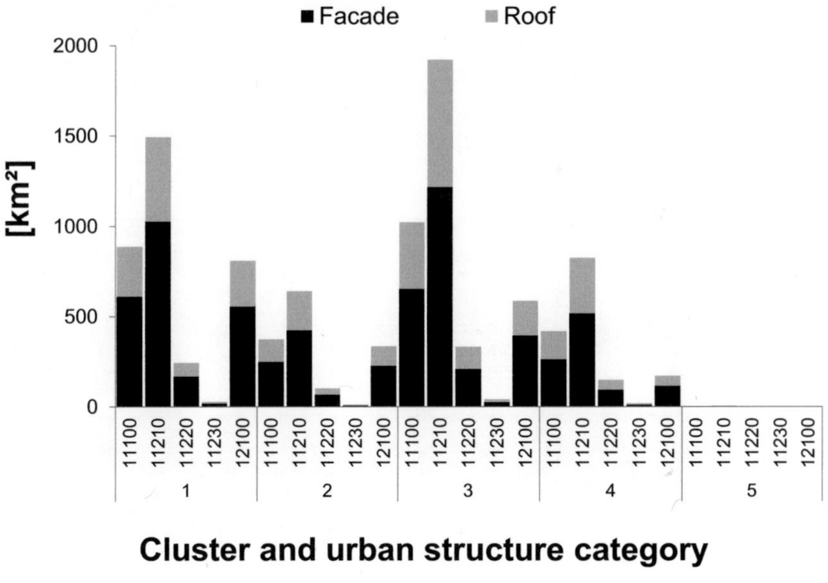

Figure 9.10: Roof and facade areas in Germany according to settlement structure clusters and urban fabric structure categories for residential buildings

In Fig. 9.10, the distribution of roof and facade areas for residential buildings in municipalities according to the cluster and urban fabric structure categories is depicted. In Figs. 9.11 and 9.12, for both residential and non-residential buildings, the distribution of facade and roof areas according to the urban fabric structures as calculated in the national potential calculation is depicted.

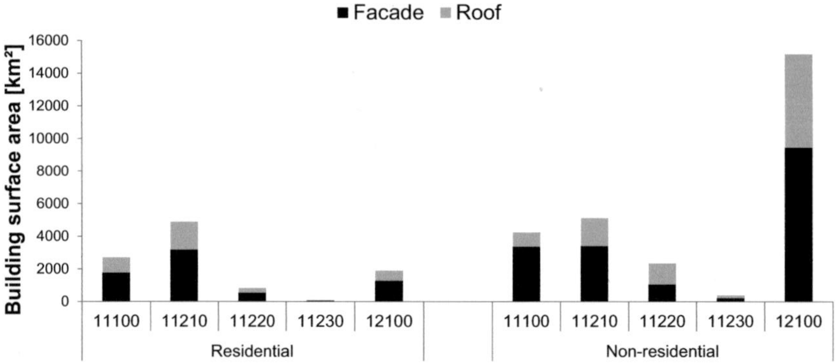

Figure 9.11: Distribution of building surface areas constituting the German theoretical potential according to urban fabric structures

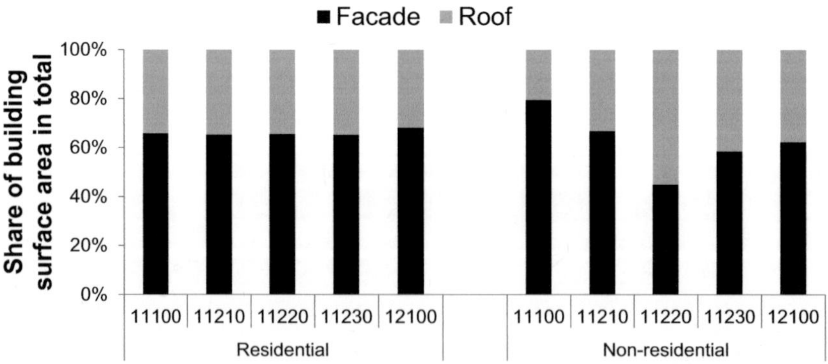

Figure 9.12: Relative share of roof and facade surfaces in the German theoretical potential for all urban fabric structures

It is clearly visible that for residential buildings, the share of facade surfaces is approximately 66 % in all considered urban fabric structures, while for non-residential buildings, the share varies between a maximum of 79 % in the most densely populated urban fabric structure category 11100 and a minimum of 45 % in the least populated urban fabric structure category 11230. The total theoretical potential amounts to 37,700 km^2, of which approximately 65 % are building facades and 35 % roof surfaces. 28 % of surfaces are on residential buildings, while 72 % are on non-residential buildings. Approximately 17,000 km^2 or 45 % of the total surface area is located in urban fabric structure category 12100 containing mainly large commercial and industrial buildings.
In Figs. 9.13, 9.14 and 9.15 the distribution of building surfaces according to building location in the identified settlement structure clusters for German municipalities is depicted.

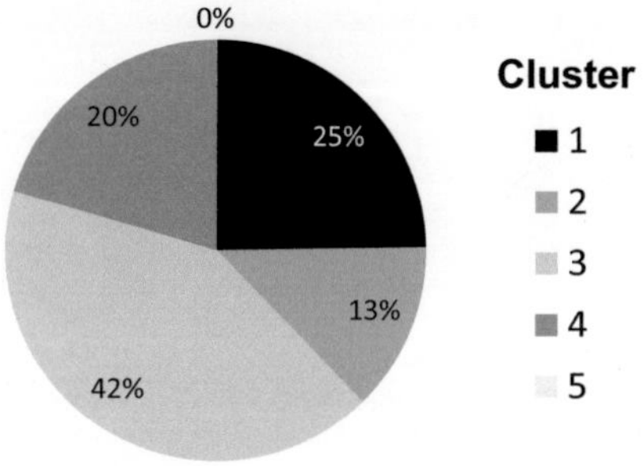

Figure 9.13: Distribution of building surface areas constituting the German theoretical potential according to settlement structure clusters

Municipalities assigned to cluster 3 contain the largest share of building surface areas, with a total area of 15,777 km^2 which is 42 % of total. Interestingly, 25 % and 13 % of total building surface areas are situated on buildings in municipalities assigned to clusters 1 and 2 respectively, although these municipalities account for only 7 % and 4 % of the total municipality surface area (Fig. 9.6). Contrary to that, the less densely populated municipalities assigned to cluster 4, accounting for 41 % of the total area, contain only 20 % of the building surface area. The share of roof and facade surfaces is almost equal in all clusters with approximately 64 % of the surface area on facades and 36 % on roofs.

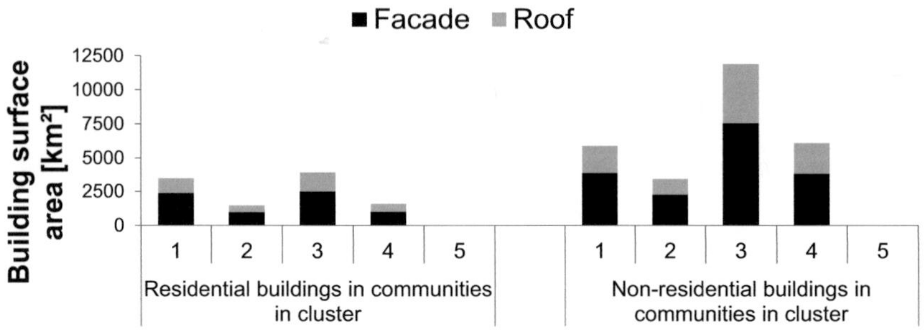

Figure 9.14: Building surface areas in municipalities in clusters

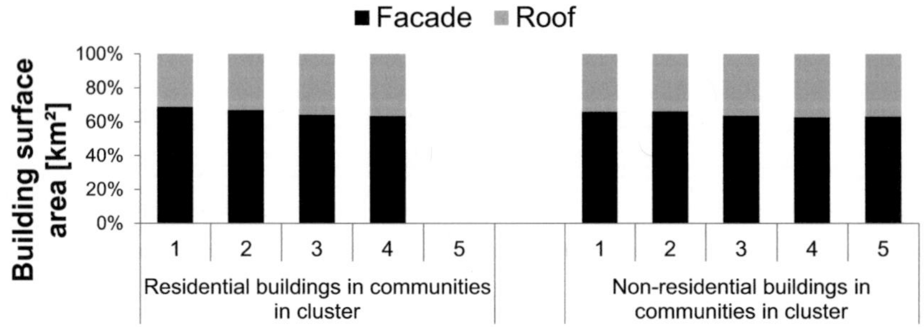

Figure 9.15: Relative share of building roof and facade surfaces in the German theoretical potential in municipalities for each type of settlement structure cluster

9.2 National technical potential

For the calculation of the technical potential based on the findings of this thesis, different options exist. In the following, these different options will be presented in detail to show the range of possible results, since the uncertainty of the final results increases with the number of considered influential factors.

9.2.1 National location potential

9.2.1.1 Methodology based on irradiation in urban fabric structures

For the calculation of a national location potential, the irradiation distribution on building surfaces calculated in Section 7.4 can be utilized. Here, the distribution of building surfaces according to irradiation classes has been determined, which can now be multiplied with the available building surface areas in each urban fabric structure category. For the calculation, the midpoint of the irradiation classes (e.g. 1050 kWh/(m^{2}a) for irradiation class 1000 to 1100 kWh/(m^{2}a)) has been used, resulting in the irradiation factors depicted in Tab. 9.3.

Table 9.3: Irradiation factors in urban fabric structures

	Irradiation factor [kWh/(m^{2}a)]	
EEA-Code	**Roof**	**Facade**
11100	829	397
11210	925	458
11220	887	481
11230	833	429
12100	924	447

Since these factors are based on the irradiation analysis of Neubrandenburg, for the large-scale assessment they were normalized with the respective average annual global irradiation for every municipality. This was determined by deriving the geographical coordinates for each municipality from the municipality boundaries to identify the relevant global irradiation data from the rasterized average global irradiation data for the years 1981 to 2000 (Suri et al. 2007). Average global irradiation values range from 952 kWh/(m^{2}a) in municipalities in North Rhine-Westphalia to 1211 kWh/(m^{2}a) in the Bavarian municipalities Rettenberg and Oberstdorf with an area-weighted average in Germany of 1014 kWh/(m^{2}a). From this approach, a location potential of 22,855 TWh results. Approximately 47 % (10,799 TWh) of the location potential is located on building facades and 53 % (12,056 TWh) on roof surfaces. 27 % (6204 TWh) of the potential is located on surfaces of residential buildings, while 73 % (16,651 TWh) are located on surfaces of non-residential buildings. In Figs. 9.16 and 9.17, the distribution of the location potential according to urban fabric structures is depicted for roof and facade surface areas on residential and non-residential buildings as absolute and relative values.

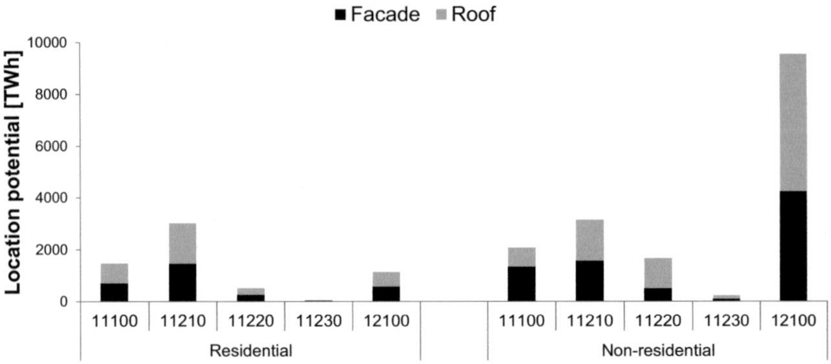

Figure 9.16: Distribution of German location potential on building surface areas according to urban fabric structures, as calculated with irradiation factors

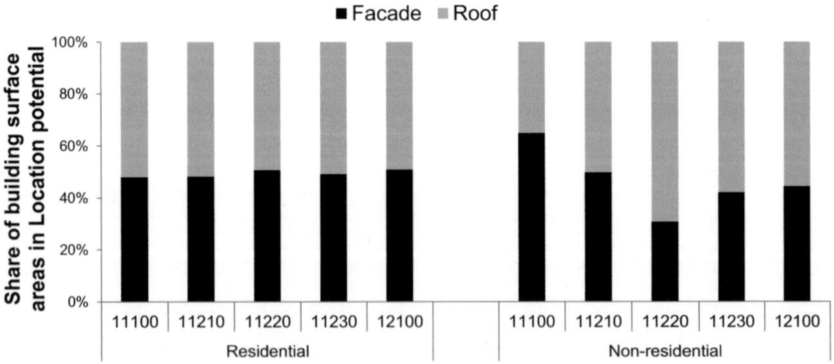

Figure 9.17: Relative share of the German location potential on building surface areas in urban fabric structures, as calculated with irradiation factors

Fig. 9.17 documents that for residential buildings, the share of the location potential on facade surfaces ranges from 48 % in the most-densely populated urban fabric structure categories 11100 and 11210 to 51 % in urban fabric structure categories 11220 and 12100. For non-residential buildings, it ranges from 31 % in urban fabric structure category 11220 to 65 % in the most densely populated urban fabric structure category 11100. As indicated by Fig. 9.16, approximately 11,000 TWh or 47 % of the total potential is located on building surface areas located in urban fabric structure category 12100 which contains mainly large commercial and industrial buildings.

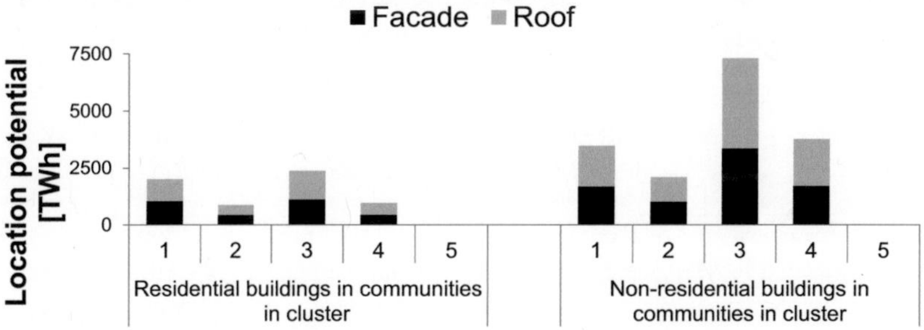

Figure 9.18: Distribution of German location potential on building surface areas in municipalities according to settlement structure clusters, as calculated with irradiation factors

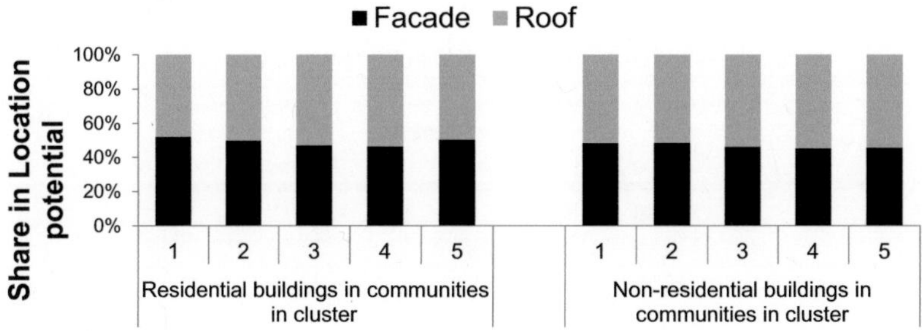

Figure 9.19: Relative share of the German location potential on building surface areas in municipalities according to settlement structure clusters, as calculated with irradiation factors

In Figs. 9.18 and 9.19, the distribution of the location potential on building surface areas according to building location in the identified settlement structure clusters is depicted.

9.2.1.2 Methodology based on shading in urban fabric structures

Based on the results of this thesis, another option for the calculation of a location potential is the utilization of the shading factors calculated in Section 7.3. For this, first the annual average global irradiation in the municipality determined as described in Section 9.2.1.1 has been multiplied by the available surface areas. For this, assumptions concerning the distribution of roof orientation and inclination have to be made, since solar irradiation varies depending on the roof azimuth and tilt angles. Here, based on a survey of roof characteristics for Baden-Württemberg by Kaltschmitt and Wiese (1992), a normal distribution of roof tilt angles with a mean of 34° (for SFH and TH) and 44° (for MFH) and a standard deviation of 3° and 7° respectively has been assumed. This approach has already been employed in Mainzer & Fath et al. (2014). Concerning the roof orientation, an even distribution over all azimuth angles has been assumed. Secondly, in order to account also for shading, average shading factors for the different urban fabric structure categories were calculated as area-weighted average values of the shading factors per irradiation class calculated in Sections 7.3.1 through 7.3.5 and are documented in Tab. 9.4.

Table 9.4: Shading factors in urban fabric structures

	Shading factor	
EEA-Code	**Roof**	**Facade**
11100	10 %	36 %
11210	6 %	26 %
11220	6 %	22 %
11230	7 %	38 %
12100	6 %	27 %

These factors have been multiplied by the calculated potential to account for the different levels of shading in the urban fabric structure categories.
Based on this methodology, the total location potential amounts to 22,839 TWh which is only 0.7 ‰ less than that resulting from the approach based on the irradiation distribution on building surface areas presented in Section 9.2.1.1. Since the two methodologies are complimentary from a mathematical perspective, this calculation serves as an additional check of calculation procedures.
In Figs. 9.20 and 9.21, the distribution over building surface areas for both residential and non-residential buildings according to urban fabric structure categories is depicted. The distribution of the location potential over building surface areas is the same (47 % on facades, 53 % on roofs) as for the other methodology. Figs. 9.22 and 9.23 document the distribution of the German location potential over building surface areas according to building location in the identified settlement structure clusters.

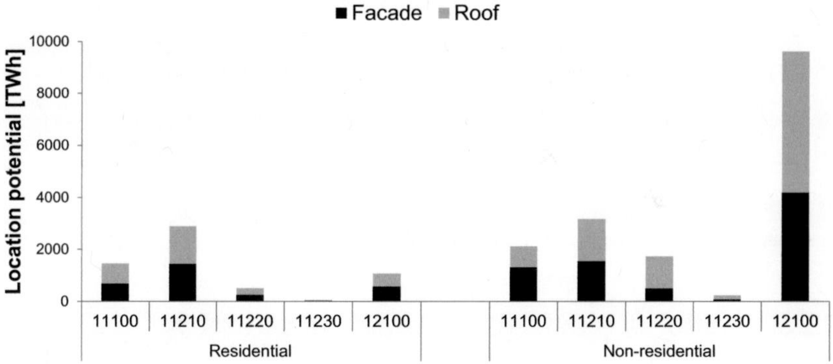

Figure 9.20: Distribution of German location potential on building surface areas according to urban fabric structures calculated with shading factors

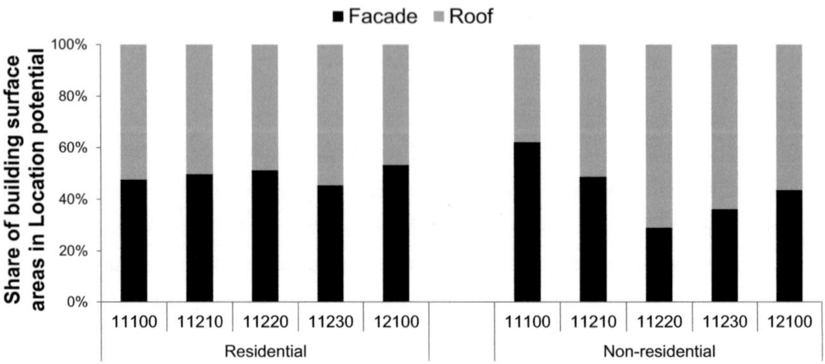

Figure 9.21: Relative share of the German location potential on building surface areas in urban fabric structures calculated with shading factors

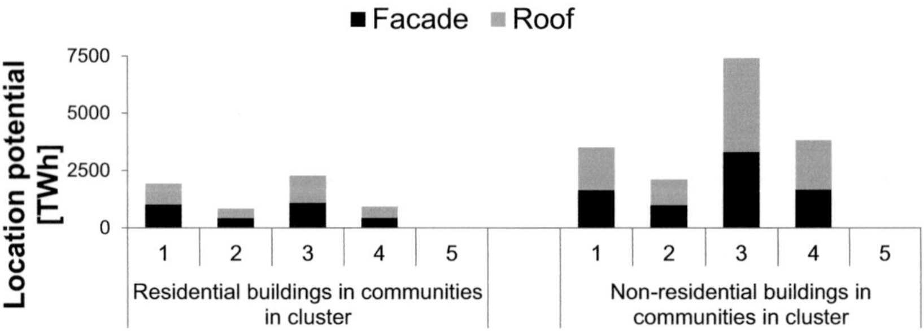

Figure 9.22: German location potential on building surface areas in municipalities according to settlement structure clusters, as calculated with shading factors

9.2.2 National electricity generation potential

For the assessment of the electricity generation potential, in Section 4.2 a methodology for detailed electricity yield simulations, accounting for low-level irradiation and temperature effects, has been presented. However, for the national potential assessment conducted in this chapter, the hourly-resolved irradiation time series are not available. Therefore, for this large-scale assessment, a simplified approach as in Fath et al. (2015) will be used. The following calculations are based on the location potential, calculated according

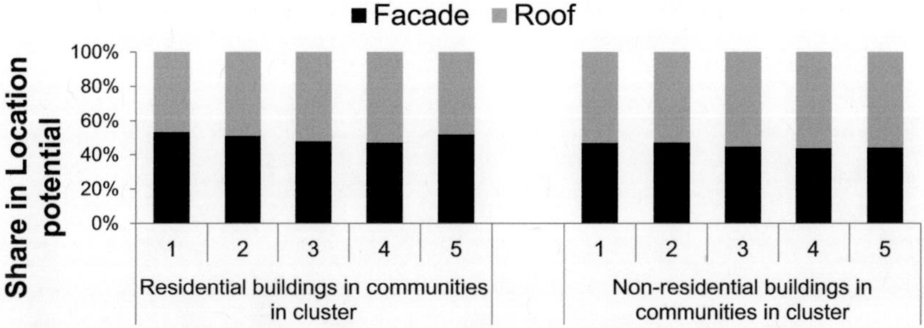

Figure 9.23: Relative share of the German location potential on building surface areas in municipalities according to settlement structure clusters, as calculated with shading factors

to the methodology based on irradiation in urban fabric structures presented in Section 9.2.1.1, since here mainly results of this thesis are used.

Based on the location potential, the electricity generation potential can be calculated by accounting for photovoltaic module and total plant efficiency. For the average module efficiency η, 15 % has been assumed, representing the industrial standard at the beginning of 2015 (Wirth 2014). The total plant efficiency is expressed as a Performance Ratio (PR) accounting for ohmic losses in cabling and the inverter efficiency in different operation modes. Here, 90 % and 80 % were assumed for PR_{roof} and PR_{facade} respectively. PR_{facade} is lower due to the assumed higher share of low-level irradiation on vertical surfaces resulting in lower module and inverter efficiencies and possibly higher temperatures due to less ventilation. By multiplying the location potential with the module efficiency and the appropriate PR, an electricity generation potential of 2923 TWh results. Due to the lower PR, the share of facade surfaces in this potential decreases to 44 % (1296 TWh). The distribution among residential and non-residential buildings stays the same with the shares of 27 % (792 TWh) and 73 % (2131 TWh) respectively.

Figs. 9.24 and 9.25 show the distribution of the German electricity generation potential according to urban fabric structures for roof and facade surfaces on residential and non-residential buildings as absolute and relative values.

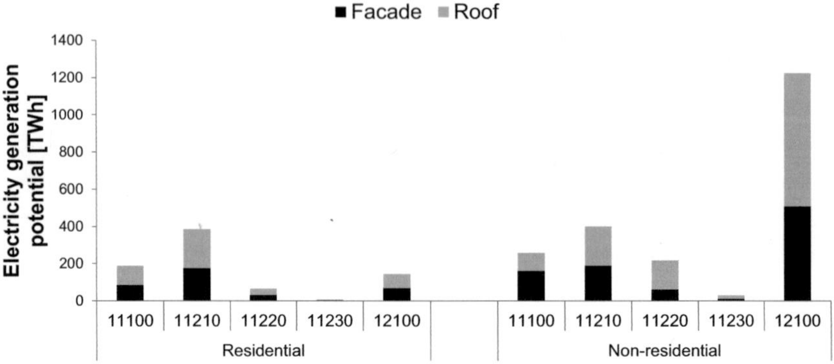

Figure 9.24: German electricity generation potential on building surfaces according to urban fabric structures

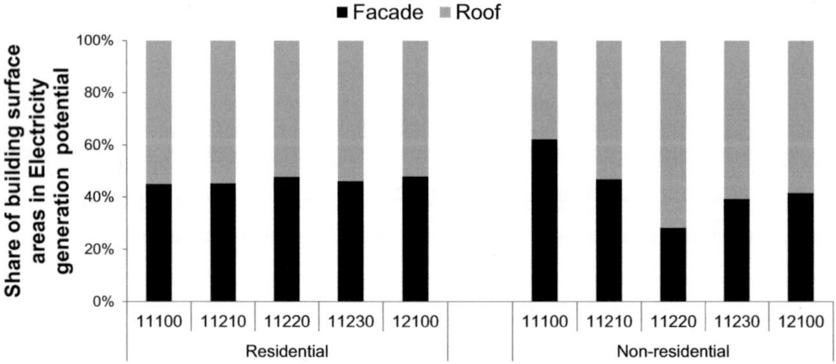

Figure 9.25: Relative share of the German electricity generation potential on building surfaces according to urban fabric structures

In Figs. 9.26 and 9.27, the distribution of roof and facade surfaces on buildings in municipalities assigned to the different settlement structure clusters is depicted.

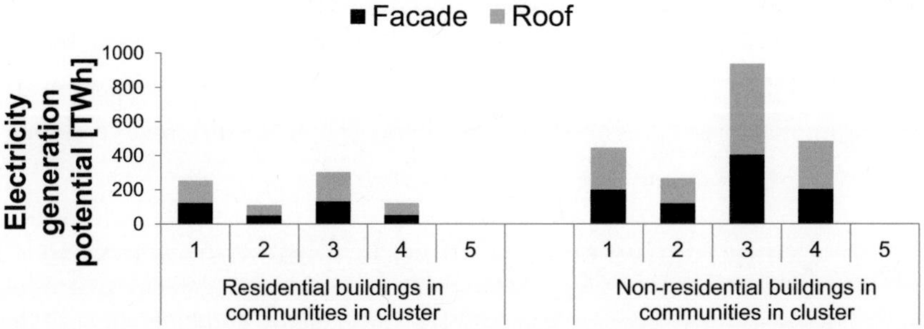

Figure 9.26: Distribution of the German electricity generation potential on building surfaces in municipalities according to settlement structure clusters

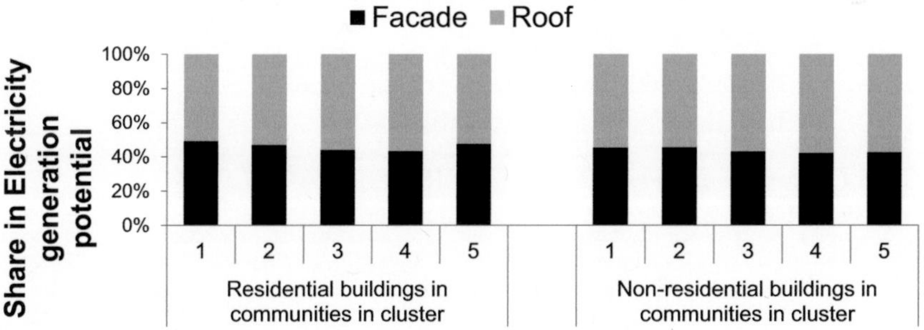

Figure 9.27: Relative share of the German electricity generation potential on building surface areas in municipalities according to settlement structure clusters

9.2.3 Conclusion on national technical potential prognosis

At first glance, the reason for the minimal deviation of the location potential based on the calculation with irradiation in urban fabric structures or the shading factor is obvious. While the first option uses the distribution of facade and roof surfaces over irradiation classes based on the results of the large-scale irradiation analysis performed in this thesis, data from a more than 20-year old assessment from literature were used for the second option. Due to the slow changes in the building stock, results based on these two assessments are still comparable.

9.3 National economic potential

As explained in Section 5, the economic potential is highly dependent on the assumptions for the economic parameters. Therefore, different economic-investment scenario combinations will be analyzed.

9.3.1 Conservative economic and investment scenario

First, the conservative economic and investment scenario combination with the following assumptions will be considered:

1. Economic scenario *Status quo* (Tab. 5.4), i.e.
   a) Interest rate 2 % or more
   b) System lifetime up to 25 years
   c) Electricity tariff up to 0.25 €/kWh
2. *Conventional investment scenario* (Section 5.6.2), i.e.
   a) I_{roof} from Tab. 5.2
   b) I_{facade} from Tab. 5.2

For the investment, in Tab. 5.2 different investments depending on plant size are given. However, in this large-scale assessment the information on installable plant size is missing. Therefore in a first scenario, photovoltaic plants with an installed power $P < 3\ kW_p$ are assumed on all residential buildings, resulting in I_{roof} of 1425 €/kW$_\mathrm{p}$ and I_{facade} of 2425 €/kW$_\mathrm{p}$. For non-residential buildings, $3 < P < 10\ kW_p$ is assumed resulting in I_{roof} of 1300 €/kW$_\mathrm{p}$ and I_{facade} of 2300 €/kW$_\mathrm{p}$.
According to the economic scenarios, under the given assumptions, a photovoltaic plant with an electricity yield of at least 460 kWh/kW$_\mathrm{p}$ has a NPV greater than zero at an investment of 1425 €/kW$_\mathrm{p}$, while at an investment of 1300 €/kW$_\mathrm{p}$ the NPV is greater than zero already with an electricity yield greater than 440 kWh/kW$_\mathrm{p}$. For the facade surfaces on residential and non-

residential buildings with an investment of 2425 €/kW$_p$ and 2300 €/kW$_p$ respectively these threshold values lie at 640 kWh/kW$_p$ and 620 kWh/kW$_p$. Applying the assumptions made in Section 9.2.2 on the relationship between the irradiation on building surface areas and the electricity generation, for a minimum electricity yield of 640 kWh/kW$_p$ or 620 kWh/kW$_p$ for facade surface areas an annual irradiation total of at least 800 kWh/m^2 or 774 kWh/m^2 respectively results. For roof surface areas for a minimum electricity yield of 460 kWh/kW$_p$ or 440 kWh/kW$_p$ an annual irradiation of at least 574 kWh/m^2 or 550 kWh/m^2 results. A summary of these figures is presented in Tab. 9.5.

Table 9.5: Investment I, minimum average electricity yield El_{avg} and minimum average solar irradiation E_{avg} on building surfaces for a NPV greater than 0 in the conservative economic and investment scenario

Buildings	Surfaces	I [€/kW$_p$]	El_{avg} [kWh/kW$_p$]	E_{avg} [kWh/m^2]
Residential	Roof	1425	460	574
Residential	Facade	2425	640	800
Non-residential	Roof	1300	440	550
Non-residential	Facade	2300	620	774

Based on the irradiation distribution on building surfaces calculated in Section 7.4, the economic potential is deduced from the technical potential.

Under the assumptions stated previously for this conservative economic and investment scenario, a total economic potential of 1766 TWh of annually generated electricity or 2457 GW$_p$ installed capacity results. Due to the assumed higher average irradiation on building roofs, the share of the generated electricity in the economic potential attributable to building roofs is somewhat higher, with 89 %, than in the installed capacity, with only 78 %. The distribution of this potential on building surfaces over urban fabric structures and municipalities assigned to settlement structure clusters are depicted in Figs. 9.28 to 9.31.

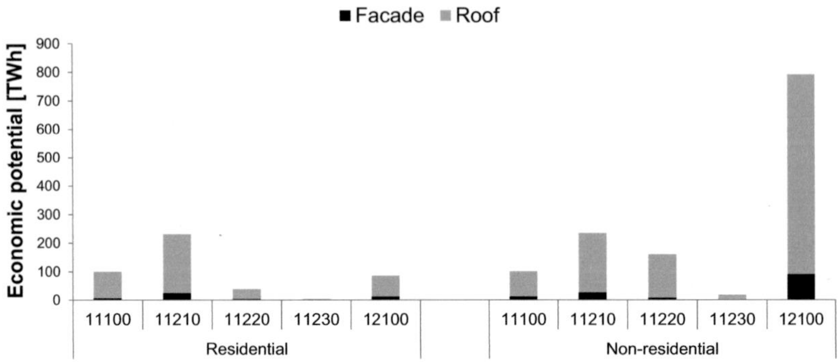

Figure 9.28: German economic potential on building surfaces in urban fabric structures for the conservative economic and investment scenario

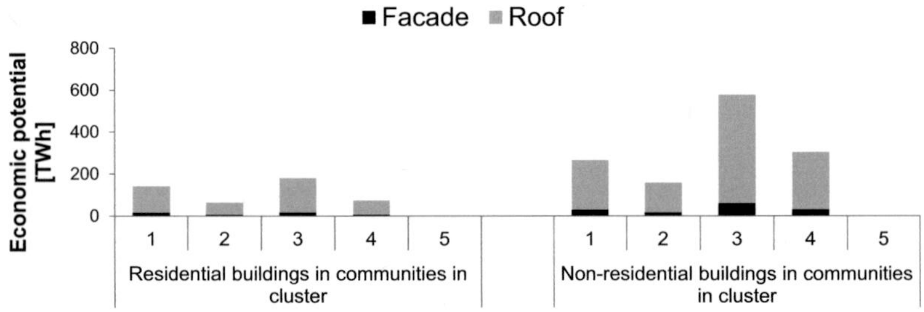

Figure 9.29: German economic potential on building surfaces in municipalities according to settlement structure clusters for the conservative economic and investment scenario

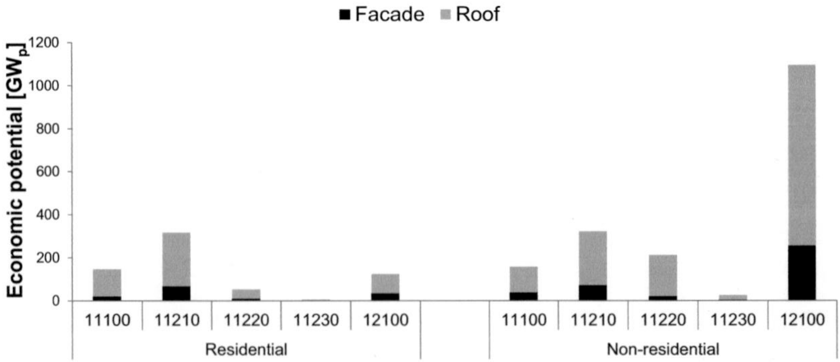

Figure 9.30: German economic potential on building surfaces in urban fabric structures for the conservative economic and investment scenario

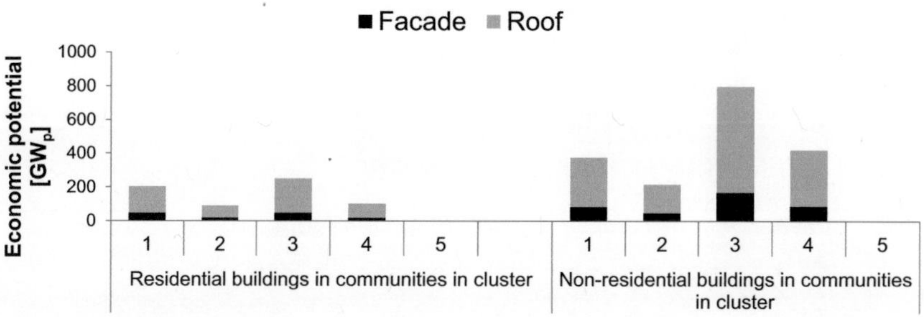

Figure 9.31: German economic potential on building surfaces in clusters for the conservative economic and investment scenario

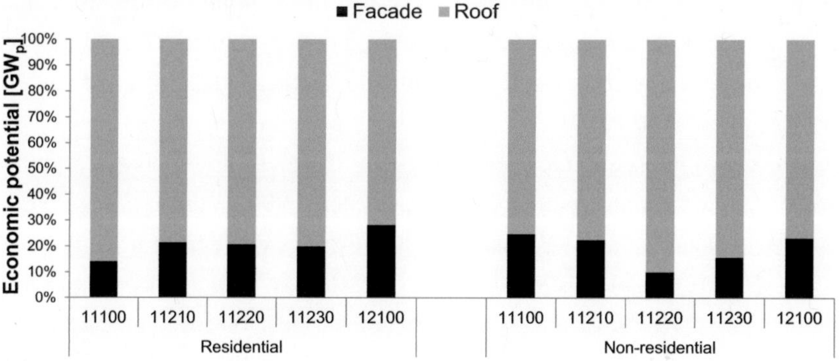

Figure 9.32: Relative share of building surface areas in the economic potential on building surface areas in urban fabric structures for the conservative economic and investment scenario

Additionally, Fig. 9.32 illustrates the relative share of building surfaces in the economic potential for the installable capacity. In comparison to the technical potential, clearly the decreasing share of facade surface areas is visible, due to the assumed higher investment for facades than roofs in this scenario.

9.3.2 Progressive economic and conservative investment scenario

Now, for comparison a more progressive economic and conservative investment scenario combination with the following assumptions will be considered:

1. Economic scenario *High potential* (Tab. 5.4), i.e.
   a) Interest rate 2 % or more
   b) System lifetime up to 30 years
   c) Electricity tariff up to 0.35 €/kWh
2. *Conventional investment scenario* (Section 5.6.2), i.e.
   a) I_{roof} from Tab. 5.2
   b) I_{facade} from Tab. 5.2

In this scenario, an installed capacity of photovoltaic plants with an installed power $3 < P < 10\ kW_p$ is assumed for residential buildings resulting in I_{roof} of 1300 €/kW$_\mathrm{p}$ and I_{facade} of 2300 €/kW$_\mathrm{p}$. For non-residential buildings, an installed capacity of $P \geq 10\ kW_p$ is assumed resulting in I_{roof} of 1140 €/kW$_\mathrm{p}$ and I_{facade} of 2140 €/kW$_\mathrm{p}$.
According to the economic scenarios, under the given assumptions, a photovoltaic plant with an electricity yield of at least 290 kWh/kW$_\mathrm{p}$ has a NPV greater than zero at an investment of 1300 €/kW$_\mathrm{p}$, while at an investment of 1140 €/kW$_\mathrm{p}$, the NPV is greater than zero already with an electricity yield greater than 270 kWh/kW$_\mathrm{p}$. For the facade surfaces on residential and non-residential buildings with an investment of 2300 €/kW$_\mathrm{p}$ and 2140 €/kW$_\mathrm{p}$ respectively, these threshold values lie at 400 kWh/kW$_\mathrm{p}$ and 380 kWh/kW$_\mathrm{p}$. The resulting minimum irradiation values are listed in Tab. 9.6.

Table 9.6: Investment I, minimum average electricity yield El_{avg} and minimum average solar irradiation E_{avg} on building surfaces for a NPV greater than 0 in the progressive economic and conservative investment scenario

Buildings	Surfaces	I [€/kW$_\mathrm{p}$]	El_{avg} [kWh/kW$_\mathrm{p}$]	E_{avg} [kWh/m^2]
Residential	Roof	1300	290	362
Residential	Facade	2300	400	500
Non-residential	Roof	1140	270	300
Non-residential	Facade	2140	380	422

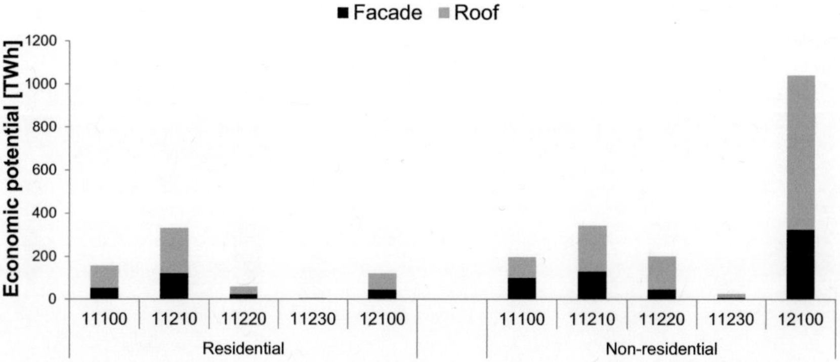

Figure 9.33: German economic potential on building surface areas in urban fabric structures for the progressive economic and conservative investment scenario

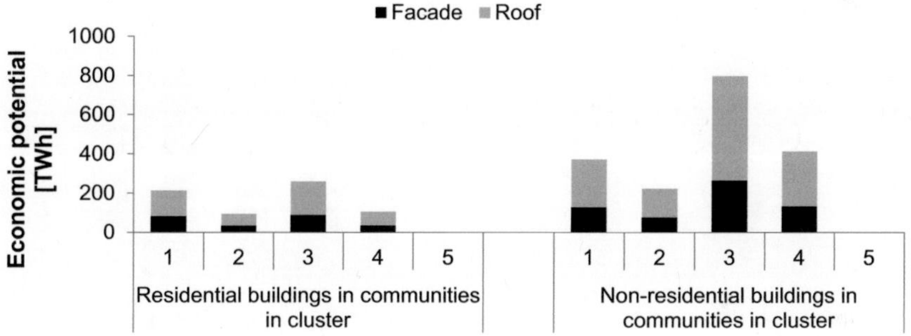

Figure 9.34: German economic potential on building surface areas in settlement structure clusters for the progressive economic and conservative investment scenario

Based on these assumptions, now an economic potential of 2482 TWh annually generated electricity or 4402 GW_p installed capacity results. The distribution of this potential on building surface areas according to urban fabric structures and settlement structure clusters is depicted in Figs. 9.33 to 9.36. In this scenario, facade surface areas account for 34 % of the generated electricity and 55 % of the installed capacity.

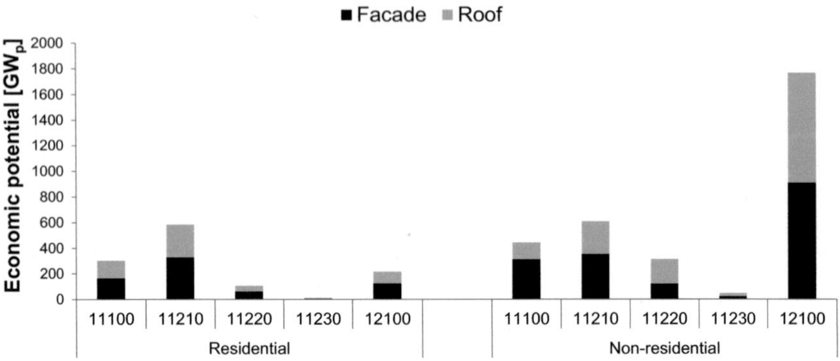

Figure 9.35: German economic potential on building surface areas in urban fabric structures for the progressive economic and conservative investment scenario

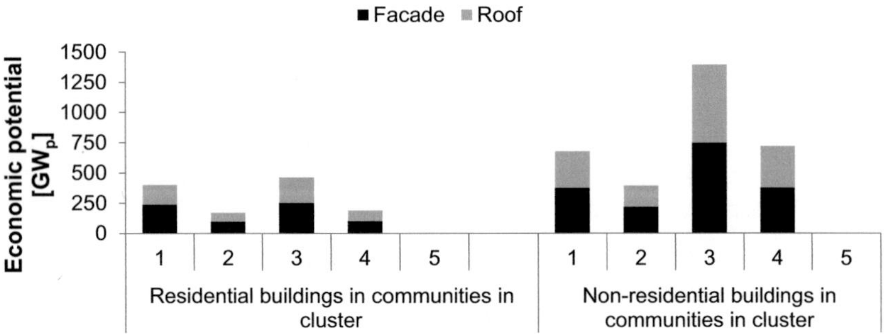

Figure 9.36: German economic potential on building surface areas in settlement structure clusters for the progressive economic and conservative investment scenario

9.3.3 Conservative economic and progressive investment scenario

In this scenario, the conservative economic conditions as well as the installed capacity on residential and non-residential buildings as in Section 9.3.2 are assumed, but for the investment, the BIPV investment scenario as defined in Section 5.6.2 is assumed, i.e.:

1. Economic scenario *Status quo* (Tab. 5.4), i.e.
    a) Interest rate 2 % or more
    b) System lifetime up to 25 years
    c) Electricity tariff up to 0.25 €/kWh
2. *Optimistic investment scenario* (Section 5.6.2), i.e.
    a) $I_{roof,BIPV}$ from Tab. 5.2
    b) $I_{facade,BIPV}$ from Tab. 5.2
    c) $P_{res} < 3\ kw_p$
    d) $3 < P_{non-res} < 10\ kW_p$

The resulting investment, minimum electricity yield and solar irradiation for a NPV greater than 0 are documented in Tab. 9.7.

Table 9.7: Investment I, minimum average electricity yield El_{avg} and minimum average solar irradiation E_{avg} on building surfaces for a NPV greater than 0 in the conservative economic and progressive investment scenario

Buildings	Surfaces	I [€/kW$_p$]	El_{avg} [kWh/kW$_p$]	E_{avg} [kWh/m^2]
Residential	Roof	1095	400	360
Residential	Facade	2095	580	464
Non-residential	Roof	970	380	342
Non-residential	Facade	1970	560	448

Based on these assumptions, an economic potential of 2352 TWh annually generated electricity or 4035 GW$_p$ installed capacity results. The distribution of this potential on building surface areas according to urban fabric structures and settlement structure clusters are depicted in Figs. 9.37 to 9.40. In this scenario, facade surface areas account for 31 % of the generated electricity and 51 % of the installed capacity.

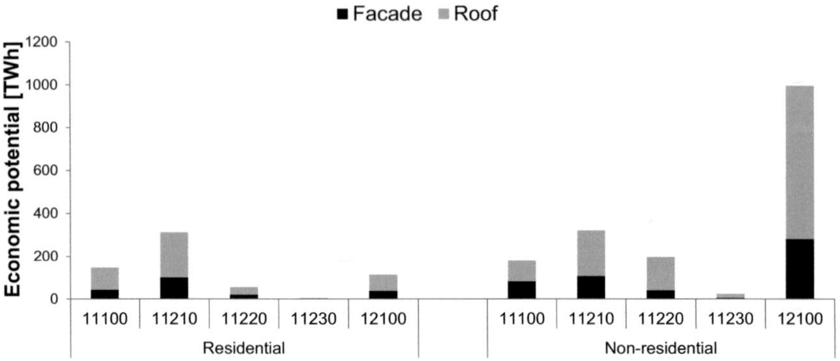

Figure 9.37: German economic potential on building surface areas in urban fabric structures for the conservative economic and progressive investment scenario

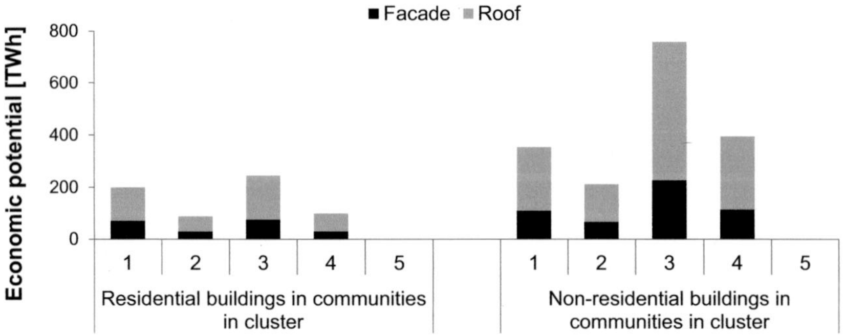

Figure 9.38: German economic potential on building surface areas in settlement structure clusters for the conservative economic and progressive investment scenario

9.3.4 Progressive economic and investment scenario

In this scenario, the progressive economic conditions as well as the installed capacity on residential and non-residential buildings as in Section 9.3.2 are assumed, but for the investment, the BIPV investment scenario as defined in Section 5.6.2 is assumed, i.e.:

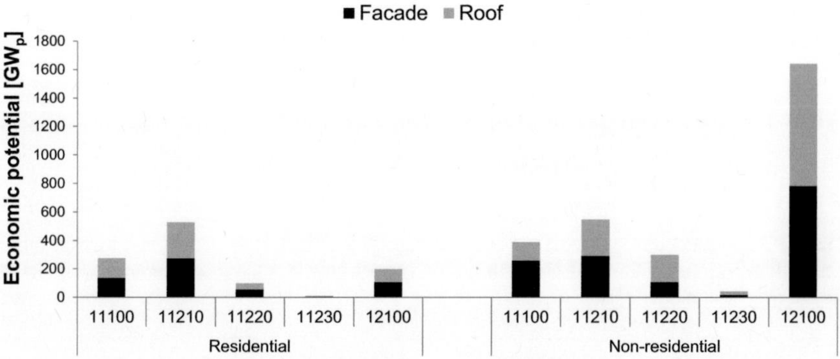

Figure 9.39: German economic potential on building surface areas in urban fabric structures for the conservative economic and progressive investment scenario

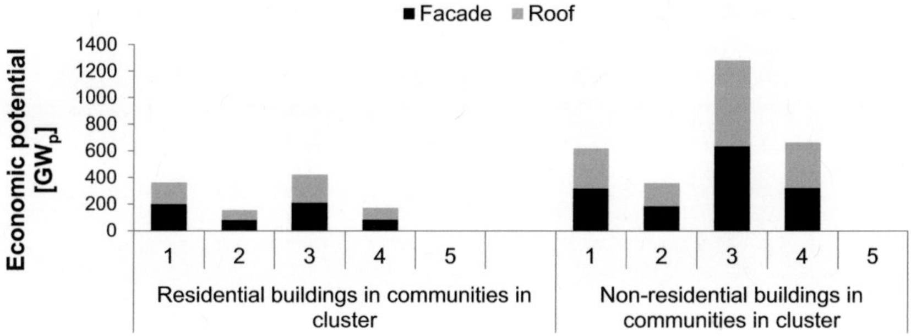

Figure 9.40: German economic potential on building surface areas in settlement structure clusters for the conservative economic and progressive investment scenario

1. Economic scenario *High potential* (Tab. 5.4), i.e.
   a) Interest rate 2 % or more
   b) System lifetime up to 30 years
   c) Electricity tariff up to 0.35 €/kWh
2. *Optimistic investment scenario* (Section 5.6.2), i.e.
   a) $I_{roof,BIPV}$ from Tab. 5.2
   b) $I_{facade,BIPV}$ from Tab. 5.2

c) $3 < P_{res} < 10\ kW_p$

d) $P_{non-res} \geq 10\ kW_p$

The resulting investment, minimum electricity yield and solar irradiation for a NPV greater than 0 are depicted in Tab. 9.8.

Table 9.8: Investment I, minimum average electricity yield El_{avg} and minimum average solar irradiation E_{avg} on building surfaces for a NPV greater than 0 in the progressive economic and investment scenario

Buildings	Surfaces	I [€/kW$_p$]	El_{avg} [kWh/kW$_p$]	E_{avg} [kWh/m^2]
Residential	Roof	970	260	208
Residential	Facade	1970	360	288
Non-residential	Roof	810	240	216
Non-residential	Facade	1810	350	280

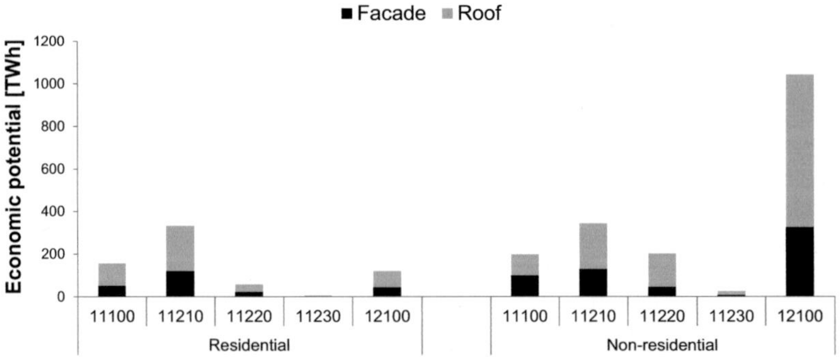

Figure 9.41: German economic potential on building surface areas in urban fabric structures for the progressive economic and investment scenario

Based on these assumptions, an economic potential of 2482 TWh generated electricity or 4402 GW_p installed capacity results. The distribution of this potential on building surface areas according to urban fabric structures and settlement structure clusters is depicted in Figs. 9.41 to 9.44. In this scenario, facade surface areas account for 34 % of the generated electricity and 55 % of the installed capacity.

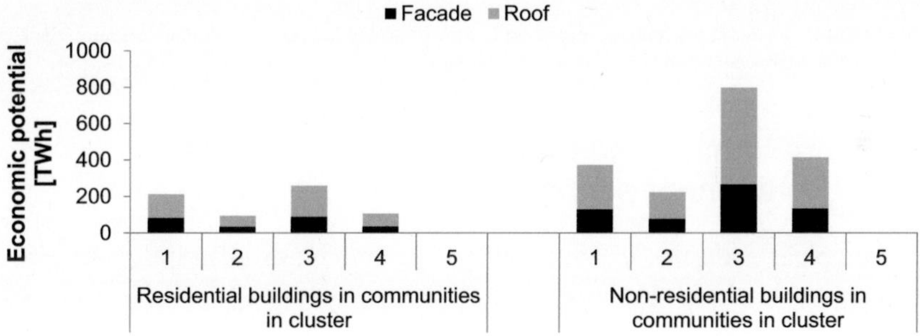

Figure 9.42: German economic potential on building surface areas in settlement structure clusters for the progressive economic and investment scenario

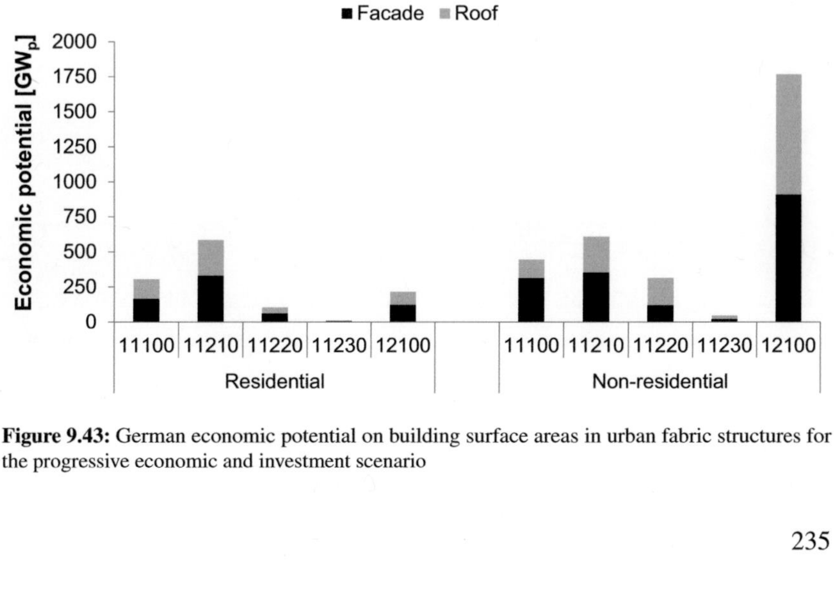

Figure 9.43: German economic potential on building surface areas in urban fabric structures for the progressive economic and investment scenario

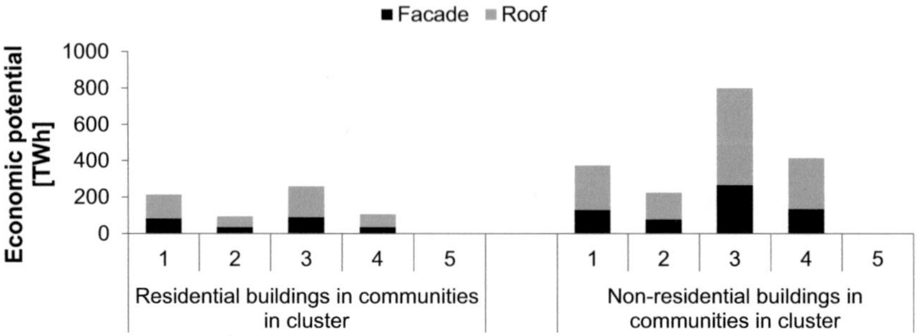

Figure 9.44: German economic potential on building surface areas in settlement structure clusters for the progressive economic and investment scenario

9.3.5 Pessimistic economic and conservative investment scenario

For comparison, the pessimistic economic conditions as well as the conservative economic conditions as in Section 9.3.1 are assumed in this last scenario, i.e.:

1. Economic scenario *Low potential* (Tab. 5.4), i.e.
   a) Interest rate 5 % or more
   b) System lifetime up to 20 years
   c) Electricity tariff up to 0.15 €/kWh
2. *Conventional investment scenario* (Section 5.6.2), i.e.
   a) I_{roof} from Tab. 5.2
   b) I_{facade} from Tab. 5.2
   c) $P_{res} < 3\ kw_p$
   d) $3 < P_{non-res} < 10\ kW_p$

The resulting investment, minimum electricity yield and solar irradiation for a NPV greater than 0 are depicted in Tab. 9.9. In this scenario, no economic potential on facade surfaces exists at all, i.e. under the given assumptions, the value of the electricity generated on facade surfaces is not sufficient to cover the investment and operating cost over the system lifetime of 20 years or less.

Table 9.9: Investment I, minimum average electricity yield El_{avg} and minimum average solar irradiation E_{avg} on building surfaces for a NPV greater than 0 in the pessimistic economic and conservative investment scenario

Buildings	Surfaces	I [€/kW$_p$]	El_{avg} [kWh/kW$_p$]	E_{avg} [kWh/m^2]
Residential	Roof	1425	1030	927
Residential	Facade	2425	-	-
Non-residential	Roof	1300	970	873
Non-residential	Facade	2300	-	-

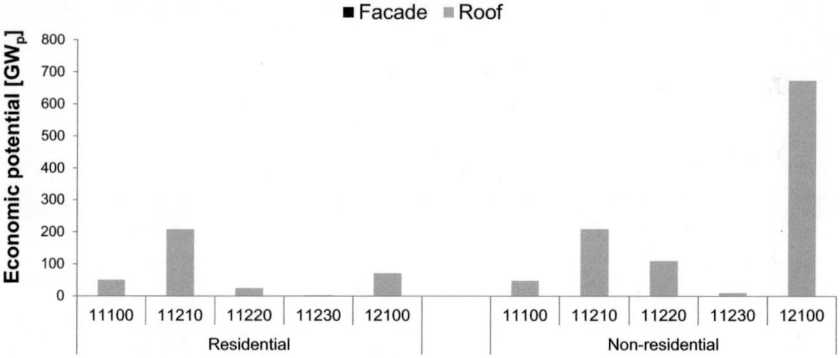

Figure 9.45: German economic potential on building surface areas in urban fabric structures for the pessimistic economic and conservative investment scenario

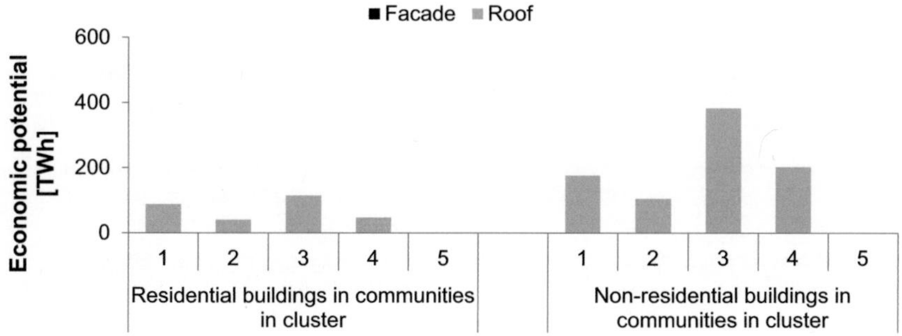

Figure 9.46: German economic potential on building surface areas in settlement structure clusters for the pessimistic economic and conservative investment scenario

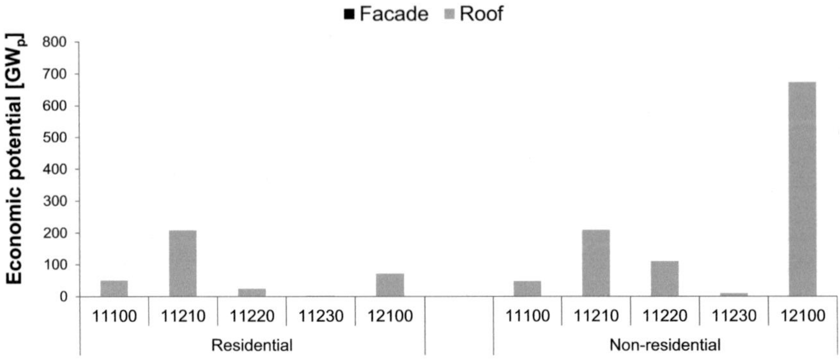

Figure 9.47: German economic potential on building surface areas in urban fabric structures for the pessimistic economic and conservative investment scenario

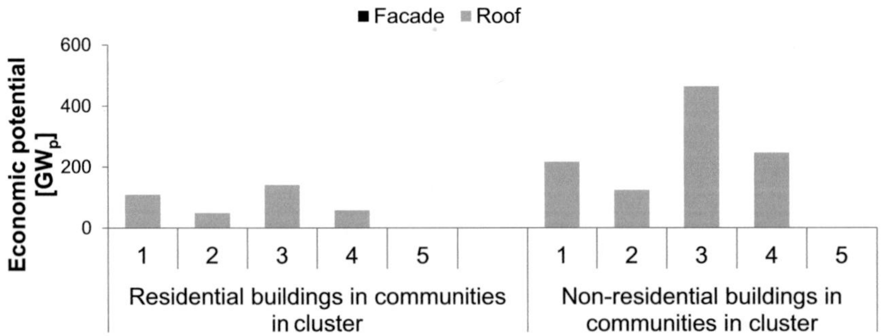

Figure 9.48: German economic potential on building surface areas in settlement structure clusters for the pessimistic economic and conservative investment scenario

9.3.6 Summary of economic scenarios

Fig. 9.49 summarizes the results for the German economic potential for the considered economic-investment scenario combinations. Taking the conservative economic and investment scenario (Scenario 1) as the baseline, the difference between the pessimistic scenario (Scenario 5) and the optimistic scenarios (Scenarios 2, 3 and 4) ranges from 52 % to 114 % for the electricity generation and from 75 % to 213 % for the installed capacity. This demonstrates the large spread inherent in economic potential calculations due to the long-term time horizon considered and the large variations in economic parameters.

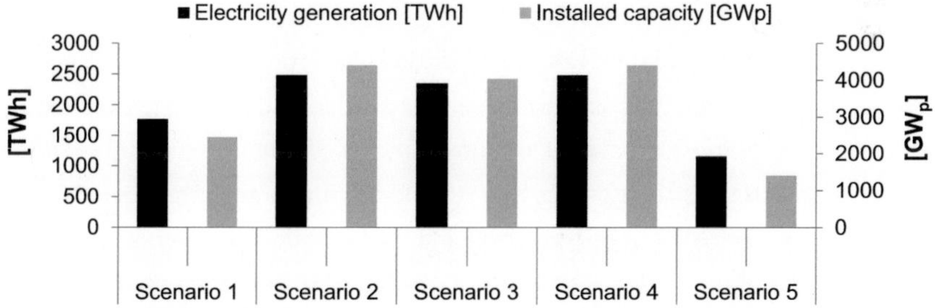

Figure 9.49: Summary of German economic potential for the (1) conservative economic and investment, (2) progressive economic and conservative investment, (3) conservative economic and progressive investment, (4) progressive economic and investment, (5) pessimistic economic and conservative investment scenario

9.4 Prognosis for national photovoltaic potential development

One objective of this thesis is to make a prognosis for the development of the potential for photovoltaic installations on buildings in Germany until 2050. Based on the results from the previous sections, scenarios for the target value in 2050 are investigated in this chapter. The development of the potential is influenced by multiple drivers: First of all, technological improvements in the photovoltaic industry such as improved materials, cell and module technologies lead to an increase in module efficiency and therefore power output. Additionally, in combination with advances in the manufacturing industry, these developments lead to a lower specific investment (VDMA 2015).

Another influential factor for the potential considered in this thesis is the change in the national building stock. Considerable research has been conducted on the expected change in the building stock considering new construction, refurbishment and demolition to derive a prognosis for the future energy consumption (Stengel (2014); Bürger and Tilman (2015)). However, for further usage in this thesis, a source with the high resolution considered, i.e. on municipality level, has been sought. From the German Federal Institute for Research on Building, Urban Affairs and Spatial Development (BBSR), a detailed list of the expected development of municipalities in Germany is available, based on the indicators of population, migration balance, employable age, available jobs, employment and income (BBSR 2014). For further calculation, the population development between 2009 and 2014 has been calculated as the minimum, average and maximum of all municipalities according to the development classification based on the above mentioned six indicators. This has then be used as a proxy for the development of the building stock in the respective municipality.

Table 9.10: Annual population growth rates in different categories of German municipalities from 2009 to 2014 (BBSR 2014) and prognosis for German population in 2050

Description	Minimum	Average	Maximum
Strongly shrinking	-2.34 %	-1.14 %	-0.36 %
Shrinking	-2.05 %	-0.66 %	0.37 %
No development	-1.09 %	-0.21 %	-0.60 %
Growing	-0.71 %	0.21 %	3.79 %
Strongly growing	-0.01 %	0.80 %	5.08 %
Population prognosis for 2050 [million]	61	85	264

The values used for the population development of the municipalities according to their classification are documented in Tab. 9.10. As a plausibility check, the resulting population has been calculated and is also included in Tab. 9.10. Considering the maximum of the population development for a prognosis of the population in 2050 would result in a total population in Germany then of 264 million, which is unrealistic and will therefore not be considered further. Instead the two scenarios based on the minimum and the average of the population development in the municipalities will be used further. In Figs. 9.50 and 9.51 the distribution of the number of municipalities and their area according to the development prognosis categorization is depicted.

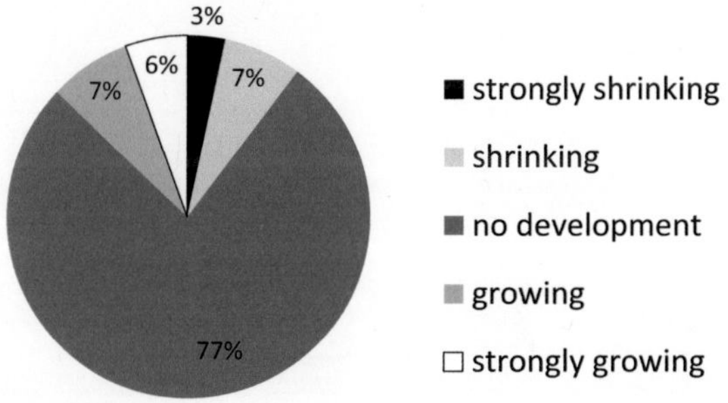

Figure 9.50: Distribution of number of municipalities in 2014 according to the development prognosis categorization (BBSR2014)

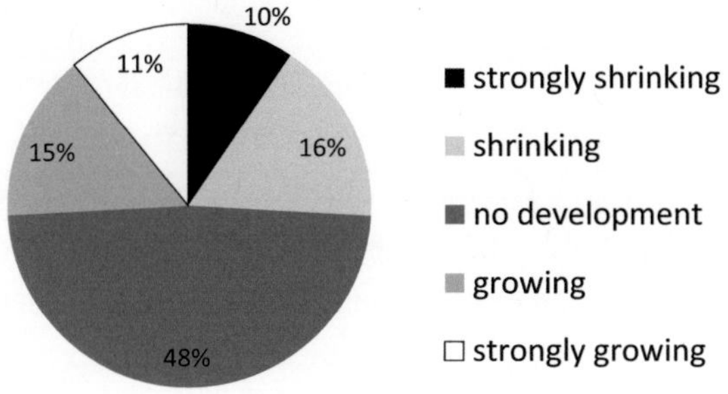

Figure 9.51: Distribution of the municipality area in 2014 according to the development prognosis categorization (BBSR2014)

9.4.1 National theoretical potential in 2050

For the calculation of the theoretical potential in 2050, the building stock calculated as described in Section 9.1 has been multiplied with the annual population development as documented in Tab. 9.10 for 35 years, taking the year 2015 with 81 million people as the baseline. Taking the average population development, for the year 2050 a theoretical potential of 37,219 km^2 results, i.e. a decrease in potential by 1 % compared with the year 2015. This decrease is due to a concentration of people in densely populated municipalities thereby reducing the theoretically available surface area per person. Taking the minimum population development, a theoretical potential of 26,639 km^2 results, i.e. a decrease in the potential of 29 %.

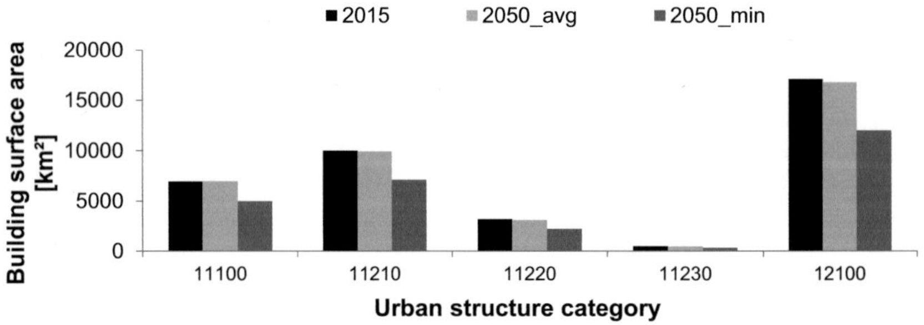

Figure 9.52: German theoretical potential in 2015 and 2050 for the average and minimum population growth scenarios according to urban fabric structures

In Fig. 9.52, the distribution of the calculated theoretical potentials for the year 2015 with and the two considered scenarios for 2050 are depicted according to urban fabric structure categories. For the second scenario, i.e. assuming a strongly decreasing population development, a decrease in theoretical potential between 28 % and 31 % can be observed in all urban fabric structure categories. By contrast, in the first scenario, the decrease in the theoretical potential is the greatest in the lowest-density urban fabric structure category 11230 with almost 4 %, while it is the least, with 0.2 %, in the densely populated urban fabric structure category 11100. Since the population development factor has been applied 1:1 to all building surfaces alike, no change in the distribution of the theoretical potential among roofs and facades can be observed.

9.4.2 National technical potential in 2050

9.4.2.1 National location potential in 2050

For a prognosis on the development of the location potential in 2050, again the methodology based on the irradiation in urban fabric structures as described in Section 7.4 has been utilized but now based on the two considered population growth scenarios for the theoretical potential in 2050. Thus, it is assumed that only a change in the building stock leads to a change in the location potential. Although there are examples of so-called solar settlements with an increased share of solar irradiation in the urban fabric structure, their share in this national study is considered negligible. In this way, the calculated irradiation factors for urban fabric structures are considered to constitute valid assumptions until the year 2050.

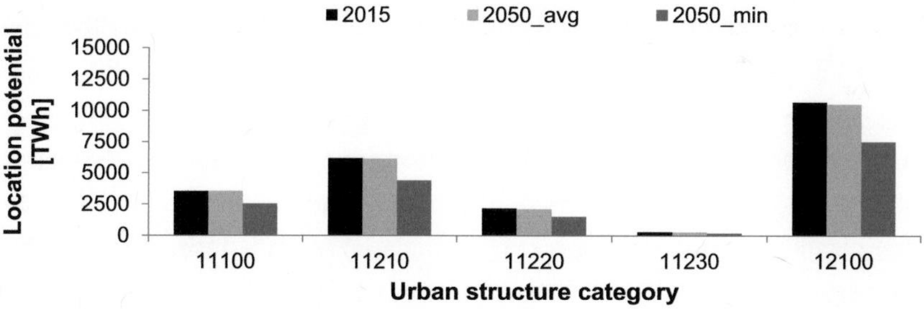

Figure 9.53: German location potential in 2015 and 2050 for the considered average and minimum population growth scenarios according to urban fabric structures

As a consequence, the prognosis for the location potential in 2050 based on an average population development is again, with 22,595 TWh, 1 % less than the location potential in 2015 (see Section 9.2.1.1). Based on the minimum population development, a location potential in 2050 of 16,185 TWh or 29 %

less than in 2015 results. A graphical comparison of the calculated location potentials is depicted in Fig. 9.53.

9.4.2.2 National electricity generation potential in 2050

In contrast to the location potential which has been assumed here to be influenced only by the change in the building stock, for the electricity generation potential, a major development can be expected until 2050 due to technological improvements in the photovoltaic industry. In Mayer et al. (2015) scenarios for future module and system efficiency as well as the associated investment are available. Due to inevitable efficiency losses associated with photovoltaic module construction, the theoretically achievable cell efficiency cannot be reached, such that in Mayer et al. (2015), a module efficiency industry standard of 24 % is assumed as a conservative assumption for 2050. Considering new cell technologies, so-called tandem and triple-junction cells, in an 'average' and 'optimistic' scenario, even 30 % and 35 % module efficiency are assumed. For the large-scale assessment conducted here, only the 'conservative' and the 'average' scenarios will be considered further. Concerning the PR, in Mayer et al. (2015) instead of an explicit scenario it is only mentioned that for bifacial modules even a PR > 100 % is feasible. Thus, in the following calculations a PR_{roof} and PR_{facade} of 95 % and 90 % are assumed respectively.

In the conservative module efficiency scenario, i.e. with a standard industrial module efficiency and assuming an average population development in the municipalities an electricity generation potential of 5023 TWh results, which constitutes an increase by 72 % in comparison to 2015. Assuming a minimum population development an electricity generation potential of 3598 TWh results which constitutes a potential increase of 23 %, thereby overcompensating the location potential decrease by 29 %.

In the average module efficiency scenario, i.e. assuming 30 % module efficiency due to the wide-spread usage of the tandem cell technology and assuming the average population development scenario, an electricity generation potential of 6279 TWh results, which constitutes an increase by 115 % in comparison with 2015. In the minimum population development scenario, an electricity generation potential of 44 % results, i.e. an increase by 54 %. In Fig. 9.54 an overview of the considered scenarios is depicted. Thanks to the differentiation between the location and the electricity generation potential, the effects of this multitude of influential factors can be analyzed in detail.

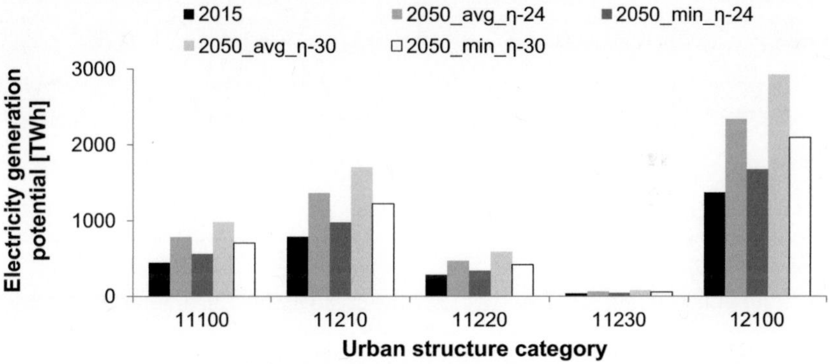

Figure 9.54: German electricity generation potential 2015 and 2050 according to urban fabric structures for the considered scenarios of population growth and module efficiency improvement, assuming an average population development

9.4.3 Economic potential in 2050

In Mayer et al. (2015), also scenarios for the investment of a photovoltaic installation in 2050 are given, ranging from 280 €/kW$_p$ to 610 €/kW$_p$. The focus of the study is on utility-scale systems, while here photovoltaic systems on buildings are considered. Therefore, it has been decided to assume a specific investment of 500 €/kW$_p$ for both roof and facade systems for the prognosis of the economic potential in 2050. Since it is very difficult to make estimates on economic parameters in such a distant future, these assumptions were made:

1. Interest rate of 5 % or more
2. System lifetime up to 30 years
3. Electricity tariff up to 0.3 €/kWh

This results in the minimum electricity yield and irradiation documented in Tab. 9.11 necessary for the investment to break even.

Table 9.11: Investment I, minimum average electricity yield El_{avg} and minimum average solar irradiation E_{avg} on building surfaces for a NPV greater than 0 in the prognosis for 2050

Surfaces	I [€/kW$_p$]	El_{avg} [kWh/kW$_p$]	E_{avg} [kWh/m^2]
Roof	500	270	284
Facade	500	270	300

The following prognosis is based on the conservative module efficiency scenario, i.e. with an industrial standard module efficiency of 24 %.

9.4.3.1 Scenario assuming an average population development

Based on the above listed economic parameters assuming an average population development for 2050, an economic potential of 4210 TWh generated electricity or 4325 GW$_p$ installed capacity results. The distribution of this potential on building surface areas in urban fabric structures is depicted in Figs. 9.55 and 9.56. In this scenario, facade surface areas account for 36 % of the generated electricity and 55 % of the installed capacity.

9.4.3.2 Scenario assuming a minimum population development

Based on the economic parameters listed above and assuming the minimum population development for 2050 an economic potential of 3015 TWh generated electricity or 3095 GW$_p$ installed capacity results. The distribution of this potential over building surface areas according to urban fabric structures is depicted in Figs. 9.57 and 9.58. The distribution of the economic potential on roof and facade surface areas is the same as in the previously considered scenario.

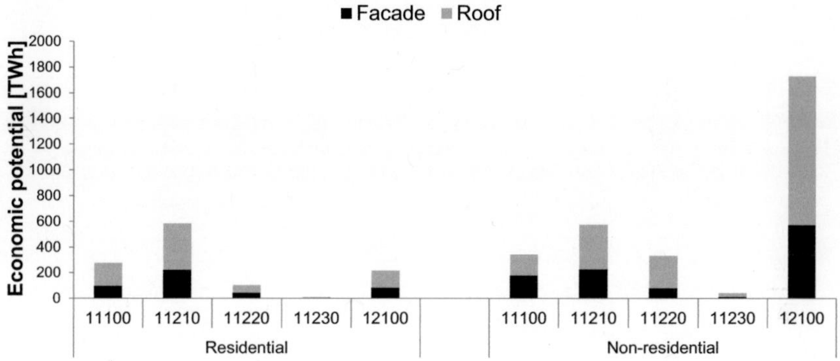

Figure 9.55: Distribution of predicted German economic potential of generated electricity in 2050 on building surface areas according to urban fabric structure categories, assuming an average population development

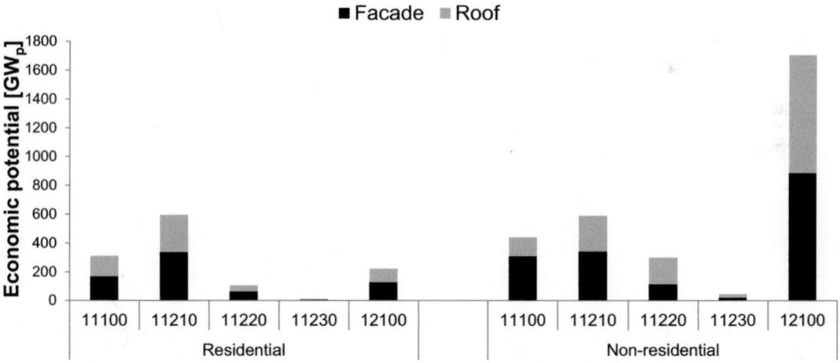

Figure 9.56: Distribution of predicted German economic potential of installed capacity in 2050 on building surface areas according to urban fabric structures, assuming an average population development

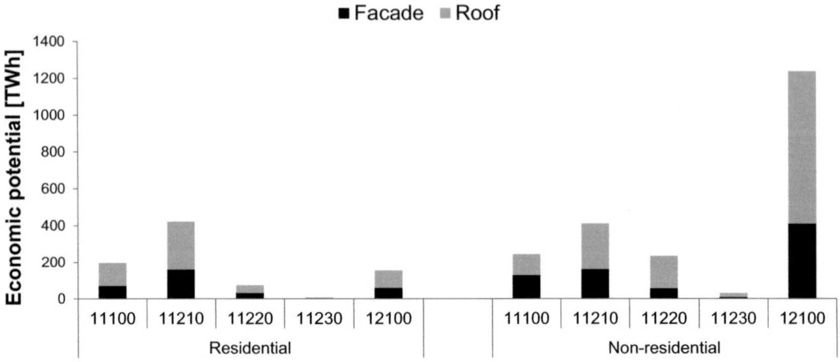

Figure 9.57: Distribution of predicted economic potential 2050 of generated electricity on building surface areas in urban fabric structures, assuming a minimum population development

The share of the technical potential on roof surfaces depicted in Fig. 9.23 ranges from 51 % to 54 %, which is more than the share of the theoretical potential due to the higher assumed irradiation on roof surfaces in comparison to facade surfaces. This distribution is almost equal to the distribution of the theoretical potential for municipalities assigned to cluster 3, which also represents the largest share (42 % or 9672 TWh) of the total location potential, with 2365 TWh or 24 % on residential buildings and 7308 TWh or 76 % on non-residential buildings. One reason for this similarity in the distribution is that the assignment of municipalities to settlement structure clusters is distributed quite evenly throughout Germany, so that there is no peak in irradiation for a certain cluster. Since the distribution of considered attributes has remained similar for each step of the performed analysis, i.e. from small-scale through medium-scale to large-scale, the transferability of settlement structural characteristics in municipalities is considered to be demonstrated.

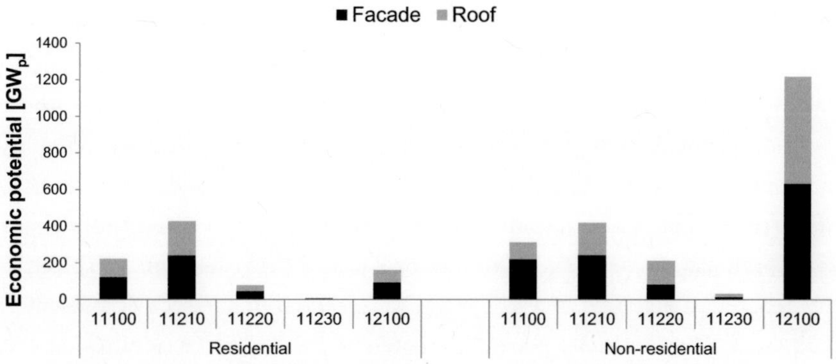

Figure 9.58: Distribution of predicted economic potential 2050 of installed capacity on building surface areas in urban fabric structures, assuming a minimum population development

9.5 Conclusion on German national photovoltaic potential on buildings

In this chapter, the solar residential and non-residential building typology for individual buildlings developed in Section 6, the irradiation analysis of urban districts performed in Section 7 and the national analysis of building stock in municipalities conducted in Section 8 have all been combined for the calculation of a German national photovoltaic potential on buildings.

Finally, a national theoretical photovoltaic potential, i. e. the surface area available on all buildings, of 37,700 km^2 results for 2015 (65 % on facade surfaces). Consequently, the national theoretical potential area for photovoltaics on buildings amounts to approximately 10 % of the German land area. 28 % of the theoretical potential is on residential building surfaces while 72 % is on non-residential building surfaces. 45 % of the theoretical potential is located on commercial and industrial buildings in commercial and industrial areas. The share of facade surfaces in the theoretical potential varies for non-residential buildings between 45 % and 80 % due to the heterogeneous nature of these buildings. By contrast, the relation of roof and facade surfaces of 65 % is similar across all building types for residential buildings.

In the next step, based on detailed irradiation simulations, a location potential of 22,855 TWh has been calculated (47 % on facade surfaces). Additionally, taking into account the photovoltaic module and plant efficiency, an electricity generation potential of 2923 TWh results (44 % on facade surfaces). With this amount the total German electricity consumption of the industrial, residential, commercial and transport sectors in 2015 could be covered four times (Umweltbundesamt 2017). Mainzer & Fath et al. (2014) calculated an electricity generation potential of 148 TWh (Tab. 2.4) on roof surfaces of residential buildings. The electricity generation potential on roof surfaces of residential buildings calculated in this thesis amounts to 418 TWh (53 % on building roofs; 27 % on residential buildings) which is almost triple the amount calculated by Mainzer & Fath et al. (2014). However, in their study average roof areas were used, as well as a utilization factor of 27 % for flat roofs and 58 % for slanted roofs due to constructional constraints (Mainzer & Fath et al. 2014). This kind of constructional constraint has not been considered in this thesis, since the analysis has been performed in LOD2, which does not include the relevant information. Also, the author has decided not to include this kind of flat reduction factor in her analysis due to the poor statistical basis. Although the study by Kaltschmitt and Wiese (1992) for the State of Baden-Württemberg had a representative coverage, here the focus was also only on residential buildings so that the application to non-residential buildings has to be questioned. By displaying the calculated potentials without reduction factors, like in this thesis, the reported potentials can also be used as basis for future studies.

For the economic potential in 2015, different scenarios have been calculated due to the strong influence of the assumptions for the economic parameters on the calculated potential. The economic potential ranges from 1158 TWh generated electricity or 1406 GW_p installed capacity in the most pessimistic scenario to 2482 TWh generated electricity or 4402 GW_p installed capacity in the most optimistic scenario.

Although the calculated economic potential appears to be very large, it should be noted that in 1987 Räuber et al. (1987) predicted an installed capacity

of 1500 MW_p for the year 2000 and 1660 MW_p for 2020 for the State of Baden-Württemberg. In Quaschning (2000), an installed photovoltaic potential of 1.8 GW_p has been predicted for 2020 in Germany and a global installed photovoltaic capacity of 18.4 GW_p.
Actually, 13 MW_p of photovoltaic systems had been installed in Baden-Württemberg in 2000 (Ministerum für Umwelt, Klima und Energiewirtschaft Baden-Württemberg 2011), but by the end of 2016 this had increased to 5393 MW_p (Agentur für Erneuerbare Energien 2017). In Germany, by the end of 2016 the installed photovoltaic capacity had reached 41 GW_p (Quaschning 2016). Globally the installed capacity had reached 228 GW_p (PVPS 2017).
Thus, all existing studies have dramatically underestimated the dynamic development of photovoltaic installations. With additional external drivers such as European energy-related regulations and a further decreasing investment, the author expects a significant share of the calculated economic potential to be exploited in the future.
Finally, based on prognoses for the population development and technological improvements in the photovoltaic industry, a prognosis for the potential development until 2050 was derived, ranging from 3015 TWh generated electricity (3095 GW_p installed capacity) to 4210 TWh generated electricity (4325 GW_p installed capacity). According to Palzer and Henning (2014), an installed photovoltaic capacity of 160 GW_p to 260 GW_p is necessary for a 100 % renewable energy system. Thus, exploitation of 5 % to 10 % of this predicted economic potential would already be sufficient.

10 Summary and outlook

10.1 Summary of photovoltaic potential assessment

In this thesis, a methodology for the potential assessment of photovoltaic installations on buildings has been developed and applied to the German building stock. The scope of existing photovoltaic potential studies has been extended in multiple ways: Firstly, in this thesis a detailed analysis of both roof and facade surfaces on buildings has been presented for the first time. Secondly, in addition to the residential building stock also the non-residential building stock has been considered on the basis of 3D and geographically referenced data. Lastly, also the economic potential has been assessed for numerous scenarios.

10.1.1 Photovoltaic potential on individual buildings

For the large-scale analysis of a national photovoltaic potential, a step-wise methodology has been developed. First, residential and non-residential buildings were analyzed with respect to their solar potential. For the residential building stock, it was possible to use an existing building typology. In absence of a comparable typology for non-residential buildings, a different approach was needed for the very heterogeneous non-residential building stock, where detailed irradiation and electricity generation simulations have been performed for 38 buildings. The individual building results were analyzed with cluster analysis resulting in five clusters of non-residential buildings with detailed statistical information on building characteristics and the photovoltaic potential. These five archetypes with detailed quantitative information provided one building block for later use in up-scaling the results to a national potential.

10.1.2 Photovoltaic potential in urban districts

In the next step, the same detailed irradiation simulations that had already been applied to individual buildings, were employed for the irradiation simulation of five urban districts with different urban fabric structures. From the results of these medium-scale analyses, conclusions on shading losses in urban fabric structures could be drawn. In particular, the large share of facade surfaces in urban areas in the location potential was established. The average irradiation on building roof and facade surfaces was used in further analysis of the national photovoltaic potential.

10.1.3 National photovoltaic potential

The results of the small-scale (individual buildings), medium-scale (urban districts) and large-scale (national building stock) analysis were all combined for the calculation of a national photovoltaic potential. For the analysis of municipalities where no information on the building stock was available, urban data mining methods have been used. Since this is connected with uncertainty, sensitivity analysis of the stability of results has been performed.
Finally, applying the documented methodology and assumptions, a theoretical photovoltaic potential area of 37,700 km^2 on buildings results for 2015. 28 % of the theoretical potential is on residential building surfaces while 72 % is on non-residential building surfaces. Then, based on detailed irradiation simulations a location potential of 22,855 TWh has been calculated. Additionally, taking into account the photovoltaic module and plant efficiency, an electricity generation potential of 2923 TWh results. For the economic potential in 2015, different scenarios have been calculated due to the strong influence of the assumptions for the economic parameters on the calculated potential. The economic potential ranges from 1158 TWh generated electricity or 1406 GW_p installed capacity in the most pessimistic scenario to 2482 TWh generated electricity or 4402 GW_p installed capacity in the most optimistic economic scenario. Based on prognoses for the population development and technological improvements in the

photovoltaic industry, a prognosis for the potential development until 2050 has been derived, ranging from 3015 TWh generated electricity (3095 GW_p installed capacity) to 4210 TWh generated electricity (4325 GW_p installed capacity).

10.2 Critical discussion

For the methodology developed in this thesis, a compromise between accuracy and valid assumptions for achieving the objective of a national potential calculation had to be found. Therefore, for the detailed irradiation simulations, available geometrical building data either in 2D format (analysis of individual buildings in Section 6.2) or 3D format (analysis of urban districts in Section 7.2) has been utilized. This data was only available in LOD2 format, i.e. without detailed information on building add-ons like chimneys, dormers, balconies and alcoves (see Section 2.1.2). These building characteristics will lead to a reduction of the calculated potentials. However, since there was no reliable information available on the amount of this reduction on a national scale, it was decided to present all calculated figures without considering them. In this way, these figures can be reduced later according to updated results.
Also, this requirement led to focusing this thesis on irradiation and electricity yield simulations without considering the consumption side. In future studies based on the detailed irradiation and electricity generation time series calculated here, conclusions can be drawn on the amount of self-consumption, possibly also including energy storage systems and feeding of electricity into the grid, as has been presented for the case of roof-installed photovoltaics in Mainzer et al. (2014). As a basis for this future research, valuable conclusions on the amount and profiles of energy demand for differing building types can be drawn from the analysis of building distribution and sizes according to urban fabric structures performed in this thesis. For this, average building footprint sizes for different building categories can be combined with average heights, e.g. from BMVBS (2013) for the calculation of building volume, floor area, and number of people employed and living in different urban fabric structure categories.

Although the calculated economic potential appears to be very large, it should be noted that photovoltaic potential studies in the past have strongly underestimated the future installed capacity of photovoltaic plants (see Section 9.5). The European building energy regulation (Energy Performance of Buildings Directive (EPBD)) requires all new buildings to be nearly-zero energy building (nZEB) by 2021 (2019 for public buildings) (Hermelink et al. 2013), such that in the future, partial on-site generation of electricity will be required. With this kind of external driver and further decreasing investment for photovoltaic installations, the author expects a further increase in installed capacity and a significant share of the calculated economic potential of building-related photovoltaics to be exploited in the future.

10.3 Outlook

In this thesis, the potential for photovoltaic installations on buildings in Germany in the year 2015 has been calculated, demonstrating a large share of economic potential yet to be exploited. The methodology developed in this thesis can be easily transferred to other countries where a similar database is available. Results can also be further refined when more detailed geographic information on the actual building stock in Germany exists. The author hopes to contribute with her thesis to greater awareness of the potential offered by buildings as the location for further installation of photovoltaic plants since they constitute an emission-free source of renewable energy with high public acceptance.

A Appendix

Table A.1: Specific investment for different plant types and size categories in €/m^2, assuming an average module efficiency of 15 %; The asterisks (*) mark the specific investment utilized in the scenario 'Very optimistic BIPV investment scenario' in Section 5.6.

P [kW$_p$]	I_{roof} [€/m^2]	$I_{roof,BIPV}$ [€/m^2]	I_{facade} [€/m^2]	$I_{facade,BIPV}$ [€/m^2]
$P < 3$	214	115 - 164*	364	265 - 314
$3 \leq P < 10$	195	96 - 146*	345	246 - 296
$P \geq 10$	171	72 - 122*	321	222 - 272

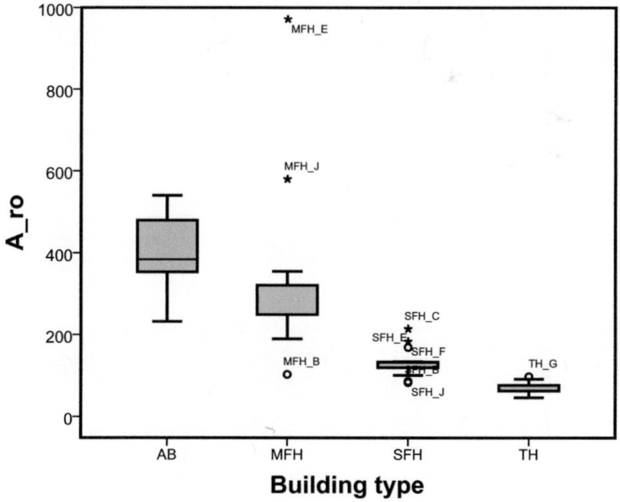

Figure A.1: Roof area A_{ro} [m^2].

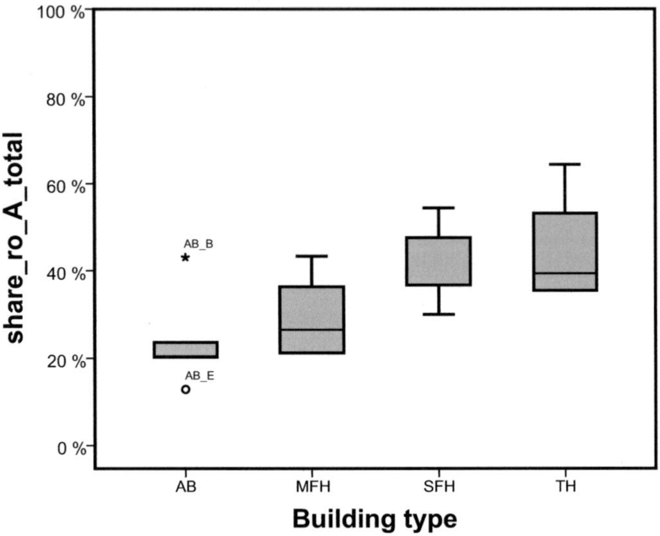

Figure A.2: Share of roof area A_{ro} in total building surface area A_{total}.

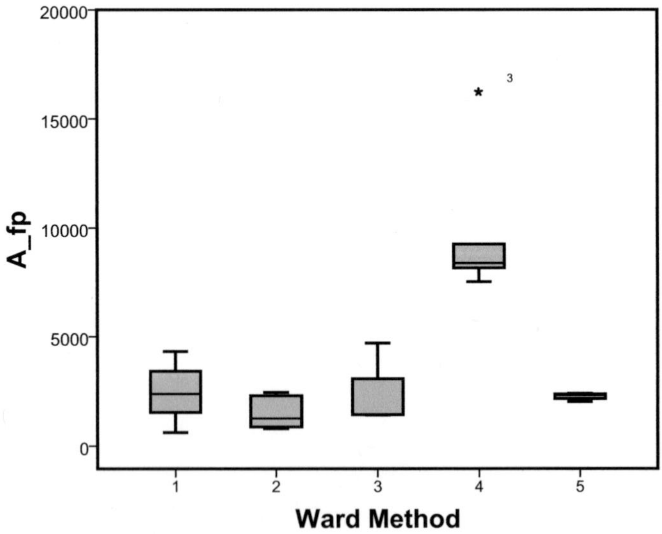

Figure A.3: Building footprint area A_{fp} [m^2].

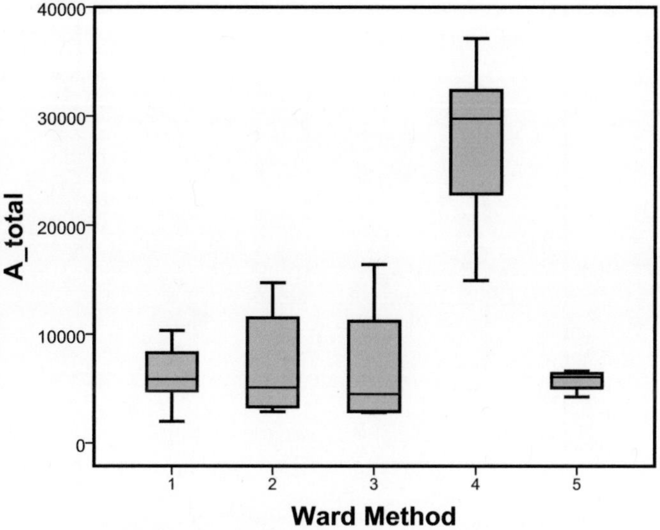

Figure A.4: Total building surface area A_{total} [m^2]

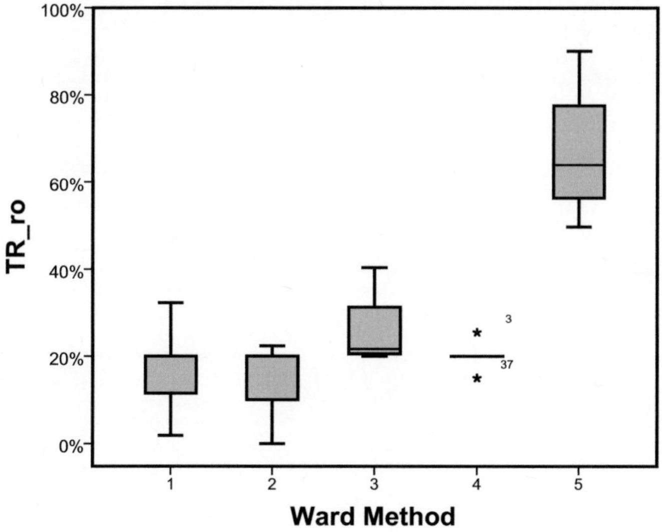

Figure A.5: Roof transparency ratio TR_{ro}.

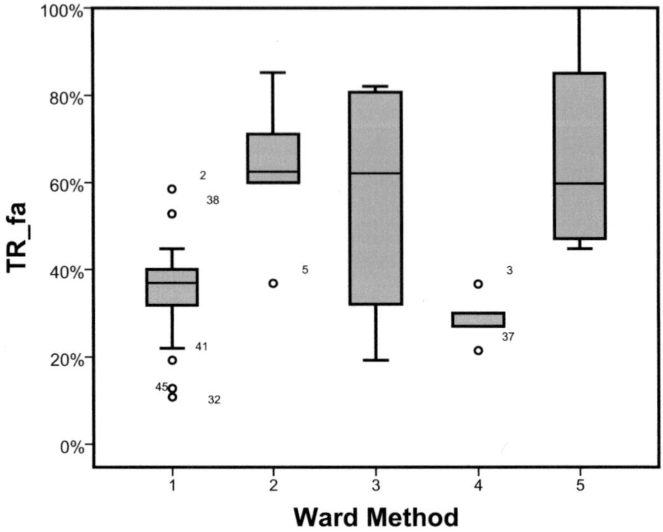

Figure A.6: Transparency ratio facade TR_{fa}

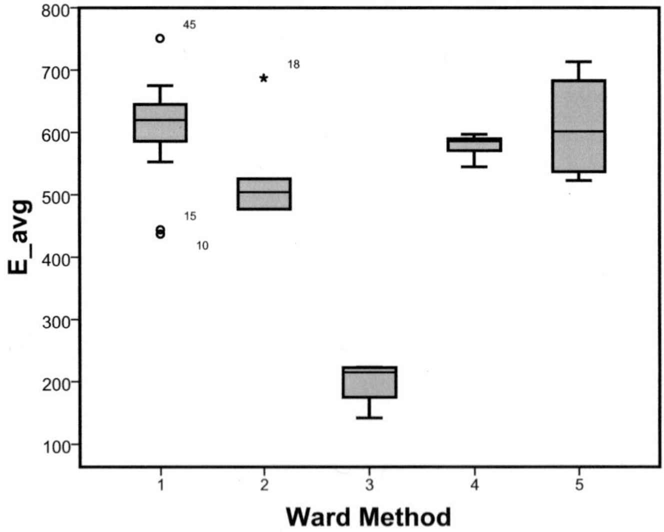

Figure A.7: Average irradiation E_{avg} [kWh/m^2].

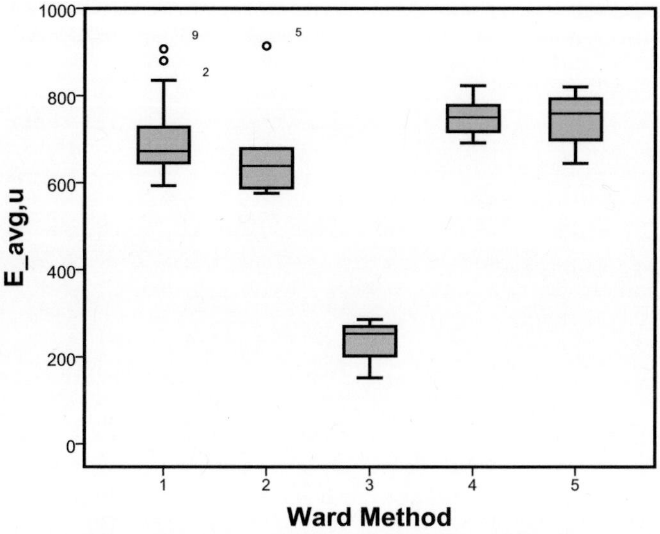

Figure A.8: Average irradiation unshaded $E_{avg,u}$[kWh/m^2]

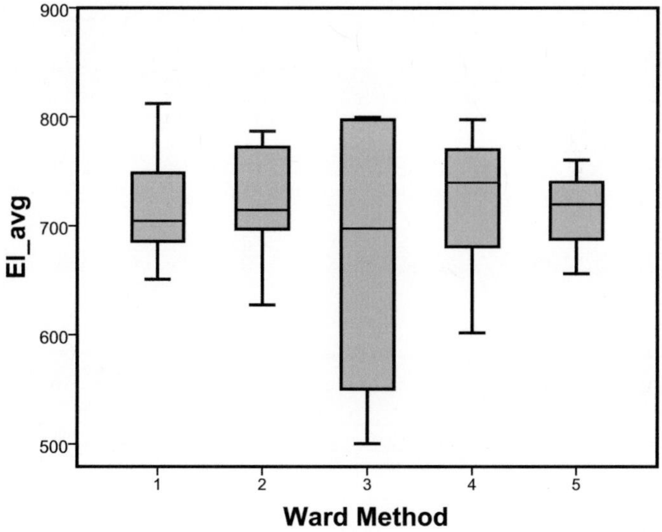

Figure A.9: Average electricity generation El_{avg} [kWh/m^2]

Table A.2: Average values of selected attributes for the five identified non-residential buildings clusters with the number of analyzed buildings N assigned to this cluster. The asterisk (*) marks the attributes used in the cluster analysis. Two asterisks (**) marks the attributes that were standardized and then used in the cluster analysis.

Cluster	**1**	**2**	**3**	**4**	**5**
Location characteristics					
pd*	973	2769	1037	2223	905
Theoretical potential					
A_{fp}*	2509	1441	2253	9015	2063
A_{ro}*	2651	1458	3871	9105	2171
A_{fa}*	3742	5645	3169	18300	3592
A_{total}	6393	7102	7040	27404	5763
TR_{ro}*	17 %	15 %	26 %	20 %	67 %
TR_{fa}	35 %	63 %	56 %	29 %	66 %
TR_{total}*	27 %	52 %	41 %	26 %	66 %
Technical potential					
E_{avg}**	607	529	199	578	610
$E_{avg,u}$**	702	672	236	752	746
El_{avg}*	718	719	674	718	714
$A'_{total,gt500}$*	4267	3458	1261	11106	3600
N	17	6	4	5	4

Table A.3: Average values of attributes used in municipality classification into settlement structure clusters according to *k-Nearest-Neighbor* algorithm with 100 % of 2876 municipalities used as training data set (*c) KNN_100%* in Section 8.4)

Cluster	**1**	**2**	**3**	**4**	**5**
Urban fabric category					
11100	4 %	4 %	1 %	0 %	0 %
11210	10 %	11 %	4 %	2 %	2 %
11220	2 %	2 %	2 %	1 %	1 %
11230	0 %	0 %	0 %	0 %	0 %
12100	10 %	8 %	2 %	2 %	2 %
N_{res} *and building age category*					
1, 2 Before 1919	10 %	6 %	10 %	21 %	18 %
1, 2 1919-1948	15 %	8 %	9 %	11 %	12 %
1, 2 1949-1978	18 %	35 %	37 %	22 %	18 %
1, 2 1979-1990	7 %	13 %	14 %	12 %	9 %
1, 2 After 1990	15 %	16 %	22 %	28 %	18 %
3-12 Before 1919	7 %	2 %	1 %	1 %	5 %
3-12 1919-1948	6 %	1 %	1 %	1 %	2 %
3-12 1949-1978	14 %	11 %	3 %	2 %	8 %
3-12 1979-1990	2 %	3 %	1 %	1 %	6 %
3-12 After 1990	3 %	4 %	2 %	2 %	4 %
>12 1949-1978	1 %	1 %	0 %	0 %	0 %
>12 1979-1990	0 %	0 %	0 %	0 %	0 %
>12 After 1990	0 %	0 %	0 %	0 %	0 %
pd	1272	1158	279	108	146

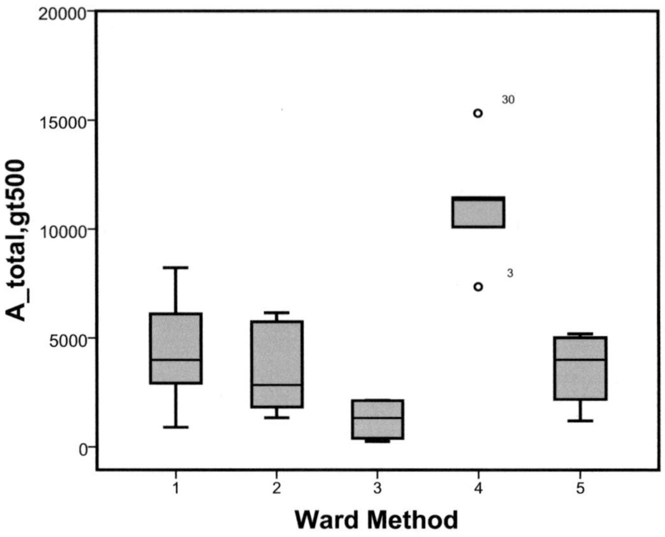

Figure A.10: Building surface area with irradiation greater than 500 kWh/m^2 $A_{total,gt500}$ [m^2]

References

AdV (2014a). Die amtlichen 3D-Gebäudemodelle in der Ausprägung LoD1 (LoD1-DE). München.

AdV (2014b). Die amtlichen Hausumringe Deutschland (HU-DE). München.

Agentur für Erneuerbare Energien (2017). Föderal Erneuerbar - Bundesländer mit neuer Energie. Berlin.

Aran Carrion, J., A. Espin Estrella, F. Aznar Dols, & A. Ramos Ridao (2008). The electricity production capacity of photovoltaic power plants and the selection of solar energy sites in Andalusia (Spain). *Renewable Energy 33*, 545–552.

Bacher, J., A. Pöge, & K. Wenzig (2010). *Clusteranalyse: Anwendungsorientierte Einführung in Klassifikationsverfahren*. München: Oldenbourg.

Backhaus, K., B. Erichson, W. Plinke, & R. Weiber (Eds.) (2008). *Multivariate Analysemethoden: Eine anwendungsorientierte Einführung*. Berlin: Springer.

BBSR (2011). *Laufende Stadtbeobachtung - Raumabgrenzungen*. Bonn.

BBSR (2014). *Wachsende und schrumpfende Gemeinden in Deutschland, Stand 31.12.2014*. Bonn.

Behnisch, M. (2008). *Urban data mining: Operationalisierung der Strukturerkennung und Strukturbildung von Ähnlichkeitsmustern über die gebaute Umwelt*. Karlsruhe: Universitätsverlag.

Behnisch, M. & A. Ultsch (2008). Estimating the Number of Buildings in Germany. In *Advances in Data Analysis, Data Handling and Business Intelligence – Proceedings of the 32nd Annual Conference of the*

Gesellschaft für Klassifikation e.V., Joint Conference with the British Classification Society (BCS) and the Dutch/Flemish Classification Society (VOC), July 16-18, 2008, Hamburg, Germany, pp. 585–593.

Behnisch, M. & A. Ultsch (2009). Urban data-mining: spatiotemporal exploration of multidimensional data. *Building Research & Information 37*(5-6), 520–532.

Behnisch, M. & A. Ultsch (2010). Urban Data Mining – Eine Methodik zur raumbezogenen Wissensextraktion. *GIS.SCIENCE 4*(135-147).

Bergamasco, L. & P. Asinari (2011). Scalable methodology for the photovoltaic solar energy potential assessment based on available roof surface area: Further improvements by ortho-image analysis and application to Turin (Italy). *Solar Energy 85*(11), 2741–2756.

Bergs, S. (1980). *Optimalität bei Clusteranalysen: Experimente zur Bewertung numerischer Klassifikationsverfahren*. Münster.

Biljecki, F. (2013). The concept of level of detail in 3D city models. *GISt Report No. 62*.

BKG (2014). *Administrative Boundaries for Germany*. Frankfurt am Main.

BKI (2010). *Statistische Kostenkennwerte für Bauelemente*. BKI-Baukosten. Stuttgart: Baukosteninformationszentrum Deutscher Architektenkammern, Rudolf Müller.

Blesl, M., S. Kempe, & H. Huther (2010). *Verfahren zur Entwicklung und Anwendung einer digitalen Wärmebedarfskarte für die Bundesrepublik Deutschland: Kurzbericht zum Forschungsvorhaben*. Frankfurt, M.: AGFW.

Blotevogel, H. H. (1996). Zentrale Orte: Zur Karriere und Krise eines Konzepts in Geographie und Raumplanung. *Erdkunde 50*, 9–25.

Blum, A. E. (Ed.) (2010). *Typologien der gebauten Umwelt: Modellierung und Analyse der Siedlungsentwicklung mit dem Strukturtypenansatz*. Aachen: Shaker.

BMVBS (2011a). *Bewertungssystem Nachhaltiges Bauen Büro- und Verwaltung*. Berlin.

BMVBS (2011b). *Typologie und Bestand beheizter Nichtwohngebäude in Deutschland*. Berlin.

BMVBS (Ed.) (2013). *Systematische Datenanalyse im Bereich der Nichtwohngebäude - Erfassung und Quantifizierung von Energieeinspar- und CO_2-Minderungspotenzialen*. BMVBS-Online-Publikation 27/2013.

BMWi (2013). *Energiedaten: Ausgewählte Grafiken*. Berlin.

BMWi (2016). *Reserven und Ressourcen*. Berlin.

BMWi (2017). *Energiedaten: Gesamtausgabe*. Berlin.

Braun, M., A. von Oehsen, Y.-M. Saint-Drenan, & T. Stetz (2012). *Vorstudie zur Integration großer Anteile Photovoltaik in die elektrische Energieversorgung*. Kassel: Fraunhofer IWES.

Breuer, B. (2010). *Urban Development in Germany*. The Hague: European Urban Knowledge Network.

Bürger, V. & H. Tilman (2015). *Entwicklungsperpsektiven des Gebäudesektors*. Freiburg: Öko-Institut e.V.

Brito, M., N. Gomes, T. Santos, & J. Tenedório (2012). Photovoltaic potential in a Lisbon suburb using LiDAR data. *Solar Energy 86*(1), 283–288.

Brosius, F. (2013). *SPSS 21*. Heidelberg: mitp.

Buchert, M., U. Fritsche, W. Jenseit, L. Rausch, C. Deilmann, G. Schiller, S. Siedentop, & A. Lipkow (2004). *Nachhaltiges Bauen und Wohnen in Deutschland*. Berlin: Umweltbundesamt.

Bundesnetzagentur (2017). *Installierte EE-Leistung 2016*. Berlin.

Bundesverband Solarwirtschaft (2013). *Photovoltaic plants 66 % cheaper since 2006*. Berlin.

Burgdorf, M. (Ed.) (2012). *Raumabgrenzungen und Raumtypen des BBSR*. Bonn: BBSR.

Carr, L. & T. Schmid (2013). Erneuerbare Energien - Potenziale und ihre räumliche Verteilung in Deutschland. *Flächennutzungsmonitoring V - Methodik - Analyseergebnisse - Flächenmanagement - IÖR Schriften Band 61*, 269 – 277.

Catita, C., P. Redweik, J. Pereira, & M. Brito (2014). Extending solar potential analysis in buildings to vertical facades. *Computers & Geosciences 66*, 1–12.

Chae, Y. T., J. Kim, H. Park, & B. Shin (2014). Building energy performance evaluation of building integrated photovoltaic (BIPV) window with semi-transparent solar cells. *Applied Energy 129*, 217–227.

Cheng-Dar, Y. & S.-S. Wang (2006). GIS-based evaluation of multifarious local renewable energy sources: a case study of the Chigu area of southwestern Taiwan. *Energy Policy 34*, 730–742.

Choi, Y., J. Rayl, C. Tammineedi, & J. R. S. Brownson (2011). PV Analyst: Coupling ArcGIS with TRNSYS to assess distributed photovoltaic potential in urban areas. *Solar Energy 85*(11), 2924–2939.

Compagnon, R. (2001). *RADIANCE: a simulation tool for daylighting systems*. Berkeley.

Compagnon, R. (2004). Solar and daylight availability in the urban fabric. *Energy and Buildings 36*(4), 321 – 328.

D-GMES (2014). *Nutzung des GMES Urban Atlas in Stadtklimamodellen*. Bonn.

Defaix, P. R., W. G. J. H. M. van Sark, E. Worrell, & E. de Visser (2012). Technical potential for photovoltaics on buildings in the EU-27. *Solar Energy 86*(9), 2644–2653.

Delaunay, J.-J., J. Wienold, & W. Sprenger (2014). gendaylit - generates a radiance description of the daylight sources using perez models for direct and diffuse components. Freiburg i.B. Fraunhofer ISE.

DesignBuilder (2014). *Daylighting calculation options*. Gloucestershire.

Didoné, E. L. & A. Wagner (2013). Semi-transparent PV windows: A study for office buildings in Brazil. *Energy & Buildings 67*, 136–142.

Diefenbach, N. (2013). *Basisdaten für Hochrechnungen mit der Deutschen Gebäudetypologie des IWU: Neufassung Oktober 2013*.

EnBauSa GmbH (2014). Städte mit Solarkataster. Tübingen.

Enquête-Kommission (2002). *Endbericht der Enquête-Kommission "Nachhaltige Energieversorgung unter den Bedingungen der Liberalisierung"*.

Esch, T. & M. Tum (2013). Einsatzmöglichkeiten der Erdbeobachtung auf dem Weg zur Umsetzung einer nachhaltigen Energiversorgung. In *Flächennutzungsmonitoring V - Methodik - Analyseergebnisse - Flächenmanagement - IÖR Schriften Band 61*, Berlin, pp. 279 – 286. IÖR.

European Environment Agency (2014). *Urban Atlas for Europe*. Copenhagen.

Everding, D. H. & M. Kloos (Eds.) (2007). *Solarer Städtebau: vom Pilotprojekt zum planerischen Leitbild*. Stuttgart: Kohlhammer.

Fath, K. (2013). Photovoltaic systems. *CONCERTO Case Study*.

Fath, K., J. Stengel, F. Schultmann, S. Mende, H. R. Wilson, & T. E. Kuhn (2012a). Impact of semi-transparent building-integrated photovoltaics on building life-cycle cost. In Strauss, Frangopol, and Bergmeister (Eds.), *Life-Cycle and Sustainability of Civil Infrastructure Systems*.

Fath, K., J. Stengel, F. Schultmann, S. Mende, H. R. Wilson, & T. E. Kuhn (2012b). Impact of semi-transparent building-integrated photovoltaics on building life-cycle cost.

Fath, K., J. Stengel, W. Sprenger, H. R. Wilson, F. Schultmann, & T. E. Kuhn (2015). A method for predicting the economic potential of (building-integrated) photovoltaics in urban areas based on hourly radiance simulations. *Solar Energy 116*, 357 – 370.

Fath, K., H. R. Wilson, T. E. Kuhn, J. Stengel, & F. Schultmann (2013). Lebenszykluskostenanalyse einer PVShade-Pilotanlage. *5. Anwenderforum Bauwerkintegrierte Photovoltaik.*

Fraunhofer ISE (2007). *Jahresbericht - Leistungen und Ergebnisse.* Freiburg i. B.

Fraunhofer ISE (2016). *Metal Wrap Through (MWT) Technologie.* Freiburg i. B.

Fraunhofer ISE (2017a). *Aktuelle Fakten zur Photovoltaik in Deutschland.* Freiburg i. B.

Fraunhofer ISE (2017b). *Stromerzeugung in Deutschland im Jahr 2016.* Freiburg i. B.

Freitas, S., C. Catita, P. Redweik, & M. C. Brito (2015). Modelling solar potential in the urban environment: State-of-the-art review. *Renewable and Sustainable Energy Reviews 41*, 915–931.

Frontini, F. (2011). *Daylight and Solar Control in Buildings: General Evaluation and Optimization of a New Angle Selective Glazing Facade.* Stuttgart: Fraunhofer Verlag.

Fu, P. & P. M. Rich (1999). Design and Implementation of the Solar Analyst: an ArcView Extension for Modeling Solar Radiation at Landscape Scales. *19th Annual ESRI User Conference*, 1–24.

Fung, T. Y. & H. Yang (2008). Study on thermal performance of semi-transparent building-integrated photovoltaic glazings. *Energy and Buildings 40*(3), 341–350.

Geißdörfer, K., R. Gleich, & A. Wald (2009). Standardisierungspotentiale lebenszyklusbasierter Modelle des strategischen Kostenmanagements. *ZfB Zeitschrift für Betriebswirtschaft 79*, 693 – 716.

Geißdörfer, K. (2009). *Total Cost of Ownership (TCO) und Life Cycle Costing (LCC): Einsatz und Modelle: Ein Vergleich zwischen Deutschland und USA.* Controlling und Management; 7. Münster: LIT.

Gernhardt, D., M. Skiba, M. Mohr, & H. Unger (1992). Strahlungsmodellierung und Potentialflächenabschätzung an Wohngebäuden in Nordrhein-Westfalen.

Gierga, M. & H. Erhorn (1993). *Bestand und Typologie beheizter Nichtwohngebäude in Westdeutschland*. Instrumente für Klimagas-Reduktionsstrategien / Teilprojekt 5 Haushalte und Kleinverbraucher ; 5,14. Jülich: Forschungszentrum.

Glantz, S. A. (1997). *Primer of biostatistics*. New York: McGraw-Hill, Health Professions Division.

GMES (2014). Urban Atlas: Understanding cities to improve our way of life.

GODI (2014). Global Open Data Initiative.

Gruhler, K. & R. Böhm (2011). *Ressourcenbezogene Kennwerte von Nichtwohngebäuden - Analyse und Aufarbeitung von Daten der Statistik "Bauen und Wohnen"*. Fraunhofer IRB Verlag.

Hachem, C., A. Athienitis, & P. Fazio (2011). Investigation of solar potential of housing units in different neighborhood designs. *Energy & Buildings 43*(9), 2262–2273.

Hair, J. F. (Ed.) (2010). *Multivariate data analysis: a global perspective*. Upper Saddle River, NJ: Pearson.

Handl, A. (2010). *Multivariate Analysemethoden: Theorie und Praxis multivariater Verfahren unter besonderer Berücksichtigung von S-PLUS*. Statistik und ihre Anwendungen. Berlin, Heidelberg: Springer-Verlag.

Hecht, R. (2014). *Automatische Klassifizierung von Gebäudegrundrissen – Ein Beitrag zur kleinräumigen Beschreibung der Siedlungsstruktur*. Ph. D. thesis, Dresden.

Held, A. M. (2010). *Modelling the future development of renewable energy technologies in the European electricity sector using agent-based simulation*. Ph. D. thesis, Karlsruhe.

Hermelink, A., S. Schimschar, & T. Boermans (2013). Towards nearly zero-energy buildings - Definition of common principles under the EPBD - Final report.

Heydenreich, W., B. Müller, & C. Reise (2008). Describing the world with three parameters: A new approach to PV module power modelling. *Solar Energy 25*(2), 2–5.

Hii Jun Chung, D., C. K. Heng, L. C. Malone-Lee, J. Zhang, N. Ibrahim, Y. C. Huang, & P. Janssen (2011). Solar radiation performance evaluation for high density urban forms in the tropical context. In *12th Conference of International Building Performance Simulation Association*, 14. - 16. November, Sydney, Australia, pp. 2595 –2602.

Hoffmann, H.-J., W. Katscher, & G. Stein (1997). *Energiestrategien für den Klimaschutz in Deutschland: Das IKARUS Projekt des BMBF; Zusammenfassender Endbericht.*

Hoffmann, V. U. (2008). Damals war's - Ein Rückblick auf die Entwicklung der Photovoltaik in Deutschland. *Sonnenenergie* (11/12), 38–39.

Hofierka, J. & J. Kanuk (2009). Assessment of photovoltaic potential in urban areas using open-source solar radiation tools. *Renewable Energy 34*(10), 2206–2214.

Hofierka, J. & M. Šúri (2002). The solar radiation model for Open source GIS: implementation and applications. In *Open source GIS - GRASS users conference*, Trento, Italy, 11-13.09.2002, pp. 11–13.

Hollander, M. (2014). *Nonparametric statistical methods*. Wiley series in probability and statistics. Hoboken, New Jersey: John Wiley & Sons, Inc.

Hoogwijk, M. M. (2004). *On the global and regional potential of renewable energy sources*. Ph. D. thesis, Universiteit Utrecht.

Hossain Mondal, A. & A. K. M. S. Islam (2011). Potential and viability of grid-connected solar PV system in Bangladesh. *Renewable Energy 36*(6), 1869–1874.

Huang, L. & J. Wu (2014). Effects of the splayed window type on daylighting and solar shading. *Building and Environment 81*, 436–447.

Hunkeler, D., K. Lichtenvort, & G. Rebitzer (2008). Introduction - history of life cycle costing, its categorization and its basic framework. *Environmental Life Cycle Costing*.

Ibarra, D. & C. F. Reinhart (2011). Solar availability: A comparison study of six irradiation distribution methods. In *Building Simulation 2011*, 14.-16.11.2011, Sydney, Australia.

IEA PVPS Task 2 (2007). Cost and performance trends in grid-connected photovoltaic systems and case studies. Paris.

IEA PVPS Task 7-4 (2002). Potential for Building Integrated Photovoltaics. Paris.

IEA PVPS Task 7-5 (2002). Building Integrated Photovoltaic Power Systems Guidelines for Economic Evaluation. Paris.

INSPIRE (2014). Infrastructure for Spatial Information in the European Union.

Institut Wohnen und Umwelt (2005). Deutsche Gebäudetypologie - Systematik und Datensätze.

IRENA (2012). Power Sector - Solar Photovoltaics. *Renewable Energy Technologies: Cost analysis series 1*(4/5), 52.

Izquierdo, S., M. Rodrigues, & N. Fueyo (2008). A method for estimating the geographical distribution of the available roof surface area for large-scale photovoltaic energy-potential evaluations. *Solar Energy 82*(10), 929–939.

Jacobs, A. (2012). Radiance Tutorial.

Jakubiec, J. A. & C. F. Reinhart (2013). A method for predicting city-wide electricity gains from photovoltaic panels based on LiDAR and GIS data combined with hourly Daysim simulations. *Solar Energy 93*, 127–143.

James, T., A. Goodrich, M. Woodhouse, R. Margolis, & S. Ong (2011). *Building-Integrated Photovoltaics (BIPV) in the Residential Sector: An Analysis of Installed Rooftop System Prices*. Golden: NREL.

Jensen, R. (2013). Bevölkerungsrückgang löst Streit ums Geld aus. *ZEIT*.

Jimenez, D. W. & W. Williams (2011). Cost of ownership and overall equipment efficiency: a photovoltaics perspective. *Photovoltaics International 6*.

Jo, J. & T. Otanicar (2011). A hierarchical methodology for the mesoscale assessment of building integrated roof solar energy systems. *Renewable Energy 36*(11), 2992–3000.

Jochem, A., B. Höfle, & M. Rutzinger (2011). Extraction of Vertical Walls from Mobile Laser Scanning Data for Solar Potential Assessment. *Remote Sensing 3*, 650–667.

Kaltschmitt, M. (2007). *Renewable energy: technology, economics and environment*. Berlin: Springer.

Kaltschmitt, M. & A. Wiese (1992). *Potentiale und Kosten regenerativer Energieträger in Baden-Württemberg*. Forschungsbericht des Instituts für Energieträger in Baden-Württemberg. Universität Stuttgart.

Kaltschmitt, M. & A. Wiese (1993a). *Erneuerbare Energieträger in Deutschland - Potentiale und Kosten*.

Kaltschmitt, M. & A. Wiese (1993b). Regenerative Stromerzeugung - Technische Möglichkeiten und ökonomische Grenzen. *etz 114*(23-24), 1432–1437.

Karteris, M., T. Slini, & A. M. Papadopoulos (2013). Urban solar energy potential in Greece: A statistical calculation model of suitable built roof areas for photovoltaics. *Energy & Buildings 62*, 459–468.

Khai, N. P. (2014). *Semi-transparent building-integrated photovoltaic (BIPV) windows for the Tropics*. Ph. D. thesis, Singapore.

Kiefer, K., D. Dirnberger, B. Müller, W. Heydenreich, & A. Kröger-Vodde (2010). A degradation analysis of PV power plants. In *25th European Photovoltaic Solar Energy Conference and Exhibition*, 06.-10.09.2010, Valencia, Spain.

Kohler, N., U. Hassler, & H. Paschen (1999). *Stoffströme und Kosten in den Bereichen Bauen und Wohnen*. Konzept Nachhaltigkeit. Berlin: Springer.

Kohonen, T. (2001). *Self-organizing maps* (3. ed. ed.). Springer series in information sciences; 30. Berlin: Springer.

Konstantin, P. (2013). *Praxisbuch Energiewirtschaft: Energieumwandlung, -transport und -beschaffung im liberalisierten Markt* (3., aktual. Aufl. 2013 ed.). Springer, Berlin; Vieweg + Teubner.

Kost, C., J. N. Mayer, J. Thomsen, N. Hartmann, C. Senkpiel, S. Philipps, S. Nold, S. Lude, & T. Schlegl (2013). Stromgestehungskosten Erneuerbare Energien - Studie November 2013. Fraunhofer ISE, Freiburg i.B.

Kuhn, T., K. Fath, C. Bales, M. Gustafsson, R. Nouvel, & R. Fedrizzi (2014). *D2.3 RES availability survey and boundary conditions for simulations*. Freiburg i. B.: INSPIRE.

La Rosa, D. (2014). Accessibility to greenspaces: GIS based indicators for sustainable planning in a dense urban context. *Ecological Indicators 42*, 122–134.

Landesvermessungsamt Baden-Württemberg (2005). *Automatisierte Liegenschaftskarte (ALK)*. Stuttgart.

Larondelle, N., Z. A. Hamstead, P. Kremer, D. Haase, & T. McPhearson (2014). Applying a novel urban structure classification to compare the relationships of urban structure and surface temperature in Berlin and New York City. *Applied Geography 53*, 427–437.

Lehmann, H. & S. Peter (2003). Assessment of roof and facade potentials for solar use in Europe. Institute for sustainable Solutions and Innovations (ISUSI), Aachen, pp. 2–4.

Leibniz-Institut für ökologische Raumentwicklung (2014). IÖR-Monitor: Kategorie - Gebäude. Dresden.

LGL (2012). AFIS-ALKIS-ATKIS (AAA). Karlsruhe.

Li, D. H. W., T. N. T. Lam, & K. L. Cheung (2009). Energy and cost studies of semi-transparent photovoltaic skylight. *Energy Conversion and Management 50*, 1981–1990.

Liao, S.-H., P.-H. Chu, & P.-Y. Hsiao (2012). Data mining techniques and applications – a decade review from 2000 to 2011. *Expert Systems with Applications 39*(12), 11303 – 11311.

Liegenschaftsamt Stadt Karlsruhe (2012). 3D-city model (Digital Terrain Model and Buildings LoD2) of Karlsruhe. Karlsruhe.

Lödl, M., G. Kerber, P. R. Witzmann, C. Hoffmann, & M. Metzger (2010). Abschätzung des Photovoltaik-Potentials auf Dachflächen in Deutschland. *Symposium A Quarterly Journal In Modern Foreign Literatures*, 1–14.

Loga, T., B. Stein, N. Diefenbach, & R. Born (2015). *Deutsche Wohngebäudetypologie - Beispielhafte Maßnahmen zur Verbesserung der Energieeffizienz von typischen Wohngebäuden.* Darmstadt: Institut Wohnen und Umwelt.

Lu, L. & K. M. Law (2013). Overall energy performance of semi-transparent single-glazed photovoltaic (PV) window for a typical office in Hong Kong. *Renewable Energy 49*, 250–254.

LUBW (2014). Potenzialatlas Erneuerbare Energien. Karlsruhe.

Lutsch, W., H. Neuffer, & F.-G. Witterhold (2004). *Strategien und Technologien einer pluralistischen Fern- und Nahwärmeversorgung in einem liberalisierten Energiemarkt unter besonderer Berücksichtigung der Kraft-Wärme-Kopplung und regenerativer Energien - AGFW-Hauptstudie - Zweiter Bearbeitungsabschnitt, Band 1.* Frankfurt a. M.: AGFW.

Lütter, F., H. Uhlemann, M. Ammonn, V. R. Otto, & M. Lohr (2009). Standortgutachten Photovoltaik in Deutschland 2009. Bonn. EuPD Research.

Mainzer, K., K. Fath, R. McKenna, J. Stengel, W. Fichtner, & F. Schultmann (2014). High-resolution determination of the technical potential for residential-roof-mounted photovoltaic systems in Germany. *Solar Energy 105*, 715–731.

Maria Cristina Munari Probst, C. R. (2011). *Architectural integration and design of solar thermal systems*. Lausanne: EPFL Press.

Martin, N. & J. Ruiz (2013). Corrigendum to "Calculation of the PV modules angular losses under field conditions by means of an analytical model" [Sol. Energy Mater. Sol. Cells 70 (1) (2001) 25—38]. *Solar Energy Materials and Solar Cells 110*, 154.

Martin, N. & J. M. Ruiz (2001). Calculation of the PV modules angular losses under field conditions by means of an analytical model. *Solar Energy Materials & Solar Cells 70*, 25–38.

Mayer, J. N., S. Philipps, N. S. Hussein, T. Schlegl, & C. Senkpiel (2015). Current and future cost of photovoltaics. Berlin. Agora Energiewende.

McKenna, R., E. Merkel, D. Fehrenbach, S. Mehne, & W. Fichtner (2013). Energy efficiency in the German residential sector: A bottom-up building-stock-model-based analysis in the context of energy-political targets. *Building and Environment 62*, 77–88.

Meinel, G., R. Hecht, & H. Herold (2009). Analyzing building stock using topographic maps and GIS. *Building Research & Information 37*(5-6), 468–482.

Meinel, G., R. Hecht, H. Herold, T. Krüger, & M. Behnisch (2013). Monitoring of Land Use Development and Building Stocks in Germany–Methodology and Results. In A. Passer, K. Höfler, and P. Maydl (Eds.), *Sustainable Buildings Construction Products & Technologies*, Graz, Austria, pp. 1569–1579.

Mende, S., F. Frontini, & J. Wienold (2011). Comfort and building performance analysis of transparent building integrated silicon photovoltaics. In *Proceedings of Building Simulation 2011*, pp. 14–16.

Meteotest (2011). *Meteonorm*. Bern.

Meyer Burger (2016). *SmartWire Connection Technology*. Thun.

Ministerum für Umwelt, Klima und Energiewirtschaft Baden-Württemberg (2011). *Photovoltaikanlagen in Baden-Württemberg*. Stuttgart.

Mittag, H.-J. (2014). *Statistik: Eine Einführung mit interaktiven Elementen*. Berlin, Heidelberg: Springer Spektrum.

Miyazaki, T., A. Akisawa, & T. Kashiwagi (2005, March). Energy savings of office buildings by the use of semi-transparent solar cells for windows. *Renewable Energy 30*, 281–304.

Moor, D., W. Krejci, & W. Laserer (2012). Economic analysis of photovoltaic shading systems in façade construction. In Economic Forum, Munich (Ed.), *7th Energy Forum on Advanced Building Skins*, pp. 67–70.

Müller, B., L. Hardt, A. Armbruster, K. Kiefer, & C. Reise (2014). Yield predictions for photovoltaic power plants: Empirical validation, recent advances and reamining uncertainties. In *29th European PV Solar Energy Conference and Exhibition*, September 22nd - 26th, Amsterdam.

Müller, B., W. Heydenreich, K. Kiefer, & C. Reise (2009). More insights from the monitoring of real world PV power plants - A comparison of measured to predicted performance of PV systems. In *24th European Photovoltaic Solar Energy Conference*, September 21st - 25th, Hamburg, pp. 3888 – 3892.

Muneer, T., C. Gueymard, & H. Kambezidis (2004). *Solar Radiation and Daylight Models* (Second ed.). Oxford: Butterworth-Heinemann.

Nguyen, H. T. & J. M. Pearce (2010). Estimating Potential Photovoltaic Yield with r.sun and the Open Source Geographical Resources Analysis Support System. *Solar Energy 84*, 831–843.

Nitsch, J. & M. Fischedick (1999). *Klimaschutz durch Nutzung erneuerbarer Energien*. Berlin: Bundesministerium für Umwelt, Naturschutz und Reaktorsicherheit.

Ordonez, E., E. Jadraque, J. Alegre, & G. Mart?nez (2010). Analysis of the photovoltaic solar energy capacity of residential rooftops in Andalusia (Spain). *Europe 14*, 2122–2130.

Palzer, A. & H.-M. Henning (2014). A comprehensive model for the german electricity and heat sector in a future energy system with a dominant contribution from renewable energy technologies – part ii: Results. *Renewable and Sustainable Energy Reviews 30*, 1019 – 1034.

Perez, R., R. Seals, & J. Michalsky (1993). All-weather model for sky luminance distribution - preliminary configuration and validation. *Solar Energy 50*(3), 235–245.

Polo, C. S. & M. Sangiorgi (2014). Comparison assessment of BIPV façade semi-transparent modules: further insights on human comfort conditions. *Energy Procedia 48*, 1419–1428.

PV-Preisindex (2015). PV-Preisindex - Aktuelle Preise von schlüsselfertigen Photovoltaikanlagen. Triefenstein.

PVPS (2017). Trends 2016 in photovoltaic applications. St. Ursen.

pvXchange (2014). Price index.

Quaschning, V. (2000). *Systemtechnik einer klimaverträglichen Elektrizitätsversorgung in Deutschland für das 21. Jahrhundert*. Fortschritt-Berichte VDI, Reihe 6, Nr. 437, VDI-Verlag Düsseldorf.

Quaschning, V. (2011). *Regenerative Energiesysteme: Technologie, Berechnung, Simulation*. München: Hanser.

Quaschning, V. (2016). *Installierte Photovoltaikleistung in Deutschland* Berlin.

Radiance-online (1997). rtrace manual-pages.

Ramachandra, T. V. & B. V. Shruthi (2007). Spatial mapping of renewable energy potential. *Renewable and Sustainable Energy Reviews 11*, 1460–1480.

Räuber, A., M. Holland, & B. Holder (1987). *Photovoltaische Energieerzeugung*. Energiegutachten Baden Württemberg, Bd. 5, Fraunhofer ISE, Freiburg i.B.

Redweik, P., C. Catita, & M. Brito (2013). Solar energy potential on roofs and facades in an urban landscape. *Solar Energy 97*, 332–341.

Rehrl, K., K.-M. Edlinger, A. Friedwagner, B. Hahn, T. Langthaler, A. Wagner, & M. Wimmer (2012). Evaluierung von Verkehrsgraphen für die Berechnung von länderübergreifenden Erreichbarkeitspotenzialen am Beispiel von OpenStreetMap. In J. Strobl, T. Blaschke, and G. Griesebner (Eds.), *Angewandte Geoinformatik 2012*, 04.-06.07.2012, 24. AGIT-Symposium Salzburg, Austria., pp. 118–127.

Reinhart, C. & O. Walkenhorst (2001). Validation of dynamic RADIANCE-based daylight simulations for a test office with external blinds. *Energy & Buildings 33*(7), 683–697.

Roth, U. M. (Ed.) (1980). *Wechselwirkungen zwischen der Siedlungsstruktur und Wärmeversorgungssystemen*. Schriftenreihe des Bundesministers für Raumordnung, Bauwesen und Städtebau: 06, Raumordnung; 44. Bonn.

Ruiz-Arias, J. A., J. Terrados, P. Pérez-Higueras, D. Pozo-Vázquez, & G. Almonacid (2012). Assessment of the renewable energies potential for intensive electricity production in the province of Jaén, southern Spain. *Renewable and Sustainable Energy Reviews 16*(5), 2994–3001.

Schaich, E. & A. Hamerle (1984). *Verteilungsfreie statistische Prüfverfahren: eine anwendungsorientierte Darstellung*. Berlin: Springer.

Schallenberg Rodríguez, J. (2013). Photovoltaic techno-economical potential on roofs in regions and islands: The case of the Canary Islands. Methodological review and methodology proposal. *Renewable and Sustainable Energy Reviews 20*, 219–239.

Scholz, Y. (2012). *Renewable energy based electricity supply at low costs*. Ph. D. thesis, University of Stuttgart.

Schulz, W., K. Traube, & H.-U. Salmen (1994). *Ermittlung und Verifizierung der Potentiale und Kosten der Treibhausgasminderung durch Kraft-Wärme-Kopplung zur Fern- und Nahwärmeversorgung im Bereich Siedlungs-KWK*. Bremen: Bremer Energie-Institut.

Siedentop, S., S. Kausch, K. Einig, & J. Gössel (2003). Siedlungsstrukturelle Veränderungen im Umland der Agglomerationsräume. Bonn. Bundesamt für Bauwesen und Raumordnung.

Sliz-Szkliniarz, B. (2013). *Energy Planning in Selected European Regions: Methods for Evaluating the Potential of Renewable Energy Sources*. Regionalwissenschaftliche Forschungen; 35. Karlsruhe: KIT Scientific Publishing.

SolarWorld (2015). *Die lineare Leistungsgarantie*. Bonn.

Sonntag, P. & P. Mittner (1993). *Kennwerte zur Charakterisierung und Bewertung des energetischen Zustandes und des Energieverbrauchs der Gebäude im Nichtwohnbereich*. Instrumente für Klimagas-Reduktionsstrategien / Teilprojekt 5 Haushalte und Kleinverbraucher; 5,14. Jülich: Forschungszentrum.

Sprenger, W. (2013). *Electricity yield simulation of complex BIPV systems*. Ph. D. thesis, Technische Universiteit Delft.

Statistisches Bundesamt (2013). "Kennzahlen Gebäude und Wohnungen" aus der Gebäude- und Wohnungszählung 2011.

Statistisches Bundesamt (2014a). NUTS-Klassifikation. Wiesbaden.

Statistisches Bundesamt (2014b). Zensus 2011 - Ergebnisse im regionalen Vergleich. Wiesbaden.

Stengel, J. (2014). *Akteursbasierte Simulation der energetischen Modernisierung des Wohngebäudebestands in Deutschland*. Ph. D. thesis, Karlsruhe.

Strzalka, A., N. Alam, E. Duminil, V. Coors, & U. Eicker (2012). Large scale integration of photovoltaics in cities. *Applied Energy 93*, 413–421.

SUN-AREA (2017). Sun-area. Weikersheim.

Suri, M., T. A. Huld, E. D. Dunlop, H. A. Ossenbrink, & S. Marcel (2007). Potential of solar electricity generation in the European Union member states and candidate countries. *Solar Energy 81*, 1295–1305.

Theodoridou, I., M. Karteris, G. Mallinis, A. M. Papadopoulos, & M. Hegger (2012). Assessment of retrofitting measures and solar systems' potential in urban areas using Geographical Information Systems: Application to a Mediterranean city. *Renewable and Sustainable Energy Reviews 16*(8), 6239–6261.

Tregenza, P. R. & I. M. Waters (1983). Daylight coefficients. *Lighting Research and Technology 15*(2), 65 – 71.

Tritsch, T. (2011). *IHK-Arbeitskreis Energieeffizienz - Gebäudeintegrierte Photovoltaiksysteme - BIPV-Systeme der Gehrlicher Solar AG*. Haar.

Umweltbundesamt (2017). Stromverbrauch. Dessau-Roßlau.

VDMA (2015). International Technology Roadmap for Photovoltaic (ITRPV) 2015 Results. Frankfurt am Main.

Volwahsen, A. B. (Ed.) (1980). *Rationelle Energieverwendung im Rahmen der kommunalen Entwicklungsplanung*. Schriftenreihe des Bundesministers für Raumordnung, Bauwesen und Städtebau: 03, Städtebauliche Forschung; 83. Bonn-Bad Godesberg.

Wagner, A. (2010). *Photovoltaik engineering: Handbuch für Planung, Entwicklung und Anwendung*. Berlin: Springer.

Ward Larson, G. & R. A. Shakespeare (1998). *Rendering with Radiance - The Art and Science of Lighting Visualization*. Morgan Kaufmann Publishers.

Westenberg, G. & K. Will (2013). Geometrieinformationen zum Gebäudebestand - die Produkte Hauskoordinaten, Hausumringe und 3D-Gebäudemodelle. In *Flächennutzungsmonitoring V - Methodik - Analyseergebnisse - Flächenmanagement - IÖR Schriften Band 61*, pp. 147 – 154. Rhombos-Verlag Berlin: IÖR.

Winkens, H. P. & Z. Günter-Dioszeghy (1985). *Untersuchung einer zum Heizöl alternativen Energiebedarfsdeckung für den Rhein-Neckar-Raum: Planstudie im Auftr. d. Bundesministers für Forschung u. Technologie u.d. Energie- u. Wasserwerke Rhein-Neckar AG, Mannheim*. Örtliche und regionale Energieversorgungskonzepte ; 4. Bonn: Bundesforschungsanst. für Landeskunde u. Raumordnung.

Wirth, H. (2014). Aktuelle Fakten zur Photovoltaik in Deutschland - Fassung vom 19.3.2014. Fraunhofer ISE, Freiburg i.B.

Wittmann, H., P. Bajons, M. Doneus, & H. Friesinger (1997). Identification of roof areas suited for solar energy conversion systems. *Renewable Energy 11*(1), 25–36.

Wong, P. W., Y. Shimoda, M. Nonaka, M. Inoue, & M. Mizuno (2008). Semi-transparent PV: Thermal performance, power generation, daylight modelling and energy saving potential in a residential application. *Renewable Energy 33*, 1024–1036.

Wouters, F. (2007). Potentiale passiver und aktiver Solarenergienutzung in den Stadtraumtypen. In D. Everding (Ed.), *Solarer Städtebau*. Verlag Kohlhammer, Stuttgart.

PRODUKTION UND ENERGIE

Karlsruher Institut für Technologie (KIT)
Institut für Industriebetriebslehre und Industrielle Produktion
Deutsch-Französisches Institut für Umweltforschung

ISSN 2194-2404

Band 1 **National Integrated Assessment Modelling zur Bewertung umweltpolitischer Instrumente.**
Entwicklung des otello-Modellsystems und dessen Anwendung auf die Bundesrepublik Deutschland. 2012
ISBN 978-3-86644-853-7

Band 2 **Erhöhung der Energie- und Ressourceneffizienz und Reduzierung der Treibhausgasemissionen in der Eisen-, Stahl- und Zinkindustrie (ERESTRE).** 2013
ISBN 978-3-86644-857-5

Band 3 Frederik Trippe
Techno-ökonomische Bewertung alternativer Verfahrenskonfigurationen zur Herstellung von Biomass-to-Liquid (BtL) Kraftstoffen und Chemikalien. 2013
ISBN 978-3-7315-0031-5

Band 4 Dogan Keles
Uncertainties in energy markets and their consideration in energy storage evaluation. 2013
ISBN 978-3-7315-0046-9

Band 5 Heidi Ursula Heinrichs
Analyse der langfristigen Auswirkungen von Elektromobilität auf das deutsche Energiesystem im europäisschen Energieverbund. 2013
ISBN 978-3-7315-0131-2

Band 6 Julian Stengel
Akteursbasierte Simulation der energetischen Modernisierung des Wohngebäudebestands in Deutschland. 2014
ISBN 978-3-7315-0236-4

Band 7 Sonja Babrowski
Bedarf und Verteilung elektrischer Tagesspeicher im zukünftigen deutschen Energiesystem. 2015
ISBN 978-3-7315-0306-4

Band 8 Marius Wunder
Integration neuer Technologien der Bitumenkalthandhabung in die Versorgungskette. 2015
ISBN 978-3-7315-0319-4

Band 9 Felix Teufel
Speicherbedarf und dessen Auswirkungen auf die Energiewirtschaft bei Umsetzung der politischen Ziele zur Energiewende. 2015
ISBN 978-3-7315-0341-5

Band 10 D. Keles, L. Renz, A. Bublitz, F. Zimmermann, M. Genoese, W. Fichtner, H. Höfling, F. Sensfuß, J. Winkler
Zukunftsfähige Designoptionen für den deutschen Strommarkt: Ein Vergleich des Energy-only-Marktes mit Kapazitätsmärkten. 2016
ISBN 978-3-7315-0453-5

Band 11 Patrick Breun
Ein Ansatz zur Bewertung klimapolitischer Instrumente am Beispiel der Metallerzeugung und -verarbeitung. 2016
ISBN 978-3-7315-0494-8

Band 12 P. Ringler, H. Schermeyer, M. Ruppert, M. Hayn, V. Bertsch, D. Keles, W. Fichtner
Decentralized Energy Systems, Market Integration, Optimization. 2016
ISBN 978-3-7315-0505-1

Band 13 Marian Hayn
Modellgestützte Analyse neuer Stromtarife für Haushalte unter Berücksichtigung bedarfsorientierter Versorgungssicherheitsniveaus. 2016
ISBN 978-3-7315-0499-3

Band 14 Frank Schätter
Decision support system for a reactive management of disaster-caused supply chain disturbances. 2016
ISBN 978-3-7315-0530-3

Band 15 Robert Kunze
Techno-ökonomische Planung energetischer Wohngebäudemodernisierungen: Ein gemischt-ganzzahliges lineares Optimierungsmodell auf Basis einer vollständigen Finanzplanung. 2016
ISBN 978-3-7315-0531-0

Band 16 A. Kühlen, J. Stengel, R. Volk, F. Schultmann, M. Reinhardt, H. Schlick, S. Haghsheno, A. Mettke, S. Asmus, S. Schmidt, J. Harzheim
ISA: Immissionsschutz beim Abbruch - Minimierung von Umweltbelastungen (Lärm, Staub, Erschütterungen) beim Abbruch von Hoch-/Tiefbauten und Schaffung hochwertiger Recyclingmöglichkeiten für Materialien aus Gebäudeabbruch. 2018
ISBN 978-3-7315-0534-1

Band 17 Konrad Zimmer
Entscheidungsunterstützung zur Auswahl und Steuerung von Lieferanten und Lieferketten unter Berücksichtigung von Nachhaltigkeitsaspekten. 2016
ISBN 978-3-7315-0537-2

Band 18 Kira Schumacher, Wolf Fichtner and Frank Schultmann (Eds.)
Innovations for sustainable biomass utilisation in the Upper Rhine Region. 2017
ISBN 978-3-7315-0423-8

Band 19 Sophia Radloff
Modellgestützte Bewertung der Nutzung von Biokohle als Bodenzusatz in der Landwirtschaft. 2017
ISBN 978-3-7315-0559-4

Band 20 Rebekka Volk
Proactive-reactive, robust scheduling and capacity planning of deconstruction projects under uncertainty. 2017
ISBN 978-3-7315-0592-1

Band 21 Erik Merkel
Analyse und Bewertung des Elektrizitätssystems und des Wärmesystems der Wohngebäude in Deutschland. 2017
ISBN 978-3-7315-0636-2

Band 22 Rebekka Volk (Hrsg.)
Entwicklung eines mobilen Systems zur Erfassung und Erschließung von Ressourceneffizienzpotenzialen beim Rückbau von Infrastruktur und Produkten („ResourceApp"): Schlussbericht des Forschungsvorhabens. 2017
ISBN 978-3-7315-0653-9

Band 23 Thomas Kaschub
Batteriespeicher in Haushalten unter Berücksichtigung von Photovoltaik, Elektrofahrzeugen und Nachfrage-steuerung. 2017
ISBN 978-3-7315-0688-1

Band 24 Felix Hübner, Rebekka Volk, Oktay Secer, Daniel Kühn, Peter Sahre, Reinhard Knappik, Frank Schultmann, Sascha Gentes, Petra von Both
Modellentwicklung eines ganzheitlichen Projektmanagementsystems für kerntechnische Rückbauprojekte (MogaMaR): Schlussbericht des Forschungsvorhabens. 2018
ISBN 978-3-7315-0762-8

Band 25 Karoline Fath
Technical and economic potential for photovoltaic systems on buildings. 2018
ISBN 978-3-7315-0787-1